Cinemaphagy

*On the psychedelic classical form
of Tobe Hooper*

by Scout Tafoya

Library of Congress Cataloging-in-Publication Data

Scout Tafoya, Cinemaphagy: On the Psychedelic Classical Form of Tobe Hooper, film history and criticism

Summary: A critical assessment of the work of film director Tobe Hooper

ISBN: 978-1-939282-46-0

Published by Miniver Press, LLC, McLean Virginia
Copyright 2021 Nell Minow

First edition February 2021

Sarcophagy
noun plural sar·coph·a·gy \sär ˈkäfəjē\
the practice of feeding on flesh

Table of Contents

Introduction

About a third of the way through writing this book on Tobe Hooper, about why his negligible legacy deserved reinforcement, how his work as an artist was overlooked by a culture that despised horror film and its outré signifiers and tonal register, about a director who practically in secret kept alive a rich tradition of effulgent Hollywood film grammar, I lost it all. All my progress... gone. My computer ate it in some mad software glitch. I hadn't saved copies of it, believing it wasn't far enough along. I tried spinning it a thousand ways so the stupid thing I'd done could be seen as secretly *great*, helpful in the long run. I decided to go get coffee to clear my head. Just as the door to my apartment slammed shut, however, I realized I'd left without my keys. My girlfriend was at work and wouldn't be home for another few hours. *Of course,* I thought. It was the bow tied on top of a catastrophic twenty-four hours. Realizing I didn't want to kill two hours at the cramped Dunkin Donuts a few blocks from our apartment, I walked the extra ten minutes to the Starbucks across from the world-famous Museum of the Moving Image. I sat down with my ridiculously expensive coffee, looked up, and saw Mark Borchardt sitting at the table across from mine.

There was no mistaking him. No one on planet Earth looks like Mark Borchardt except Mark Borchardt. It was just an insane coincidence that brought the Milwaukee-based filmmaker to that Starbucks in Queens that hour, on that day. So I introduced myself to the *Coven* director and almost immediately he asked me to sit down.

"What are you doing here?" he asked, as if he were familiar enough with my routine to know that it was weird that I'd be at this Starbucks around now.

"I locked myself out of my apartment... I've been distracted... I was writing a book and lost it all last night."

"You'd better sit down," he said, genuine worry in his sticky, sweet Midwestern voice. "That sucks, man."

I tried explaining the silver lining theory I was pursuing, but he stopped me.

"Don't bullshit yourself, man. You've gotta suffer. Then there's nothing else to do but get back on the horse."

What a beautiful, hard-won, Midwestern way of looking at things. There was nothing else to do but feel the hurt that I'd earned through my choices. I'm guessing Mark learned that through years of living in the coldest place in the United States. He was right. I'd made a mistake and I wasn't going to get around it by lying. How are your successes going to feel different or special if you don't allow yourself failures?

Mark asked me why I wanted to write a book about Tobe Hooper and it was a question I realized I'd been ignoring all through the months of writing I'd done. Why should people reappraise a director that Western criticism had mostly written off? He seemed bowled over by the idea that Hooper was a long-lost Golden Age studio filmmaker when I explained it to him. His confusion was nothing new to me. I experienced a little of it myself when I first saw *The Texas Chain Saw Massacre* in 4th grade. *Just what* is *this?* my young mind asked the assault of images and sounds. And these days, I experience it every time I stand up for *The Mangler* or *Spontaneous Combustion*. Defending him means explaining who he was to most people, and then explaining he's not the disappointment his legacy suggests.

Why does no one see Hooper the way I do? *The Texas Chain Saw Massacre* is one of the greatest American films of all time (or it is according to filmmakers Rob Zombie, Raya Martin, Wes Craven, and Takashi Miike, as well as critics Veronika Ferdman, Budd Wilkins, David Flint, Paul Duane, and myself, according to a poll conducted on the website They Shoot Pictures, Don't They?) and we've more or less gotten to the point where it's no longer seen as "just" a horror film. From Ryan Gilbey's obituary in the Guardian:

Like George A Romero's Night of the Living Dead and Wes Craven's The Last House on the Left, the film used horror to express the discontentment of a country reeling from Vietnam and widespread social unrest. Fans included Ridley Scott ("It shocked the hell out of me"), Stanley Kubrick, who bought his own print, and William Friedkin, director of The Exorcist, who said it "transcended the [horror] genre."

If Texas Chain Saw is "more" or "better" than just horror, then his other works (which are proudly and purely genre despite their asymmetrical shape and bold form) are somehow not as worthy of canonization or respect. They're cult items and curate's eggs, notable only for having been the strange things that the director of one of the most famous American horror films got up to in the years after. And because Texas Chain Saw Massacre has risen to Citizen Kane levels of fame/infamy, nothing its creator did would ever live up to that standard. And so, as so many did with Orson Welles, we continue to imagine that the man who made an American masterpiece could never possibly reclaim the highs of that "first" film that put them on the map and ensured a lifetime fighting to flee from its shadow.

Hooper's legacy, it seems, was too unwieldy and our mainstream critical body rejects that which isn't tidy. He couldn't be both a genius and a failure, so we kept the genius of Texas Chain Saw Massacre and discarded the failures over and over again. When the Poltergeist debacle unfurled, when a journalist claimed to see Steven Spielberg directing it on set and not Hooper and Americans were asked to choose who they believed directed it, the more popular entertainer won out. You now can't talk about Poltergeist's artistry without debating whether Hooper actually directed it. That's a level of artistic hijacking with which Welles could have sympathized.

And we all let it happen because we don't feel the same connection to Hooper that we do to Spielberg (or even to Carpenter or Craven) despite the fact that his films have spawned legions of remakes (three of Texas Chain Saw alone), prequels, and sequels, and his creations are still being cribbed from to this day. Hooper was never put forward in publicity the same way a lot of American directors are.

And yet, here I was starting this book from scratch after losing months of work, believing firmly enough in Hooper's artistry to do the whole thing over again. He's an artist who deserves better, more than the little space we've granted him in our discourse. Nakedly political, earnestly outsized and unsubtle, and interested in the beauty of visuals as an end unto themselves, Hooper, like so many studio directors of the '70s, has become a footnote. His last film, the marvelous 2013 film *Djinn*, was laughed out of a distribution deal and wound up quietly streaming on Netflix. The reviews seemed astonished, as they always do, that the man who directed *The Texas Chain Saw Massacre* had stooped to this.

Our culture had greedily consumed his work for years and spit out his bones, making it nearly impossible for him to make a living in the US as an artist (*Djinn* was shot overseas with international backing, after Hooper had spent decades making exclusively mid- to low-budget film and TV throughout the '90s and 2000s). This kind of cowardly anti-aestheticism must come to an end. Just before his death, he was still able to direct and direct well. Yet his films had to sneak in front of audiences. The time for Hooper to take his place as one of the great American artists was long ago, but now will have to do. He's gone, but the work is, thankfully, timeless.

So what is the book you're about to read? It's a couple of things: there's a little information about his working life—his biography as it coincides with the movies he made. This is not an attempt to draw the most complete version of Hooper's life. He passed away before I got a chance to interview him, and I did not speak to his family and so this will not be a remotely thorough look at his life as a person, husband, father, or any of the other social roles he fulfilled throughout his incredible life. Rather, this is the first serious analytical manuscript on Hooper's complete works as a director, consisting of essays on every single film and TV show he directed that can be found. Currently his pilot for the 1998 television series *Prey* remains only accessible at the UCLA Film and Television archive and thus it was not within my means to watch it for research. The rest are accounted for and slotted into, what I hope, is a complete portrait of the working methods and form of one of the most interesting and neglected artists who ever worked his way through the American studio system. This is a critical and technical study, analyzing every camera movement, every homage to classic Hollywood and horror, every recurring motif; this is a portrait of a man drawn in his obsessions and each of his decisions behind the camera. Hooper was never treated like other directors, and this is an attempt to give him serious consideration. The irony that this book was turned down by thirty other publishing houses, including university presses, is not lost on me. People fought tooth and nail to keep Hooper from being treated like an artist. That stops now.

Scout Tafoya

Chapter 1:
The Cave (1964–1974)

While talking to Laura and Kate Mulleavy for *Interview Magazine* in July of 2014, Hooper claimed that his mother went into labor in a cinema, his first attack on the comforts a movie house ostensibly provides. The cinema was his womb and, just as his arrival burst the fictitious bubble of whatever film his mother was watching that day in 1943, he would puncture the safety the movie house is meant to engender by breaking the unspoken agreement of safety provided to moviegoers. His movies depicted the perversion of plentiful womb spaces. When they'd destroyed the safety of every character, his movies would practically crawl off the screen and ensure that no one left untouched by the machinery of his extrasensory filmmaking. His movies left scars.

This is a biographical sketch from collaborator LM Kit Carson from the late summer 1986 issue of *Film Comment* magazine about his experience with Hooper making *The Texas Chainsaw Massacre 2*:

> "I was a fanatic film fan from before birth. My mother had to be taken out of the State Theatre in Austin straight to the hospital in labor. Probably it was one of those good, good black-and-white Michael Curtiz pictures she didn't want to leave. My mother and father loved movies. As soon as I was out of the hospital, I was taken with them to the movies. And I literally grew up in the movies." … "After my folks split up, I lived with my mother. But my father became

terminally ill when I was a teenager, and I moved to Grand Prairie [near Dallas] to be with him for his last four years. There I made my first 16mm film, $1100 budget, called The Abyss. Things were kind of dark around me in those days watching my father dying." After his father's death, Hooper returned to Austin and into the University of Texas Film Department (population, 2: Tobe Hooper and the Film Instructor). Hooper got a part-time job making 20-minute sales-tool shorts for a local insurance company—insidious little dramas to pitch fear into families. Like what happens after Dad gets mashed to death in a three-car accident: lose the home; the dog runs away; finally the 12-year-old daughter hits the streets hooking. Like what are the Odds For The Future: a hundred little golden plaster of Paris men standing on a wonderful wide horizon; 95 of these figures abruptly explode; that's the odds; don't bet on it, pal. After he'd made almost 50 of these bum trips, Hooper got a call from the insurance company president congratulating him for helping to boost sales—plus a suggestion that Hooper start studying the obituary columns so he could go shoot telephoto footage of real grief-filled funerals. Hooper quit. Then, unaccountably, the insurance prez called Hooper back. He had been truly impressed with Hooper's work in scaring lots of money out of insurance buyers. He offered to bankroll a short film, no joke.

Carson left out his first marriage to Maev Margaret Noonan, which resulted in the birth of Hooper's only son William Tony Hooper, who would later work as a makeup and model maker on Hooper films *The Texas Chainsaw Massacre 2*, *Spontaneous Combustion*, *Lifeforce*, and *The Mangler* where he worked on the titular Mangler. Hooper and Noonan divorced in 1969, and in 1983, after *Poltergeist*, Hooper married Carin L. Berger, daughter of actor William Berger (whom Hooper would cast in *I'm Dangerous Tonight*). They would remain married until 1990, but Carin would work on the later Hooper film *Crocodile*. He got married a third time in 2008 to Rita Marie Bartlett who worked as a production assistant on *Spontaneous Combustion* and was more involved as producer and consultant on *Night Terrors* and *The Mangler*, but they divorced in 2010.

Hooper began as a radical filmmaker whose experimental technique was a mirror of the psychedelic music being made in his home state of Texas. Bands like Bubble Puppy, The Red Krayola, and Josephus were trying deconstructive and exciting things with feedback, distortion, song structure, instrumental tone, and carnivalesque atmospherics learned and adapted from albums by Pink Floyd, The Yardbirds, and The Rolling Stones. The mix of heavy rock and roll and blues with the purposeful shapelessness of free jazz created a trancelike sound that became a late '60s touchstone. Hooper's camera, soundtrack, and editing bay shared this mix of the precise and the wild. He had a playfully bleak sense of humor and the willingness to try any technique just for the sake of seeing what outcomes might be achieved. Never fully abandoning his radical origins, his later films would play like the psychedelic answer to the studio films of the '50s and the art house films of the late '60s—recognizable techniques left out in the sun, lights turned up a little too bright, gallows humor galore.

To a degree, every Tobe Hooper film concerns one big fish eating a smaller one. Conflicting ideologies meet and the meaner one wins. He started out making films about people seeking shelter from American society through the "hippie" lifestyle. Folk music and commune living were blankets kids could wrap themselves in to avoid contact with the outside world. Rejection was a political policy that seemed to be the only way to survive in the age of the draft, in which kids were involuntarily pressed into service to fight the Vietnam War. But as beautiful as he may have found the idea, his movies depicted the impossibility of fully insulating oneself the ugliness of America's hungry political machine. It would find you and when it did, it would not have any interest in talking peace or learning your language. Hooper's early films show free spirits eating themselves from the inside or being eaten by bigger forces. The hippies in Hooper's films form a communal organism incapable of protecting itself, or of even detecting a predatory threat when it finds them.

In the late '60s and early '70s, he made documentaries, and, though most of them have been lost, a few, including one about the folk trio Peter, Paul, and Mary, survive. Called *The Song Is Love*, it climaxes with stock footage of soldiers in Vietnam in double exposure over top of the cherubic folkies peacefully harmonizing, before the songs and the intensity of their performance builds without warning. Suddenly we hear them belting "kill the traitor" during the chorus of "Great Mandala," and the footage of soldiers marching becomes ironically galvanizing. It's unnervingly effective given how bluntly it presents its contrasting ideas. Unconsciously, it asks how anything beautiful could coexist with something so horrific, while more obviously showing the things that the folk movement existed to question. How can you expect to meaningfully interact with the hideous tendencies of society, even if that just means resisting, when you haven't properly reckoned with the boundless capacity for cruelty and violence inside men's hearts? As late as 2013, he was still asking whether it made sense to hide one's head in the sand rather than face political realities for the sake of one's sanity. The question of how to be a politically engaged citizen pops up again and again in his work, which further sets him apart not just from horror directors but from all Americans.

Hooper's psychedelic trickery would stay with him all his life, black clouds waiting to subsume the easy rhythms of cozy generic trappings. The weird and the unearthly would rise up to eat anything wholesome, suburban, and expected. Hooper was an agent of chaos between poles. He would dream up scenes of picturesque innocence and then horror would ruin them like a burst of feedback from an electric guitar. Of Hooper's more than two dozen feature films, almost none can be said to have a "happy" ending. For all the beautiful artifice on display, he remained a realist at heart, and never strained to help us accommodate the contradiction.

The Heisters (1964)

Hooper's earliest surviving film is the short work *The Heisters*, which is about three medieval thieves squabbling with each other in a cave; ten minutes of unhinged technique lavished on top-notch cinephile in-jokes. It's a live-action Warner Bros. cartoon ("This theatre is proud to announce that the following presentation is ridiculous," reads the opening crawl), parodying the house styles of Hammer films (an English studio renowned for reimagining Universal monster movies like *Dracula* and *Frankenstein* in color, with high quotients of gore and sexuality) and American International Pictures (a pioneering low-budget genre studio, whose ethos of art from trash is located most purely in the Roger Corman–directed Edgar Allen Poe adaptations starring Vincent Price from the early 1960s). The almost overbearing presentational lighting and color used to frame Price in tableaux that externalized his deteriorating mental state, not to mention Corman's budget-conscious production management, would find their way into most of Hooper's work after *The Texas Chain Saw Massacre*. Hammer's brand—classy-but-trashy English revisions of age-old horror characters and tropes—wasn't worlds away from Hooper's own work. Both Hooper and Hammer ladled gorgeous production design and art direction over stories borrowed from existing ideas to make them their own.

Hooper shot *The Heisters* when he was 21 and he already demonstrated an incredible formal control. It was shot without synchronized audio (what film industry lifers call MOS, an abbreviation of the German saying "mit-out-sound") and all the post-production sound is perfectly over-the-top. Set to a jittery silent comedy piano, three bickering thieves in old-timey costumes run through the woods pursued by the sound of dogs barking. Two of them bash each other with switches, to which the soundtrack attributes fierce whip-cracking noises. They retreat to a cave to regroup and divvy up the spoils. Once they enter the cave, the gags begin right away. One of the thieves eats a gingerbread man and the crunching sounds so obnoxious that his companions are moved to sickness. After a few loud bites, he removes a tiny bone from his teeth and adds it to a pile of similarly miniature skeletal parts in a small barrel. The music punctuates every movement, a strain of film composing called "Mickey Mousing" with an instrumental flourish for every one of their movements, a seasick violin accompanying the turning of a head and so forth.

The events of the film bear little relation to each other. Unhappy with his share of the loot, one of the heisters fights with an ornate papier-mâché statue in the corner, each cut placing him in a new flamboyant combat pose, while debris explodes all around him like visual guitar distortion. Another uses his junior alchemy set to increase the size of a beetle, which is later strapped to a block and tortured *Pit and the Pendulum*-style. Dancing girls waltz into frame carrying a giant diamond, which will turn out to be made of ice. As payback for the diamond ruse, a knight's gauntlet is deployed like a dueling glove. In the shot that sets up the gag, a man is slapped with the metal hand. In the punch line answer shot, a bunch of big fake teeth land on the ground, followed by the man's eyebrows. A ten-pace duel is fought with pies. The loser activates a Rube Goldberg machine to reveal a man-sized pie into which he walks before it can be deployed. The whole thing ends with a keg of explosives going off, in fine *Looney Tunes* tradition.

For all its silliness, *The Heisters* is absolutely stunning. Ronald Perryman's Technicolor photography is crisp and clear, showcasing the elaborate lighting scheme, which would become an invaluable piece of Hooper's arsenal as a director. Blue, green, and purple lights on the surfaces behind the actors in some of the shots and the on-screen lighting of torches and lightning are equally as arresting. It looks genuinely like the American International Pictures and Hammer films it apes. Hooper's editing is a joy, and a good faith impression of Chuck Jones, Tex Avery, and/or Frank Tashlin, the animators responsible for the golden age of *Looney Tunes* shorts, with its wacky sound design and frenetic cutting to build jokes. Its cumulative effect could only be achieved through filmmaking.

Hooper's framing is incredibly beautiful and precise. The cave is a recurring theme in Hooper's work: the deceptive comfort of the womb space as portrayed by caverns, cobwebbed basements, or uninhabited houses. There are many false shelters sought by so many of his naïve heroes who wish to return to a time predating responsibility and adulthood. And, conversely, to a time of supposedly idyllic but regressive politics associated with the country's postwar infancy in the 1950s.

The Heisters is in many ways the film Hooper would remake throughout his career. Everything from his loving decoration and careful lighting to the womb-like hideout setting to the grimly funny tone would become leitmotifs throughout his work. It's also a story he'd explore many different ways: that safety is impossible, no matter how well you think you've hidden from the forces that want you dead. There is a certainty to Hooper's ideology—it isn't enough to hide from what scares you.

Down Friday Street (1966)

If *The Heisters* was Hooper's film announcing his intentions as a director of action, *Down Friday Street* was the film that just as earnestly enunciated his intentions as a director of time and space. This ten-minute short is a catalogue of editing strategies and distortion settings. The music by Ray Lynch and The Merlin Tree is a bombastic psych-rock explosion to match his electric montage and images, juxtaposing under-exposed shots of an Austin street at night and day. He catches cars, the silhouettes of men in telephone booths, signs for everything from parking to live nude girls, and ugly fluorescent-lit hallways. As in the later *Eggshells*, he vacillates between stillness, the natural world, sped-up time, the excitement of an urban environment, and the promise of life represented by people in urban environments. There is a sense, produced by the busy sound design (insistent dripping sounds, traffic, a beeping electronic device) in concert with incongruous images like empty streets and a spider eating a bug in its web—of impending dread. A voice on a loudspeaker encourages people to take cover. It's as if the film were meant to be a warning about what to do in the event of nuclear war, down to the air raid siren that plays over kids in their 20s nonchalantly walking and riding bikes down the streets.

This work is free of narrative but rather subsists on raw visual energy, on the power of unnerving images of cobwebbed corners and rain-struck parks. It's like William Klein's 1956 short *Broadway By Light*, which similarly captured the energy of a time and place without a word of dialogue or much input from any human responsible for the images. Hooper's first decade is sketched here. There's the abandoned infrastructure and buildings that set the table for *Texas Chain Saw Massacre*, to say nothing of the focus on insects, the lovingly appointed old manor that sits in the center on *Salem's Lot*, there's the avant-garde blasts of sound to accompany images of destruction in *Eggshells*, and there's the angular and oppressive soundscape of *Eaten Alive*. The film mimics explosions by zooming in with one camera in a double exposure, while the other one sits still and a sound of crunching rocks crackles. It's Hooper's film of pure sensation, no story or object to dominate his attention. It's simply the world he saw with the rushing rhythm of a sudden high coming on. Between this and *The Heisters* is the bedrock of his diction and obsessions, a full style split in two.

Eggshells (1969)

Eggshells, Hooper's first independent feature-length film, is a mix of fiction and nonfiction. It's about the denizens of a commune in Austin, Texas and their slow dissolution and implosion. Crucially, it's the forces inside the house and the group that prove to be their undoing more so than anything they're rebelling against or from which they're hiding. Hooper sees beauty in the freedom with which they attempt to live but knows it's an unstable and incomplete ethos. The movie is largely a series of aimless vignettes but the most important plot point involves one of the kids awakening some kind of evil force in the basement which then destroys the members of the commune who don't escape. None of the characters have names, which makes identifying the actors playing them difficult. The point is that the characters are meant to be interchangeable, a youthful revolutionary class destined to be destroyed as one. *Eggshells* is, along with the more obviously counterculture courting *Easy Rider* by Dennis Hopper about bikers on a road trip making a drug buy, about the death of a short-lived idealism that gripped young America.

It opens on a flock of birds captured in silhouette against a brilliant yellow sunrise before cutting to a girl in the back of a pick-up truck, an image will be duplicated in the end of *The Texas Chain Saw Massacre*—the films frequently seem like mirror images of each other. Hooper is the film's cinematographer and he shoots in a bleached-looking 16mm that washes the colors to hazy pastels. Through Hooper's camera, dead grass looks purple and sweltering Austin looks ready to melt into the sickly green sky. In the heart of town, there's some form of nationalist rally taking place with American and Texan flags flapping under the white sun. The girl from the truck skirts the festivities, which look disconcertingly like the erupting crowds in front of the 1968 Democratic National Convention captured in Haskell Wexler's *Medium Cool,* released the year before. Some easy Texan freak folk chugs away on the soundtrack. A coffin painted in red, white, and blue is carried through town opposite a banner that reads "The government is violent—not us." The gleaming white shirts of the attendees almost blind the camera.

Hooper's subject, the girl from the truck, is apart from the demonstration. She and her commune-dwelling friends don't take part in what's happening on the streets so near their home. They hide from the action, the violence, and the marches. Implicitly, they hide from the Vietnam War.

Hooper finally rests on the commune itself. The heat of the sun is visibly oppressive. Hooper stares at the sun through foliage, then dead leaves blown by wind before finding a paper airplane abandoned in a gutter. It flies at the house and explodes like a kamikaze, landing next to a barefoot commune kid with red hair, the sudden incongruous burst of flame provoking an uneasy laugh. It's a warning: the violence is coming. It won't be ignored. This is the first of many bursts of slightly surreal metahumor Hooper performs with his camera in *Eggshells*.

We're given an ecstatic tour of the house where Hooper tries every angle and movement he can think up. It's an exciting flurry of activity that ends in the kitchen where breakfast is being cooked. The sounds of the house—bacon frying, the gas range, warbling bluegrass—grow into a cacophonous wail. And then, just as suddenly, they all go quiet. Hooper messes with the edit and sound design like he's mixing a psych album.

"That's enough of this god bullshit, let's eat," says one of the girls at the table.

The early parts of the film capture the real discussions of the kids in the commune and cut them up and lay them over top of each other in anarchic double exposures. Characters, stray elements, and sounds come in and out of focus that, while very overwhelming, gives a brief summation of the feeling of the house itself.

"Can you believe anything you see on TV?" a girl asks.

How can you believe anything when your life is this hectic? It's empathetic filmmaking on the one hand, but also equally alienating. The pace and random order of life in the house is too much to quite accept as normal, so Hooper's gently hallucinatory approach to their lives feels both apt but also geared toward wanting us to leave the house and return to real life.

There's a funny little tangent where one of the kids tells a ghost story and is met with a sarcastic rejoinder from a boy with an afro and glasses (Allan Danziger, who'd follow Hooper to *Texas Chain Saw*): "Vincent Price was there." Hooper probably didn't plan the exchange, it feels too tossed off, but it's a funny parallel to *The Heisters*, which deliberately recalls Vincent Price's work in the films of Roger Corman for American International Pictures.

Eggshells sticks to a rhythmic formal pattern: there will be a documentary-style sit-in with the communists, then Hooper will take over with an overtly psychedelic aside. It's an identical strategy to the one used in the Texas psych-rock hallmark *The Parable of Arable Land* by The Red Krayola. The tracks alternate between real songs and what were called "free-form freak-outs" of noise and experimentation. The first of Hooper's freak-outs is a stop-motion race around and through the house. The sequence, made up of seconds-long snapshots of the house strung together like Claymation, is set to a warbling woodwind and Jew's harp—very disorienting. The camera winds up in the basement. Hooper's lighting in this sequence reinforces the film's color scheme: purple, green, and red.

The nonfiction relief from the freak-out is two of the kids in a bathtub talking about communism: "You don't know what communism is." Their politics are useless because they haven't educated themselves. Putting them in the tub emphasizes their childishness as they talk in circles. His camera is very still during their exchange, letting the actors guide the scene with just their words.

The next of the freak-outs is brief: the redhead who dodged the exploding paper airplane considers some sinister portraiture hung on his walls and stacked in a corner of his room. Next, Hooper plants his camera at the bottom of the house's staircase and jump cuts between different members of the commune walking up and down. Between the random cutting patterns and the sound of footsteps on the stairs, it's like the cinematic equivalent of a drum circle, compounded upon by the uncentered subjects, the diagonal angle of the stairs, and the z-axis of the hallway on the left. They create directionality, like little movies inside the frame. Whatever else is true of his approach during these "freak-outs," Hooper's experimentation took time and a lot of control. The seemingly drunk movement of the camera in some of the sequences only seems woozy because of the care with which he places the camera during the rest of the movie.

We follow the redhead to the basement for a little game that would have fit comfortably in *The Heisters*. He kicks a can of glitter into an improbably placed sword, which he immediately picks up and starts swinging. The scene drips with portentous metaphor. The basement is a womb, a place the redhead retreats into during a party in the commune. A retreat from a retreat that places him back inside the mother he rejects by living outside of society. When he starts swinging the sword around, he notices that when he lashes out, his mirror image jumps onto the receiving end of the blow to counter it. He begins sword fighting with himself. Hooper's editing here is top-notch, maintaining continuity even through camera moves and zooms. With its exaggerated clanging sounds, it plays like a trippy spin on the Ray Harryhausen Claymation fights with sword-wielding skeletons from *The Seventh Voyage of Sinbad* or *Jason & The Argonauts*.

The fight concluded, one version of the redheaded boy's inner self defeated, the basement begins to glow, beckoning him further into the womb, sword at the ready. He discovers a light through a pinhole, through which a proboscis emerges and licks his face—the first image of Hooper's that directly recalls H. P. Lovecraft (also the name of a psych band from this era), with its primordial tentacles emerging from other dimensions as in his stories *The Call of Cthulhu* and *At The Mountains of Madness*. The light dances for him, in a circular display, before turning into an eyeball-like bubble. We're denied the conclusion of this episode, as we return upstairs to the party, but the eye will return. (Though the menacing light show and emergence of tentacles/tongues from other dimensions would return in different forms in both *Poltergeist* and *Invaders from Mars*.) That night, the redheaded boy has a nightmare featuring dozens of balloons released into the sky like little projections from the eye as he slowly gives into it.

We see something resembling the eye in the next scene: the two lovers from the bathtub lie under a protective glass bubble in a field, literally shielding themselves from anything outside of their conception of what is good and natural. The girl ribs the boy gently by saying the only reason he loves her is because "I do the dishes and cook all the meals and pick up all your shit..." Their relationship seems to, at least partially, resemble the domesticity of their parents. "I may stay in this Plexiglas bubble all my life," she says. Hooper seems to believe that they're clearly trading one version of complacency for another, the bubble keeping in their mistaken belief that there could be another way of life in the simple act of refusing their parents' lifestyles.

They even travel with the bubble over the car, like a halo keeping out toxic bad vibes just as it does the dust their car kicks up. Hooper's camera floats around the inside of the car as they drive around, observing the squares downtown from the safety of their bubble. As they talk about a spare room in need of fixing, Hooper's edit takes us into the future as they paint it, then abandon the project in favor of painting each other's naked bodies. The room literally paints itself (through stop-motion animation) to resemble a night sky while they pay attention to each other. They're too distracted to notice the walls coming alive and designing themselves.

The next freak-out is a tie-dyed sex scene, one of the few in Hooper's body of work that isn't thwarted by something malevolent. He plays with light, focus, lenses, rhythm, shapes, and time during this scene, uninterested in sex as anything but an opportunity to present the melding of forms. It's unmistakably sex (there's even symbolic tantric sitar on the score), but it's deeply and purposefully unsexy and difficult to parse who's involved—it could be anyone. It careens into straight psychedelic collage towards the end. The nudity in the film is presented as an extension of their childish approach to their existence. This is their garden of Eden, as the naked people piled on top of each other smoking pot spell out. One of the girls plays "Edelweiss" on the soundtrack, a song linked to Nazism and the Germany soiled by the rise of fascism. Every gesture hints at the end of their peaceful existence and the rise of Nixonian conservative politics.

While the denizens sing in warbling, uneasy harmony, the redheaded boy is seen alone, increasingly at odds with the rest of the commune. He goes back down to the basement, called by the glowing eye. It glows angrily, purple light and smoke churning inside. A portal sucks the redhead inside like a giant mouth. When he returns, he's brought an odd arrangement of furniture with him: chairs with hairdresser-style orbs above them. He sits with his head inside of one while Hooper brings us inside his mind: a collection of dust speckles dancing around the screen that harkens back to the work of avant-garde pioneer Stan Brakhage. Upstairs, his roommates, oblivious and sibilant, get high and talk nonsense, fiddling while the house conspires against them.

Hooper plays a funny little trick of perspective, showing an orb in what looks like an actual womb, but turns out to be a doctor's bag. The eye has apparently given birth. The redhead takes the orb and walks upstairs, covered in ominous violet light. The whole house is now coated in oppressive light as he leaves, as if he's been spat out into an alternate version of the commune (alternate realities will reappear in *Poltergeist* and *Djinn* among others). Or maybe he sees things the rest of the childlike communists can't. The redhead takes the bag to a public park in downtown Austin where he spies a young girl in nearly erotic repose with a tree being watered by a nearby sprinkler; the jets create the illusion of bars around the boy. He watches her, stroking the bag with a far-off look in his eye, planning something sinister. He follows her through a field of balloons, projections from the eye, his dream imagery made real. They both accidentally gather dozens of the balloons as they walk, an image that calls to mind bacteria.

The next scene of ordinary talk is set in a room with three windows. Hooper has adjusted his iris to let in enough light to blur the edges around the people in the room. He'd use this light quality again during the early scenes of *The Funhouse*, both passages flirting with the trap of domesticity and marriage. A doe-eyed naïveté gazing at potential suburban bliss. Everyone is taking part in a fitting for a wedding dress, a succession to ordinary life. One of the men (played by co-writer and producer Kim Henkel) picks up on the vibe the dress sends and confesses he hates what it symbolizes. It's a betrayal of their lifestyle. In response, he drives the car with the plexiglass bubble out to a field and destroys it with an ax. The lie of their safety has been exposed and he reacts violently, setting fire to the automobile filled with all his belongings and clothing inside (in front of a symbolic ant colony, it begs pronouncement)—a naked Adam running from an exploding car, rejecting Eve.

The two central couples bathe and Hooper cuts between them (the one that will get married and the one that rejects marriage) to show that their essential aimlessness remains the same. The wedding takes place on a lawn almost like a concert, but the crowd all wears suits or pantsuits, artifacts of ordinary life surrounding them like the parasitic balloons of the redhead and his dream lover. The parallels are fairly clear—there are two ways out of the commune: marriage or...

Back at the house, the writer who burned the car types while a storm gathers around him, lighting his face with shades of orange, green, and purple before he's drawn to the basement. He grabs his girl and they run down to the eye, pursued by balloons. Their rejection of marriage has only made them prey for the force in the basement. They sit in the odd helmets, transfixed by whatever knowledge is being imparted to them by the eye.

The next scene of bizarre, passive violence could be read a few different ways. One is that no matter how hard you try to stay away from tradition, it will find and devour you. The chairs that the eye produces for the hippies to sit on consume the kids and turn them to liquid; it is magically waiting for them in a park being bulldozed to make room for a greater municipality. The chair and helmet-apparatus could symbolize anything—a soul-sapping career path, Vietnam, growing destitution and dereliction when their Eden is foreclosed upon—but it spells the end of their way of life. Hooper's inclusion of the Vietnam footage in *The Song Was Love* suggests someone keenly aware of the machinations of the US government and the many traps laid for young people, but uninterested in an easy answer. His next fiction film would literalize the struggle of the country's innocent to remain alive. Hooper's hippies didn't know how dangerous the world had become while they were indoors, safe from harm. The world had continued to spin and it had gotten meaner.

Through its beautiful abstraction and disturbing visual metaphors, *Eggshells* showed the crumbling resolve of youth resistance from the inside out. It wasn't even necessarily that Vietnam or a violent police force would externally scuttle the dreams of the '60s. The dreamers had never settled on an end goal, so their own lifestyle and shelter consumes them in the end. And because they were never organized, they never presented any real threat to the government (unlike the Black Panther party or the Weathermen). The straight establishment only had to wait until they tore themselves apart and started over as squares.

Hooper's antagonists are essentially political and historical in nature. They're representatives of the kind of American spirit threatened by the new optimism of '60s radicalism. Working class values cemented in post-World War II America couldn't keep up with changing attitudes, population expansion, and a sometimes-violent reaction to conservative designs on the future of the country. The "villain" of *Eggshells* is a house older than the crew of people inhabiting it and the inescapability of bourgeois life planning. If they leave the house, they become ordinary blue-collar Americans. If they stay, they're claimed by an ancient, Lovecraftian force hiding in the basement. That same force, a kind of metaphorical malevolent stand-in for the mistakes made by politicians who developed and deployed nuclear weapons and ensured the seemingly endless Vietnam War, is the secret villain of every Hooper film. The antiquated, violent ideas that were once an accepted way of life stand in stark contrast to the lifestyle of Hooper's peer group. The emerging new class couldn't control or escape the tradition of masculine violence and certainty that possesses his human villains and/or the objects that come to have a hold on his hapless heroes. Hooper envisioned an America perpetually haunted by its past.

The world that Hooper's characters inhabit has finite dimensions and no permanent shelter. The ghosts of Eisenhower's America strut around reclaiming land that was never theirs to begin with. Hooper watched firsthand as hope and love were abandoned over and over again and the world got crueler and smaller during the Nixon presidency and again during the Reagan and Bush years. Which may partly explain why Hooper turned to harsher material to explore the era's roiling tides. Hooper may never have experimented as openly as he did in *Eggshells* ever again, but he remained a florid, bold stylist, a sort of foil to the tightly coiled craft of John Carpenter (whose career started with the similarly weed and claustrophobia inspired *Dark Star*). Hooper did, however, beat Carpenter to the punch in creating a film that all of America knows by name: *The Texas Chain Saw Massacre.*

Peter Paul and Mary: The Song Is Love (1971)

Hooper's early documentaries were straight-forward delivery systems of sights and sounds, if their *incident* was a little more difficult to describe. As *Down Friday Street* was *about* a street in Texas but was more than that a kind of cinematic guitar solo, *The Song was Love* is *about* the celebrated folk trio Peter, Paul and Mary but it's a little harder to describe the cumulative effect of its images and sounds. There's a little biographical information about the band but largely he was out to capture their essence by filming them in performance, at rallies, in staged interviews, and alone with each other. It's a tiny thing but the group does reveal itself in the hour Hooper invites us to spend with them.

Hooper's allegiance to the spirit and letter of the folk movement never waned, even if his tastes evolved. He was one of the few directors who listened to the currents of music, who never needed to be told what was hip. When not commissioning lush orchestral work from the likes of Henry Mancini, he rode the waves of industrial metal, post-punk, and new wave. Hooper's musical choices occasionally pinion the movies to their respective moments (Billy Corgan's metal music for *Dance of the Dead* and the cheaper synth scores for some of his '90s work have aged equally awkwardly) but his selections were never because he strained to pick what he imagined was cool. He knew what music defined a moment, and more importantly what fit the tone of his pieces and their implications. All this to say it may in hindsight seem strange that a man known for his work making gory horror ever worked with harmonizing folkies Peter, Paul and Mary, but they have much in common from an ideological perspective. Indeed the trio allowed Hooper to make a number of political points in a more naked and obvious fashion than he frequently allowed himself to in his fiction.

The Song Is Love would be the last feature film Tobe Hooper made before he became an internationally known filmmaker, as famous as he was infamous. There's just such tidy and elegant irony to the fact that the last film he directed before making a movie as violent and horrifying and deliberately grotesque as *The Texas Chain Saw Massacre* was a documentary about the cherubic folk act Peter, Paul, and Mary, practically a synecdoche for the feel-good folk revival of the '60s. *The Song is Love* is also the final film Hooper got to make that relies on documentary tactics—handheld camera, ironic juxtapositions of footage, street scenes, loose montage—and gets near to avant-garde. Hooper never fully lost his yen for the experimental, but it was a testament to his ambition and respect for studio filmmaking that the minute he was able to afford a studio lighting setup and camera crew, he never ever did less. He loved the old-school feel of classic movies and even when making thankless work for television in the '90s for no money, he'd always do the most professional job imaginable. Hooper's work frequently rockets in relative quality but he never stopped caring about the work. Working for his lowest budget, he still directed like he was Billy Wilder in the 1950s.

The Song is Love opens with footage of people on the street as the folk trio, Peter Yarrow, Paul Stookey, and Mary Travers sing their first song. It's a brief exegesis on the function and form of socialist art—the music, the people the music is for and about. Hooper's street scenes, handheld camera whooshing around city streets and parks clogged with people of many races, ages, and types, are wonderfully disorienting. Years later Andrzej Żuławski does the same thing as he narrates the missing passages of his sci-fi epic *On The Silver Globe*, showing the people of modern Poland, the people who would have been impacted by the political crisis his movie ostensibly dramatized. By showing the people that the folkies' art was designed to bolster and radicalize, they perform the most basic humanizing purpose of film. Hooper takes the theoretical purpose and impact of Peter, Paul and Mary's music and melds it with real people. Hooper even films a goodly sum of the footage of their performance from a low angle just beneath the stage, as if he too were just an audience member.

Throughout Hooper slyly places himself in our shoes, seeing what we would see, unifying spectators, which is what their music was designed to do. He'll later interview Stookey in a rowboat, one of the most canny POV choices in Hooper's early career—literally stuck with this man rowing and interviewing him. There's a lot going on in the scene. Stookey talks about how when you pay too much attention to the music industry and its current, that becomes your life and that becomes your art, and that's not what the point of folk music is. He wants the real essence of life to pervade the music, just as Hooper cannily films him doing actual physical labor by having him row the boat to give the illusion of work, equating art with labor. To prove his point Stookey puts his hand in the lake and throws water in the camera, and Hooper lets it sit on the lens until the guitarist offers him his sweater to clean the moisture off by hand. Art in genuine conversation with art without losing the thread, without becoming intolerable or removed.

Hooper cuts to a press conference Travers gives somewhere near the stage, relishing in placing her surrounded by the anxiously listening figures here to interview her. It has a similar quality to the footage of the student union meetings that open Michelangelo Antonioni's *Zabriskie Point*, another landmark counterculture text, though a more radical, abstract, and violent one. Hooper and Antonioni both seem interested in the business of living lives in the shape of revolutionary ideas while embedded a deeply corrupt capitalist organization—in *Zabriskie Point*, a young radical daydreams a dozen mansions exploding while Pink Floyd plays in the background. Hooper has a slightly more serene design in mind. He cuts from Travers discussing her bandmates to a shot of Stookey in the green room reading a book and smoking a cigarette while Travers whistles and sings behind him, a picture of beatific calm. The trio then starts to rehearse and plan. Hooper emphasizes their ordinariness, their little neurotic tics, senses of humor, and the way they plan out their set; he keeps them human so that when they seem like stars later we remember their humanity, as when Hooper cuts seamlessly from the rehearsal of "The First Time Ever I Saw Your Face" to the group playing it on stage.

Hooper frames Travers during the performances as close to the glow of stage lights as possible, lens flares and spots illuminating her magnificently. He's fascinated by the potential for lighting to qualify and change the nature of his portrait photography, as he is by its capability to suggest the otherworldly in his fiction. Just like the water on the lens it's a way to make the audience aware of a camera's practical function, the way a camera is like a paintbrush, a tool for making art wielded by a person. Hooper never lost touch with the purpose of his art. Years later he'd direct a two-part pilot for a conspiracy theory alternate history TV show called *Dark Skies* set at the start of the folk movement, closing the chapter satisfactorily on his own place inside the modern protest art movement in America. He always tried to use his movies to awaken people to their place in systems, to the way they're being robbed and lied to and controlled. In essence he became like Bob Dylan or Woody Guthrie as much as he was like Orson Welles: people who simply wanted to make art that changed people's minds lost in great, hungry systems out to rob them of their individuality.

Hooper cuts to a protest in the street in Memphis, Tennessee, letting his camera linger on the faces of black protestors before landing on Yarrow helping light someone's cigarette with his. The police are nearby and the press assembled watch anxiously as hostility is threatened. Hooper gives over several minutes to watching the assembled crowd sing "We Shall Overcome," proving the voice of every person is as important to Hooper's cinema. Yarrow is here to sing protest songs with them and sure enough the camera finds him singing "Blowing in the Wind" in his suit while the crowd claps along. Hooper then starts editing in footage of the assembled mass marching together, which includes Yarrow holding a little girl's hand in the crowd. Hooper cuts to yet another protest where all three members march before they lead the thousands in a sing along of "Give Peace a Chance," complete with a sea of swaying arms.

In another assembly Yarrow tries to explain that the revolution will involve everybody, there's no way to opt out of putting your body on the line if you believe in change. Hooper makes this literal in the next number, the showstopping closing number, "Great Mandala." Hooper shoots as much in tight close-ups to ratchet the intensity as he brings in images of soldiers in Vietnam overtop of their faces, the peacenik image having been slowly dropped for the idea of these three as real cultural workers concerned about the future of this country. The song's final passage, in which they sing "kill the traitor" over and over, is haunting. He follows it up with the image of the concert hall empty of its patrons—a world of ghosts killed by war.

It was Hooper's last peaceful plea for reason and understanding, a final warning that if we do nothing, we'll be destroyed. And if we had any questions about how that destruction might come about, well he had the answer for that, too—*The Texas Chain Saw Massacre*, five of the most evocative and shudder-inducing words in the American canon. *The Song Is Love* is one of the most interesting looks at the spirit of revolution of the time and how fundamentally ill-equipped it was to deal with the power structures they were combating with gesture and protest. The ideas here are all strongly enunciated, but the problem is simply that they were fighting a war with songs. If American evil wanted to take your life, nothing, certainly not peaceful protest, would stop it.

Scout Tafoya

The Texas Chain Saw Massacre (1974)

The Texas Chain Saw Massacre, which is about five kids who are stalked and mutilated by a family of serial murderers, was a sort of lightning rod for post-'60s paranoia, like a lot of Hooper's art. Its images are shot through with signifiers and symbols that Americans probably recognized without quite being able to specify the origin. Like Wes Craven's rape revenge movie *Last House On The Left* (a low budget shocker that played just as dirty), it was a refraction of every nasty thing nagging away in the back of the American unconscious: Vietnam, Charles Manson, Kent State, Ed Gein... Hooper took the major symbols and ideas that had become the waking nightmares of a nation, broadcast night after night on television and making their way into an increasingly bleak national cinema, and put them in a blender. Its claims to reality are, of course, nonsense, but the feeling of mistrust, fear, and hopelessness it produces is no joke. What the film is actually based on is Hooper's realization that Americans could imagine all of this to be true in the early '70s and he plays his audience like a violin.

Even just by calling the film something so vivid, he's ensured that an audience will have done half of the work already. It's why the film's gore quotient could remain so low. As in the famous shower sequence in Alfred Hitchcock's *Psycho* (1960), we're prepared for the worst and imagine things we haven't seen. With the exception of the shot of Leatherface's leg in the film's final minutes, we never see chain saws burning through flesh. But it's more than easy to conjure a mental close-up based on the violent insanity we've been privy to. Which isn't to say that the film is as down and dirty as its milieu and subject matter suggest. It's one of Hooper's most precise feats as a director. The blueprints for his career as a studio-bound craftsman are drawn here. He relies on carefully orchestrated dolly shots, confident editing strategies, and remarkable production design. It's an incredibly upsetting work, but Hooper constructs his nightmare daytrip with as sure a hand as Orson Welles created *The Magnificent Ambersons* (1943), itself a tale of incompatible family units in conflict while progress renders their ways of life obsolete.

Texas Chain Saw is supposedly rooted in the life and behavior of Ed Gein, the Butcher of Plainfield who killed several women and robbed the graves of even more, constructing furniture out of their remains. It also recalls at times the crimes of Charles Manson, a failed folk musician who'd sent his drugged-up followers to murder a record producer, which they tried to blame on Black nationalists. This became the crime of the century as it was revealed that Manson had brainwashed his homeless charges into the crimes by telling them a race war was on the horizon. The murders made "hippies" into a national boogeyman. *Chain Saw* has a character (Edwin Neal's Hitchhiker) who seems to have been chosen for his superficial resemblance to the deranged Manson, and the characters all look like they could have sprung out of the Manson commune, Spahn Ranch, a former movie set in California. But more than taking cues from any real events, *Texas Chain Saw* implicitly mocks the structure of both Joseph Conrad's *Heart of Darkness* and explicitly Flannery O'Connor's *A Good Man Is Hard To Find*. From the former, there's an inexorable journey towards a small regressive colonial state fueled run by a man who still believes in empire-building and exceptionalism, who has brainwashed his followers into committing violent acts on his behalf. From the latter, there's a family road trip interrupted by car troubles and a psychopath that ends with a pile of corpses. (There's even a pit stop for barbecue!) *Texas Chain Saw* is what happens after the bubble from *Eggshells* bursts and commune kids venture out into the nasty world.

After an über-portentous opening narration (read by a pre-fame John Larroquette), we're treated to some of the most iconic opening credits in history. Tobe Hooper (whose work here is one of three times he would compose the music for his own films, along with *Eaten Alive* and *The Texas Chainsaw Massacre 2*) and fellow composer Wayne Bell's violin scraping accompanies the flash of a camera taking Polaroid pictures of a barely glimpsed foul deed. Someone's robbing graves. The fiddle scraping sound is perfect because it sounds like every horrible thing you can imagine. Bones being twisted, cellar doors creaking open, skin being torn, eerie smiles slowly creeping up faces, the violins in *Psycho* during Marion Crane's fateful shower. It's profoundly evocative and sets the stage for the horrifying things to come better than the snapshots of the yellowing fingers and the teeth of the dead.

The location is evidently a fictional place called Muerto (in English "Death") County, and we quickly learn it's been hit by serial grave disturbers. Hooper and cinematographer Daniel Pearl's first proper image is a slow dolly back from the bodies that have been pulled from their resting places and posed as if one was giving the other a piggyback ride. The air is yellow and full of steam and the image is as beautiful as it is nauseating.

After a credits sequence that contains solarized footage of what look like volcanic eruptions of sunspots, we see the result of the amazing heat: an armadillo dropped dead under the yellow sun by the side of the road. Our heroes drive by in a big green van. They all seem familiar types from the commune in *Eggshells* (Allan Danziger actually was, playing van driver Jerry)... all except highly-strung Franklin (Paul A. Partain), confined to a wheelchair and not riding the same good vibes as the rest of the kids in the van. Along with Jerry and Franklin, there's Franklin's sister Sally (Marilyn Burns, who'd later appear in Hooper's *Eaten Alive* as well as playing Linda Kasabian in *Helter Skelter*, strengthening this film's connection to the Manson Family), Kirk (William Vail, who'd work for Hooper again in *Poltergeist* before becoming a professional set decorator), and Pam (Teri McMinn, who basically retired from acting after this film). During a lovely dolly shot, Kirk lays out some boards so that Franklin can exit the van and pee into a coffee can. A passing truck scares him and he rolls down the hill. This is the first of many embarrassments and mortifications poor Franklin will suffer.

Pam reads from a book about zodiac signs while they drive. The unforced, naturalistic, overlapping dialogue has the same docu-realistic feel as the commune scenes in *Eggshells*. When they arrive at their destination (a graveyard), Hooper and editors J. Larry Carroll and Sallye Richardson overwhelm the audience with information. Drunks passed out on the ground, a dolly in on Franklin in the van, Sally walking towards her grandfather's grave—their ostensible purpose here is to make sure it wasn't among those disturbed. Hooper's documentary roots dictate a lot of how we receive visual information. He wants these events to hit with real force, giving us a panoramic view of the weird scene. When Sally's voice appears on the soundtrack, clearly back in the van, it's a comfort to be out of the cemetery, but it's no relief. The van passes a cattle farm and Hooper and Bell give us a quick cacophonous montage of the sweltering, sad-looking bovines. Franklin's explanation of how to best kill a cow does nothing to comfort the nerves of the weary travelers.

"Well I think we just picked up Dracula," says a nonplussed Franklin.

The Hitchhiker the kids pick up looks like Charlie Manson with heatstroke: a bloodred stain running down his face. Edwin Neal, playing the Hitchhiker, looks like a sketch artist's rendering of Manson come to life. Hooper and Pearl frame him in a medium close-up from below, placing the audience far too close to him. Neal was a Vietnam vet and is supposed to have said that filming parts of *Texas Chain Saw* were worse than the combat he saw overseas. This would become something of an unfortunate recurring theme for Hooper.

The Hitchhiker is just as interested as Franklin in the best way to murder cows. He liked the old way better—the new way, with a captive bolt pistol, put people in slaughterhouse killing floors out of a job. This will prove relevant when we learn that the anthropophagous barbecue stand was plainly a response to a failing economy. Better to adapt to a new climate than change your business model or look for a new trade. Technology pushes the cattle workers (who could just as easily have been steel mill workers or coal miners were the film set elsewhere) out of a job and their response is to dig in and use the Americans who represent the changing landscape as food, a more literal interpretation of Hooper's cannibalistic America than the one in *Eggshells*.

There's a little of Gein's story in the frustrated economics of *Texas Chain Saw*. According to Moira Martingale's *Cannibal Killers: The History of Impossible Murders*, Gein's house was also stuck in the past: "As if stuck in a time-warp, it appeared to have been untouched since the death of Gein's mother twelve years previously." The family in *Chain Saw* is developmentally trapped in more prosperous times. On top of all the remains of their victims fed into their barbecue business, they've also kept the moldering (but still living) body of the former patriarch in the attic. No part of the family's former glory can be forgotten or the insanity would come to a screeching halt. Not only did the family hang onto a bygone era through their psychopathic pragmatism, they also held onto the people who thrived in that bygone era.

This part of Texas, a distant memory from Sally and Franklin's childhood, is not used to their kind. It's a hardscrabble life where people like this lunatic walk around in hundred degree heat and derelicts drink themselves into a stupor down at the cemetery. Life isn't kind anymore and these kids never learned that lesson of keeping to themselves. Muerto County will prove to be their Vietnam and the Hitchhiker the welcoming committee.

The Hitchhiker wears out his welcome quickly, cutting himself with Franklin's pocket knife, then cutting Franklin for good measure after playing a weird trick with a photograph and some gun powder. The trouble is naturally economic in nature. The Hitch-hiker takes a picture of Franklin and then asks for money for it. Franklin refuses to pay. The old way of supporting himself—the slaughterhouse—is gone, and Franklin is between him and his daily pay. He has the last laugh, rubbing his bloody arm on the side of the van as they abandon him in the hot sun.

"That's the last goddamned hitchhiker I ever pick up," says Jerry.

He's not wrong.

"Listen to Franklin's horoscope," offers Pam. "Travel difficulties, long range plans, upsetting persons around you could make this a disturbing and unpredictable day."

The mystical prediction will come true even as the other trappings of their lifestyle work against them. Sally's horoscope is also apt: "There are moments when we cannot believe that what is happening is really true. Pinch yourself and you may find out that it is."

There's an in-scene vignette as poignant as anything in James Joyce when the kids stop at the gas station run by the old man (Jim Siedow). The gas station window washer (Robert Courtin, whose forehead is bulbous and red, one laceless boot stretched out in antsy discomfort) stares at the sun in the black sky. Hooper and Bell's sound design takes a dive into the guts of a piano. This poor man's world is just as in thrall to the heavens as the kids and their ominous zodiac warnings. During the scene, there's a pitch-black joke right out of a silent comedy throughout the conversation with the old man. The window-washer will walk behind him, bucket in tow, as if restarting his job whenever his boss approaches the car. This is part and parcel with the ingrown habits of Hooper's outdated working class. The worker, baked by the sun to the point of listless instinct, exists to perform the same menial task for his overseer.

The sign above the gas station (just below the perfectly placed Coca-Cola logo) reads "We Slaughter Barbecue." Siedow, the man who owns it, looks like a Kentucky-fried Richard Nixon to go with the not-quite Charles

Manson look of the Hitchhiker. Franklin asks about his grandfather's house, a place he and Sally visited in their youth, now bequeathed to their father. The man warns them, with a crooked smile on his face, to stay away.

Hooper's camera reverts to *Eggshells*-style disorienting space exploration as the kids, unbeknownst to them, seal their fate. His camera stations itself at a low angle of the girls by the vending machine, dollies outside the gas station, and spins handheld in the van just as in the Plexiglas bubble car, cutting between all of the characters. The sound design is at an even keel throughout. He's mapping every inch of the location, trying to slow down time and capture every banal detail of the moment when they decide to forge ahead to the old house anyway. It's almost modernist, finding importance in the sounds and behavior of people in moments that prove accidentally fortuitous. The scene has Hooper's documentary rhythm, allowing us insight into every minute detail at the gas station.

"I bet that's some of that guy's blood," muses Franklin, considering his knife.

Hooper and Pearl dolly with the van, rendering it almost animalistic in its dumb progress towards the unknown, watching it recede down the road like one of Franklin's cows towards the slaughterhouse.

The purpose with which Hooper frames the van arriving at the decrepit old manor is stunning. The soundtrack goes dark, rumbling with menacing noise like one of Red Krayola's freak-outs. The film's psychedelic credentials are in order, even if the film is less noisily experimental than *Eggshells*. The opening explosions and solar flares could adorn a Blue Mountain Eagle album cover. Even the bold title feels like the title of a forgotten psych-rock album like Blues Magoos' *Electric Comic Book*, Jefferson Airplane's *Surrealistic Pillow*, or Joe Byrd and the Field Hippies' *The American Metaphysical Circus*. It has a compositional similarity to a lot of psych songs. Listen to Blue Cheer's cover of "Summertime Blues" or Josefus' cover of "Gimme Shelter." They maintain the structure of straightforward rock songs, but in the margins are darker, thinner guitar tones prone to screaming just outside the song's key, big, hollow-sounding drums moving at erratic rhythmic patterns, and a sweaty humanity in the wailing vocals.

Chain Saw looks at first like a film about kids having a bad day before the same atonal, erratically paced weirdness creeps in, warping the ordinary. Hooper's grammar is a melding of elements that operates in the same

31

fashion: his traditional technique—the smooth dolly shots, clean, patient composition and pacing—is slowly melted by his more experimental elements—the documentary-inspired editing, the abrasive sound design, the black humor—until it no longer resembles the normalcy of its quiet moments. Hooper twists conventional filmmaking like the knob on an effects pedal. His camera's movement through tall grass observing the exodus from the van is like the rhythm section on a Can or Ant Trip Ceremony album, carrying the film along in deceptively smooth fashion.

Franklin and Sally's grandfather's house is the inverse of the property across the yard occupied by the old man and his family. It's gone to pieces, ravaged by time and abandonment. It's the honest representation of what's happened to the minds of the old man, the Hitchhiker, and Leatherface (Gunnar Hansen), who have also been abandoned in this part of Texas. In the corner of one bedroom, Kirk finds an orgy of daddy longlegs spiders, clacking unnaturally while he stares in disgust. After the psychologically presentational scene of the spiders, its back to handheld naturalism as Sally discusses the wallpaper in her childhood room. The juxtaposition of the two is Hooper's psych-rock milieu in miniature: a freak-out, then a return to the ordinary. Franklin, confined to the wheelchair, can't take part in the fun the rest of the gang is having. Their laughter echoes through the house, taunting him. Feeling sorry for himself, he offers Pam and Kirk directions to the swimming hole he remembers from childhood... just before he notices the bones hung from the doorframe and the odd sculpture made from animal remains someone has left in the house. The lunatics across the yard have infected this place too.

The water hole is dried up, like all other signs of life, but Kirk hears a motor, which means fuel, which means gassing up the van to leave. Hooper and Pearl mess with point of view ever so subtly on the walk to the house across the yard. First, we're behind Pam and Kirk, dollying as they walk, the sun glaring down at the lens turning the rest of the frame a dull orange. Then the camera moves through some brush, as if taking on the kids' perspective. The *tone* of this shot is undoubtedly frightening/frightened, which isn't an easy thing to get right in a seconds-long shot without the aid of the perfectly insistent and "ordinary" sound design.

Everything about the property screams "unusual." There are art pieces made of old objects hung from trees, old cars under a tarp, and a generator supplying power to the property. Pearl's camera swivels and zooms, revealing the dimensions of the yard and its strange design by remaining calmly demonstrative. The camera comes to a halt on Pam, alone on the porch while Kirk knocks on the door to ask for help, framed through the chains of a lonely but recently retouched swing. Kirk's knocking dislodges a tooth stuck somewhere in the wood in the front of the house. He uses it to scare Pam to the swing. Kirk knocks again and the door slides open. The shot of Kirk in the doorway is gorgeous. The hazy, rough white light of the outdoors framing him in the middle of the room. The staircase is made of dark wood glowing blue thanks to the light streaming in the open door. The walls on the opposite side of the frame are dull white and covered in pelts. It's just normal enough to invite Kirk inside when he hears something like the squealing of a pig.

He trips up a little homemade ramp and into the frame steps a burly man in a pink shirt, a dirty, off-yellow apron, a blue tie, and a mask made out of a cured human face. The following grotesque confrontation is a triumph of sound design: a grimy mix of realism and expressionism. There's a sickeningly moist crunching sound as the man hits Kirk in the head with a sledgehammer—the Hitchhiker's cow story echoing faintly in the back of the viewer's mind—and then Kirk's legs start kicking as he bleeds from the head. Recognizing the nervous movement of the feet, the burly attacker hits him again, drags him inside the room, and slams shut a steel door. At which point, a low rumbling organ takes over the soundtrack.

Pam hears the sounds and approaches. Pearl's camera dollies under the swing and behind her while the house dwarfs her like a monster; Pam walks towards it, but it looks like she's been pulled inside. She doesn't realize she's about to feed herself to it. The opulence of the house is surreal and unnatural. All the accumulated objects of passersby, like tributes to a king, surrounded by a desert of poverty and a sun that drives the drunken lower class to madness. Inside the labyrinth of abandoned cars and possessions is a minotaur named Leatherface. His living room resembles descriptions of Gein's house when the police finally stopped him (though, if anything, Leatherface was far less creative than his real-life inspiration). There are feathers all over the floor, presumably thanks to the chicken living in a cage suspended from the ceiling. Bones and teeth litter the floor, hang from the ceiling, and adorn the furniture in ritualistic design. It's a grizzly scene that

Pam flees as quickly as she can, but the man in the mask catches her, brings her inside, and hangs her on a meat hook. Pam's screams are troublingly believable. She fights to dislodge herself while Leatherface fires up a yellow chain saw and begins dismembering Kirk right in front of her.

The ways in which *the Texas Chain Saw Massacre* seems to comment on the Vietnam War, and indeed feels like a metaphorical reenactment of the American invasion of Vietnam, don't feel labored or overdrawn and could well be accidental, but the parallels are there and, to quote Sally, "everything means something, I guess." Siedow, with his Nixonian looks and uncomfortable attempts at charm, oversees a system where innocent people are sent to uncharted territory to be slaughtered in the most brutal fashion imaginable. Pam, and later Sally, will have their concept of humanity shattered by the sudden intrusion of a man wearing his victims like a fashion accessory, not dissimilar to stories of ear necklaces from the frontlines of the war. The ideological identity of the Vietcong (and, for that matter, Americans during the Revolutionary War) was intractable. The Vietcong had an identity that no amount of American intervention was going to change. The surrender-or-die mentality is in evidence in Muerto County: the family is "dug in too deep" to quote Michael Herr's narration in Vietnam ur-text *Apocalypse Now*. Leatherface, possessing the intelligence of a child, doesn't understand anything about human politics, let alone the concept that he'd need to change his lifestyle to fit a different economic climate.

Franklin is losing it back at his grandfather's house, whining and complaining to his sister. Jerry, the last cool head in the group, sets off towards the swimming hole to find Pam and Kirk. With the sun going down, turning the landscape a lovely shade of orange, Jerry arrives at Leatherface's house and is drawn in by weird sounds, just like Kirk was. He gets further than either of his friends, discovering a still-kicking Pam in a big freezer. He has time for one high-pitched scream between Pam leaping out of the freezer and Leatherface clubbing him with the big hammer. Leatherface's reaction to his own work is to run and check the window for more visitors. He looks guilty, nervous, and harried, yet completely oblivious to what he did on any other scale except the one devised in this private corner of the county. His nervous eyes and body language have something of King Kong about them. Specifically, after the giant ape kills a dinosaur midway through the 1933 movie and moves its mouth curiously, considering its mortality. Leatherface only has the vaguest idea how the world works and where he fits into it. He's more naïve than his victims, even if he's been sculpted into a killer by his family and grim circumstance.

Franklin and Sally, bickering like cats, get tired of waiting for Jerry and walk into the woods to find him. Pearl and Hooper rely on nothing but real light, first from the van's headlamps, then from a flashlight, making us feel just as lost as the characters. The camera dollies through the woods, keeping pace with the siblings as they push onwards into the dark. Sally struggles mightily with Franklin's wheelchair, making him whine with more intensity. The atmosphere is relentlessly downbeat during these scenes, making them feel considerably longer than they are. Hooper's tonal orchestration is masterful. There are few movies with this high a dose of pathos, pity, and repulsion towards its characters. Franklin stops Sally just in time to announce Leatherface's presence with the flashlight and a loud buzz. Exit pursued by the man with the chain saw.

After a few near misses with the chain saw in the woods, she finds Leatherface's house. The only place she can think to hide is the attic, where grandpa (John Dugan) and the bones of grandma are kept. The parallel editing here is superb, showing her progress and Leatherface trying to break into his own house with the chain saw. She decides to jump out a window when he breaks in and falls two stories to the ground, the sound design making us feel every scrape and bump on her way down. The faintest hint of music finally creeps onto the soundtrack: a weird mix of delayed, distorted guitar and clanking percussion. Pearl's lenses make the distance between Sally and Leatherface seem a matter of inches in the dark. Sally, running for her life, has become a twisted fairy tale character, like Jennifer Jones in Powell and Pressburger's subtextually loaded *Gone To Earth,* about a woman who refuses to join the society emerging around her feral life.

Sally reaches temporary safety in the old man's barbecue stand, but it's only minutes before she understands how deeply doomed she is. He's the brains of the operation, the Colonel Kurtz of Muerto County. When he promises to go pull his truck around to drive her to safety, he returns with a straightjacket. A newsreader on the radio describes the mutilated corpses from the cemetery just as Sally looks into the old man's furnace and sees body parts slow roasting. He also mentions 98% humidity, as if we needed a reminder.

With the truck's windows in center frame, Pearl dollies in as the old man puts a bound Sally in the shotgun seat, then dollies back out again as he walks around to the driver's side, stopping when he remembers he needs to lock up and turn the lights out, a realistic touch. "Cost of electricity enough to drive a man out of business," the old man claims. Money is his only concern, preserving his privilege.

He sees the first of his kids, the Hitchhiker, when he makes the driveway. He beats the Hitchhiker with a broken broomstick, framed in the eerie blue light of the truck's headlights. Shots like these illustrate the care and patience that Hooper took in his craft, even shooting in the intense heat. He knew every image was an opportunity to do something memorable. Hooper's chronicling of the old man capturing Sally and berating his son has the deranged intensity of film noir: patient and purposeful as things spin further out of control. Appropriately, his dusty diction in these passages would resurface in neo-noir like The Coen Brothers' *Blood Simple* and John Dahl's *Red Rock West*, films that flirt with bloody chaos but remain cool on the outside.

"Look what your brother did to the door!" The old man's gurgling cry rings out.

When we get back to the house, Hooper uses the space of the house and the many accidental frames created by doorways to create memorably warped tableaux, lit dimly with weak lamps. There's a truly lovely zoom and dolly as Leatherface and the Hitchhiker bring Grandpa into the dining room, bones on strings gliding gently by the frame. Hooper's spatial mapping through montage, movement, and framing is superb. Sally passes out after the Hitchhiker cuts her finger so Grandpa, a pretty excellent piece of makeup/set design himself, can suck her blood like a desiccated vampire, the first of Hooper's many vampire figures. She wakes up just in time for dinner.

J. Larry Carroll and Sallye Richardson indulge Hooper's psychedelia-tinged experimentation during dinner. You could say that the climax of the film is one of rising grammatical indulgence, remaining patient and coherent until finally letting loose a full-on free-form freak-out a la *Eggshells*. Sally, tied to a literal *arm*chair (right out of the accounts of Gein's furniture collection), is tormented mercilessly by the cackling, howling family. Leatherface, painted up like his best approximation of a woman, and the Hitchhiker tease her and press themselves as close to her face as they can. Leatherface's female presentation doesn't feel like a political choice, but rather his attempting to replace the absent female touch in the house and specifically around the table. His ever-present apron also suggests a working mother from another era simply trying to get food on the table. The grandmother moldering in the attic and the absence of a mother figure in the all-male household says that they desperately miss a female touch. The film critic Willow Maclay describes this scene as being "Like Norman Rockwell eviscerated." The edit jumps between several shots of Sally writhing in agony and the faces of her tormentors. Pearl zooms in and out, giving us close-ups of Sally's deep green eyes blinking furiously, unable to fathom what's happening. The soundtrack cranks up the scraping noise from the opening grave-robbing sequence. Sally's horoscope drifts to mind: she'd probably pinch herself, if only her hands weren't bound.

The subject turns to killing Sally, and the old man admits that the killing the household does is out of a misbegotten sense of value.

"Some things you have to do...don't mean you have to like it."

He'd rather allow his maniac sons to murder people than give up his way of life. They agree to give Grandpa the honors of killing Sally. After all, he was once a prize cattle killer from the days of killing floors staffed by men with hammers. He's the metaphorically incestuous, fallow remains of a proudly xenophobic working class, decaying American royalty, and he can no longer hold the hammer, let alone hit Sally with it. Sally escapes when the Hitchhiker tries to take the hammer and finish the job himself. She flies out the nearest window once again, and the grey dawn light outside feels almost alien after the horrors of the nighttime.

Bloodied and wide-eyed with terror, Sally limps to the road, Leatherface and the Hitchhiker close behind. A passing truck driver grants Sally mercy, first by mowing the Hitchhiker down, then by throwing a wrench at Leatherface, which cues up the sickening insert of the saw chewing up his flesh through his pant leg. He limps after his quarry, who narrowly escapes in a passing pick-up as the sun rises over the road. Leatherface dances around angrily, chain saw in hand, enshrouded in lens flare.

The images of the Hitchhiker cutting Sally's back to ribbons with a straight razor have the rawness of a snuff film, all the more impressive considering how clearly and simply Hooper frames the action. He's brought us into his movie, and its reality is too convincing to write off safely as fictional. *Chain Saw* nearly orchestrates a case of Stendhal Syndrome, the sense of being subsumed or stranded literally in a work of art, in the viewer. Its excellent, understated special effects, mean-spirited realism, downbeat tone, escalating insanity, and, more than anything, the look in Marilyn Burns' eyes as she fails to make sense of this turn of events are too overpowering to compartmentalize as "just a movie."

Hooper's direction and the work done by his postproduction team are elegant and finely tuned. There's a continuity of movement and action that sets it apart from the tide of both character studies and horror movies from around that time. A random sampling of either shows just how raw and strange it must have been to watch for the first time in 1974, compared to even something as good as *Black Christmas* (Bob Clark's Canadian proto-slasher film). While the atmosphere is thicker in a more deliberately decadent way, it has nothing on Hooper's honestly earned dread and single-minded purpose. Other notable American breakthroughs that year—Steven Spielberg's *The Sugarland Express,* Michael Cimino's *Thunderbolt and Lightfoot,* John Waters' *Female Trouble,* Francis Ford Coppola's *The Godfather II* and *The Conversation,* and Roman Polanski's *Chinatown*—have nothing much in common with Hooper from a tonal or craft standpoint. No one had his mix of fearlessness, cohesive, chaotic ugliness, and ambitious experimentation mixed with calm classicism. In fact, the only film that year to meld sweaty realism with naked presentational excesses with quite the same fervor might be Robert Bresson's *Lancelot Du Lac,* a film that shares with *Texas Chain Saw* a surfeit of blood and little else. *Texas Chain Saw* is now seen as one of the great works of American art, but Hooper's reputation as an artist more or less stops with it, as if he was never this invested or careful again. This is not true. He'd prove over and over and over again that his artistic life only really *started* with *Texas Chain Saw.*

In point of fact, the only film that serves a comparison (as well as a kind of legend for Hooper's later work) is Maya Deren's *At Land,* made in 1946, three years after her watershed Freudian legend *Meshes of the Afternoon.* It might now be useful to explain the entirety of *At Land* because its motifs and emotional logic will come up time and again throughout Hooper's work. *At Land* begins with a brunette (Deren) washing up on a beach, chewed up and spit out by the ocean, it seems. Like Sally, she's a victim of the earth's roiling, uneasy temperament and the people who've dug in. Deren's been brutalized by something, so says the far off look in her eyes, as she gazes at the indifferent sea birds circling overhead. Deren crawls up a nearby fallen tree and, when she lifts herself up to see what's on the other side, finds herself looking down a table of well-dressed white men smoking cigarettes in a banquet hall. This mirrors Sally's being placed in a masculine realm, forced to fight for survival. She will not be the last Hooper heroine who undergoes these trials, and many of them will even have Deren's nest of curly dark hair.

As Deren crawls along the table, she's placed in direct opposition to their looks of disdain and keeps returning, in brief flashes, to the beach, a relatively safe haven. The banquet hall is like the womb spaces Hooper will continue to create in his many movies. Deren tries to crawl out of it like a newborn, dreaming of the natural world outside of it, but the men around her offer no help. Hooper's female characters run furious gauntlets looking for ways out of the male-created womb environment. And, frequently, the final images of his films are of women running down tunnels or hallways, escaping crumbling meccas of male depravity.

Deren finds herself looking at a chessboard at the end of the table, and then drops a piece of the game into a stream back, in reality, on the beach. The chessboard motif also appears throughout Hooper's work, as does the creeping feeling that his characters are playing a game they are not meant to win. When she reclaims the chess piece, Deren finds herself walking on a desolate road (as Sally does when she tries to escape Leatherface's home and family) when a man comes up and speaks to her. The film is silent, so his words are deliberately kept from us. She tries to keep up with him on the road, but he leaves her behind before entering a dilapidated cabin that would feel at home in *Chain Saw*. It holds some clue to her past, but also eerily seems to capture her future: quiet, loneliness and decay.

On the floor lays an old man covered by a sheet like he was a piece of furniture (old men blending in with forbidding environments, orchestrating the fate of women, will appear throughout Hooper's work). She rejects the sight of him and climbs as high into the house as she can, finding herself once more on the beach. She dives onto a rock face (shades of Stretch climbing the treacherous landscape in *Texas Chain Saw 2*) and tries to make her way to safety, buffeted by the hard rocky structure. When she turns around, the rocks have been replaced by wooden scaffolding—set design as shape-shifting villain, which we'll see again in *Texas Chainsaw 2* and *The Mangler*. Deren finally takes off down the beach by herself, transformed by her encounter with unfeeling male presences, their phallic architecture, and gamesmanship.

   The Texas Chain Saw Massacre by virtue of being Hooper's first major movie, was only an introduction to his fetishes and obsessions. His love of Deren and indeed the whole of his bone-deep cinephilia would find richer expression as his budgets grew and he in turn grew more generous to his influences and heroes.

Chapter 2:
White Picket Fences (1976–1982)

If you ever doubt that horror directors have it harder than anyone else in the business, look at the fortunes of Tobe Hooper following *Texas Chain Saw Massacre*. The distributor that purchased the film was a mafia front, so no one involved in the making of the film was properly paid after the film wrapped. Then, while the film made a killing at the box office, Hooper's next offer was a production with even fewer resources. He would be given offers to direct *The Dark* and *Venom*, both of which he walked out on to be replaced by similarly disreputable directors John "Bud" Cardos and Piers Haggard. The truth is that neither *The Dark* (about an alien who murders people with a laser eye) nor *Venom* (a hostage thriller complicated by a poisonous snake) were the right match for Hooper. Both were essentially action films with genre elements and the resulting messes made by his replacements say it was unlikely he would have been able to come away with anything resembling a coherent follow-up to *Chain Saw*. The system as it was had no place for Hooper, an artist who happened to be very good at rewiring horror movies into zeitgeist Rorschach tests. They are loaded with symbols, faces, and gestures that could refer to any number of current events (for instance Jim Siedow's superficial resemblance to Richard Nixon in the *Chain Saw* movies) but are so thoroughly harrowing and grotesque it can be difficult to stop and take notice. *Texas Chain Saw Massacre* and *Eggshells* were films about what it meant to be a kid in America during and directly after the Vietnam War.

Hooper wasn't totally stymied by the less-than-perfect shooting conditions of his next film. He honed his craft and discovered the elements of studio shooting that would come to be his chosen working method. A few years after *Texas Chain Saw Massacre* failed to net the promising career he was owed, Hooper would find himself spending big studio money on lavish design elements. But first, he had to claw his way out of the minor leagues by rehashing elements of his one success.

Eaten Alive (1976)

Joe Ball was a hard-living veteran of the First World War. When he returned from the front lines, he sold bootleg liquor until the end of prohibition. Joe moved back home to Elmendorf, Texas and opened a legal bar called The Sociable Inn. Its star attraction was a hand-dug alligator pit with five of the great reptiles fighting for space. He and the locals would make a game of finding local vermin and tossing them into the pit to watch the ensuing carnage. Joe never had much social grace—reports from neighbors said he was fond of threatening people with a pistol and his waitresses never hung around long, which led the community to speculate that he must have been feeding them to his gators. That part wasn't true but he did murder a goodly number of women and bury them around the county, blackmailing and bullying locals to help dig the graves. When the police came for him, Ball grabbed a gun and shot himself. This meant he never got around to disputing the rumors about feeding barmaids to hungry gators, so his legend grew to the point where they gave him nicknames like The Alligator Man or The Butcher of Elmendorf, just as people called Ed Gein the Butcher of Plainfield.

Tobe Hooper's second horror film *Eaten Alive* bears only the faintest resemblance to the story of Ball but is nevertheless the story of a deranged hotelier who feeds his guests to his pet alligator. *Texas Chain Saw Massacre* didn't have *much* to do with Ed Gein either, so there's at least a kind of symmetry to the two films' backstories. The production similarities include a soundtrack by Hooper and Wayne Bell, and then promptly end. The rumors fly fast and furious about this one, including Hooper squabbling with his producers to the point that he would occasionally show himself off the Melrose Avenue studio and hand the reigns to director of photography Robert Caramico (who also shot exploitation anti-classics like *Spawn of the Slithis*, *The Happy Hooker Goes To Washington*, and *Blackenstein*). The film wants for a number of Hooper touchstones like the assured fluid camera work and the purposeful, rhythmic editing, and their absence could be chalked up to fatigue and frustration. Or they could be evidence that Hooper was happy to let the film become a parodic cabaret of the absurd and uncomfortable, but that takes a larger leap of faith.

The simple truth is *Eaten Alive* is nowhere near as good or interesting as *Texas Chain Saw*, and it feels like the kind of film one makes when better opportunities have failed to arrive. The performances aren't attuned to one another, the set is not as evocative or carefully designed, the music isn't as memorable, the violence isn't as visceral, and everything feels cheaper even though the budget was higher. It's dirty, sloppy, and mean, but somewhere in the muck is the Hooper touch. Look for it in the confused electronic score he and Bell put together, a woozy, drunken thing. Look for it in the cast, filled with up-and-coming exploitation stars (Marilyn Burns, back for round two, Robert Englund, Janus Blythe, Roberta Collins, and William Finley) and heroes of cult cinema Hooper would have fallen for as a young obsessive (Stuart Whitman, Carolyn Jones, Mel Ferrer, and Neville Brand). Look for it in the overheated, odd behavior of his characters and the obvious, but heavy, production design and art direction. (You could choose to see it in the dearth of subtlety, but that wasn't yet part of Hooper's stock-in-trade, so that could be a red herring.) And more than anything, look for it in everything that the film *isn't*. On paper *Eaten Alive* is "*Texas Chain Saw* in a bayou motel," but in execution, it's a far weirder proposition.

The dramatic and imagistic similarities between this and *Texas Chain Saw* feel like the demands of one of the film's half dozen producers—give us what made so much money last time. Hooper, meanwhile, is not the guy to go to for grimy, low-down exploitation. He's too good, too interested in what his new production reality affords him as an artist. Look again at the film's competition in the grindhouse circuit that year. There were dozens of indie horror efforts: William Girdler's *Grizzly*, Jeff Lieberman's *Squirm*, Charles B. Pierce's *The Town That Dreaded Sundown*, Joel M. Reed's *Blood Sucking Freaks*, Richard Ashe's *Track of the Moon Beast*, Michael Findlay's *Snuff* and Joy N. Houck, Jr.'s *Creature From Black Lake*, all of them orbiting *Eaten Alive's* swampy, murderous milieu. Each of those films has a straightforwardness in their direction that *Eaten Alive* has no interest in achieving.

Eaten Alive's contemporaries are all relatively normal movies, grammatically speaking (with the exception of *Town That Dreaded Sundown*, which has an element of "mockumentary" about it): there are monsters attacking a community dealt with by characters we spend a decent amount of time getting to know. Ordinary setups, rhythm, and compositions are employed and the filmmakers' chief concerns are trying not to let the cheapness of monster suits derail tension. Even the weirder films from the above list like *Blood Sucking Freaks* and *Snuff* are shot and edited in ordinary, cheap ways. The banquets of grotesquerie served up by Reed and Findlay just sit in front of the camera for the viewer to gawk at.

Hooper's film is an entirely different beast. The camera movements all feel too ambitious and wind up confusing for that reason. The crane his camera rides during most of the interior scenes feels like an indulgence he insisted upon because he wanted to make films like his heroes. The character choices are eccentric and he allowed his cast to swing for the fences. It's weird, aimless, theatrical, empty, and barely works as a piece of dramatic narrative filmmaking. But it's also completely singular as a piece of grindhouse trash. It's almost Rainer Werner Fassbinderian in its affectation and contempt for technical realism. Like, for instance, Fassbinder's western *Whity*, it understands what a genre movie is supposed to do, it just doesn't have any interest in behaving that way. In being asked to replicate his only major success, Hooper maintained his integrity by making the film as stylistically contrary to *Chain Saw* in every way except in his willingness to try new things. Where *Chain Saw* is precise and humane in its objective dramatic shape, *Eaten Alive* is all jutting edges, bizarre choices, and obvious fakery. Hooper gave the world *Chain Saw 2.0* without once repeating himself.

"Name's Buck and I'm rarin' to fuck," says a young, weasely Robert Englund, years before he became Freddy Krueger for Wes Craven (who was still directing porn under the pseudonym Abe Snake to make ends meet at this point in time). The location is a brothel that defines "dingy." Buck's ideas are a little too exotic for the girl he paid for, Roberta Collins' Clara.

Collins' once-promising career was in the middle of a slow fade to black that ended in the mid-'80s. She seems drugged, dazed, or both as Clara. Her violent reticence in the face of Buck's demands comes close to rape before the house mistress intervenes. Miss Hattie (Morticia Addams herself, Carolyn Jones, also of the 1950s iterations of *Invasion of the Body Snatchers* and *The House of Wax*, directed by future Hooper actor André De Toth) defuses the situation from beneath a gambler's visor and then shows Clara the door.

The lighting in the house, Hooper's first encounter with a studio setup, is reminiscent of his design for *Eggshells*: deep neon shades of yellow and purple are splashed across the brothel's stairwell over the greens of Hattie and Clara's clothes. The zoom in on Clara speaking to the house maid Ruby (Betty Cole, later of 1978's *The Toolbox Murders*, which Hooper remade in 2004) feels of a piece with his curious camera in *Texas Chain Saw*, but the drama is obvious and old school. Ruby seems like a mammy character right out of a '30s melodrama, offering money to the poor white prostitute who's off to pursue her dreams. At this point, it might be productive to wonder if Hooper had decided to make *Eaten Alive* a kind of Brechtian joke.

Bertolt Brecht, the German playwright, is an important formal forebear to Hooper. Brecht introduced or at least popularized art that spoke directly to the audience and shattered the comfortable façade of the relationship between art and audience. The object talks right to the viewer. Hooper was a director who always gave the impression of knowing the audience was a few inches away from images he created, whether by literalizing the closeness to the TV set in *Poltergeist* knowing a good number of Americans would later watch the film on the same TV or restaging *Psycho*'s shower scene with a plastic knife in *The Funhouse*. He put himself in the shoes of the viewer as often as he asked us to play the voyeur, erasing the safe boundaries the screen usually provides us from fiction.

Eaten Alive is a Brechtian work on a number of levels. There's the casting of faded heartthrobs like Ferrer and Brand as dueling kings of a swamp. There's the obvious falseness of the sets, which were built so the camera could easily move around in them. And then there's that the narrative, which deliberately mangles depression-era stories of women striking out on their own. Here a city girl comes to the swamp to make it big, instead of the other way around, as you'd see in movies made in the early 1930s. And then there's the cuddly farewell Ruby gives Clara as she leaves her life of sex trafficking. Paul Verhoeven tells a variation on that joke twenty years later in 1995's *Showgirls*, a deliberately vulgar riff on depression-era musicals choreographed by Busby Berkeley like 1933's *42nd Street*. In *Showgirls*, exotic dancer Nomi Malone (Elizabeth Berkley) makes it to the big leagues and her old boss (Robert Davi) comes to check out her Vegas showcase and wistfully wonders "It must be weird, not having anybody cum on you." Both *Showgirls* and *Eaten Alive* take classic romantic filmmaking notions and turn them knowingly rapacious and disgusting. They turn the American cinema against Americans. Just look at what happens to poor Clara...

When Clara arrives at this film's version of the Sociable Inn, The Starlight, it becomes immediately clear just how set-bound the production is. Hooper and Caramico are able to capture most of the scenes in awkward, uncertainly staged two-camera setups. *Eaten Alive* behaves like a televised play, and the cardboard sets help solidify this impression.

On the wall of the outside of the inn are ads. One is for Coca-Cola, just like the one above *Texas Chain Saw's* gas station. The light inside puts a shadow on the front door that draws Clara towards it, even as she's frightened—not every hotel has an alligator in the front yard, after all. The owner of the shadow opens the door and steps aside, leaving the doorway mysteriously empty. This is Judd (Neville Brand, a highly decorated World War 2 veteran and character actor with a career that started basically as soon as he was discharged) and it takes about one second in his company to gather that he's lost his mind. He's like a mix of the hitchhiker and the old man from *Chain Saw*. He's got one wooden leg, loves laughing at his own jokes, and recoiling from his own actions. He puts together that Clara is a prostitute from little more than the sight of her, and it sends him into a kind of murderous trance. First, he grabs her violently, then hugs her softly in apology, then tears at her clothes and throws her down the stairs. Hooper and Caramico hadn't figured out the dimensions of the set enough to stage this struggle with any grace, so they sort of hide at the bottom of the stairs and wait for it to end, inserting the occasional, unhelpful close-up. Judd grabs a rake to finish off poor Clara (the electronic soundtrack whizzes to life with each stab of the garden tool) and then throws her off the porch for his gator. We're already miles away from the psychological and social realism of *Chain Saw* and *Eggshells*. The pet monkey caged on the porch says we won't be seeing them anytime soon.

Eaten Alive is a maximalist externalization of Judd's diseased mind. Brand's performance is an unhinged, rusty delight. He sings and talks to himself, wears symbolic broken glasses, and hobbles around, playing a hunched, murderous Igor to his own genial Dr. Frankenstein (another Hooper motif). Caramico's lighting is all overpowering blues, reds, greens, and purples—chosen from the then-developing Hooper swatch book—and it makes us acutely aware that no matter the flimsy façade Judd throws on for his guests, the world is still at war in his mind. Many of the colorful tableaux are *almost* beautiful, but they're haphazardly composed and lack the satisfying geometry of his early work.

A couple, Faye and Roy (Marilyn Burns and William Finley, who'd follow Hooper to *The Funhouse*), arrive at the Starlight with their young daughter, Angie (Kyle Richards). Her dog almost immediately finds his way into the gator pit. Everyone falls about screaming, including the innkeeper, who rushes them inside to deal with their newly traumatized daughter. The scene has all the insanity of the dinner with Grandpa and none of the intensity—it's only twenty minutes into the movie, which is a little early for everyone and everything to go completely bonkers. Roy, recognizing that this isn't the first time he's messed things up, cracks completely, screaming quietly and throwing his hand uselessly at Faye.

The next guests are Clara's father, Harvey (Mel Ferrer) and his other daughter, Libby (Crystin Sinclaire). When they produce a photo of Libby, Judd thinks they're looking to spend the night with one of Miss Hattie's whores, compounding Harvey's worry mightily. They leave just in time for Roy to run downstairs to kill the gator with a shotgun he's been keeping in the trunk—the backstory of miserable, crazy Faye and Roy is left tantalizing unexplained. Judd experiences a PTSD flashback, grabs a scythe, and cuts Roy to pieces, giggling like a fool, before the gator jumps up through the fence on the porch and drags Roy into the murky water. It's a bluntly effective scene, the suddenness of the gator puppet so potent and Finlay's performance so enormous and perfectly pitiable, proving Hooper, even under dire circumstances, hadn't lost his ability to shock. There's maybe even something to the shoddiness of the surroundings allowing us to let our guard down, so that the sight of a cheap plastic alligator jumping into frame and biting a man's neck works better than we expect it to. Judd takes himself down off of his violent high with what looks like Sulfa powder but could just as easily be cocaine.

Faye, unaware that her husband has met a sticky end, draws herself a bath. There's a kind of seedy poetry in this shot as she unhooks her stockings in the oppressive red and purple glow of the room. Judd comes upstairs to wrap her up in a trash bag, bind her hands, and beat her up, allowing Angie, her little girl to run and hide under the porch. "Judd knows...he knows what he knows," Judd mumbles to himself. A good portion of *Eaten Alive* is dedicated to observing Brand talking to himself while his incautiously maintained life crumbles all around him. The script never bothers to wonder how long someone this clearly insane could possibly have kept a functioning motel in a swamp if this is his idea of a normal business day.

Harvey and Libby have sought the help of the sheriff (Stuart Whitman, a perennial sleaze who played second fiddle in the first accidental slasher film, Andrew L. Stone's *The Decks Ran Red*, which shares with *Texas Chain Saw* a critique of libertarian manifest destiny as well as a hulking boogeyman), but he's not much help. He's more interested in making an impression on Libby than he is looking for a missing girl. He twirls a cigar and suggests hitting the brothel to check for signs of Clara. The sheriff's office looks to be one of the other rooms of the set quickly and lamely converted, so Hooper shoots the whole thing in medium close-ups to hide the details of the room.

When the trio question Hattie, the brothel keeper hugs the sheriff like an old friend, which makes for a nicely sick social ecosystem in this corrupt little backwater. There's a little normalcy in the grammar as Harvey and the Sheriff trade knowing looks, captured in close-ups, as Hattie prattles on about Judd's alligator. It's the first sign of life from editor Michael Brown, who before now just let the film's long takes spin their wheels, barely cutting except when facial reactions are needed.

Back at the inn, Judd has crawled under the porch with the scythe, looking to finish off Angie. The moody lighting and heavy cobwebs as the camera moves with the two bodies in the blue moonlight are redolent of some of the scenes in the murder house in *Chain Saw*. Harvey is subject to a particularly violent death when he's dropped off moments later.

Libby and the Sheriff go get a beer in town, and the choreography in the bar has some of Hooper's rhythm to it. It's as if he blocked the scene in this way because he knew cutting it together would be a hazard if left up to the producers. We see two rednecks talking at the bar, then Buck walks behind them to order two beers (setting up his trajectory to wind up at the inn with a woman) and exits the frame just in time for the sheriff and Libby to enter from the back of the frame. Then it stays on Buck and Lynette, his chosen girl (Janus Blythe, who, like Englund, worked for Wes Craven in both *The Hills Have Eyes* and its sequel), shooting pool. It's not Howard Hawks, but it's an in-scene representation of the editing of the scenes at the graveyard and the gas station in *Chain Saw*. Lynette and Buck watch a flamboyantly weird bar fight start and diffuse while the sheriff tries to talk to Libby.

Buck brings Lynette to the inn after the sheriff berates him in front of the rest of the bar. Viewed from far away on the set of the inn, we now see he's wearing the same outfit that Kirk wore in *Chain Saw*: denim shirt and jean flares. Judd tries to tell him to go, but Buck and Lynette bypass him, steal some room keys, and head upstairs. A few seconds later, the sheriff drops Libby off. All of our major players are in place, and Judd knows it. He sits in the waiting room, listening to the fornicators overhead, the muffled shouting of Faye tied to the bed, the screams of poor Angie under the porch, and the country music on the radio he cranks to drown out all of the noise. In interviews, Hooper had said that at base *Chain Saw* is a film about a bad day. Everyone in the film has one, even Leatherface. This is also true of *Eaten Alive*. It's tough not to feel a little bad for Judd, just waiting around for the next thing to go wrong because he can't control his violent personality or temper.

There's something essentially gothic and romantically and sexually depraved about the situation. It's as if William Inge and Tennessee Williams tried collaborating on a Republic Pictures B-movie in their final days, bombed out of their minds on corn liquor. The staircase separating the reptile from the tenants has something of a Tennessee Williams' *Orpheus Descending* quality to it. In that play, a woman carries on an affair while her jealous and ailing husband silently observes from his bedroom on the second floor of their house. And who is Buck if not a classic Williams hustler who's finally settled into small town life, someone Brando would have made a meal of in the '50s and '60s? There's most certainly an Inge-ian business and darkness in the full inn's worth of Southern problematic types quarrelling, screwing, and suffering upstairs while Judd loses his mind below: the devil in hell to the conflicted purgatorial rooms above. Each room is host to a different domestic parable of abuse and misery, like Tracy Letts plays colliding with one another. It's no wonder no one has ever known what to make of this film.

In the edit, Michael Brown rockets between the rooms and their miserable occupants with increasing frequency. Hooper never once takes his camera off the tripod or crane, so he can't get close to his subjects, denying the film any of the visceral impact of *Chain Saw's* similarly cut-crazy ending. Buck goes downstairs and discovers Angie under the porch. But Judd pushes him into the gator pit, ending the rescue attempt in its infancy. Lynette inquires after the noise and Judd follows her into the misty woods for a brief, moody retread of the chase between Leatherface and Sally in the climax of *Chain Saw*. She too is rescued by a passing motorist. After gratuitously undressing, Libby discovers the bound and gagged Faye next door. Judd knocks them both around but winds up in the gator's mouth when the two women team up against him. The sheriff arrives in time to find Judd's wooden leg floating in the red and green waters.

Salem's Lot (1979)

It's telling that Hooper's biggest production, three movies into his career, was for television. He still seemed less than a sure thing for big movies and he wouldn't get his "break" for another few years. He was wild yet. *Salem's Lot* would be proof that he could play nice with big demands from a high profile book by America's new favorite novelist Stephen King. *Salem's Lot*, which is about an author moving back to his suburban New England town as it falls under the influence of a vampire, was and remains one of Hooper's most straightforward films. This is thanks mostly to its suburban setting, traditional villain, and King's white-bread dialogue. But it's also a roundabout return of sorts to Hooper's vicious clarity and the next step in his evolution into an old-school studio craftsman. Those AIP and Hammer films hiding in *The Heisters* hadn't left his memory and he was slowly reaching the point where he could direct with the sideways voluptuousness of Terence Fisher, Michael Powell, Roy Ward Baker, and Roger Corman in the early '60s.

The prologue is notable because right away we get a glimpse of the eccentric art direction Hooper would later adopt as his standard. Production Designer Mort Rabinowitz and Set Decorator Jerry Adams craft the church where the heroes, teen Mark Petrie (Lance Kerwin) and author Ben Mears (David Soul, TV's Hutch of *Starsky and Hutch*), hide out with an eye towards kitschy expressionism. Petrie and Mears are both tanned to within an inch of their lives, their sandy blonde hair linking them in beautiful destiny. Petrie looks destined to become Mears. The camera, manned by Jules Brenner shooting in academy ratio to fit TV broadcast standards, changes from a high angle of their hands filling bottles of holy water to a low angle looking at their grim faces. Its beautiful swooping motion lets us know that Hooper will be back in propulsive craft mode after the wonky detour of *Eaten Alive*. The holy water in the church cistern glows magically blue, letting the two know their unseen foe has found them. It's a less garish lighting choice than the oppressive reds from *Eaten Alive* and it has a narrative point. Hooper worked *with* the production restrictions this time.

Harry Sukman's music (aping Bernard Herrmann with a tin, '70s TV-orchestra timbre) brings us into the town of Salem's Lot, two years earlier. Mears, a writer like King, grew up here and it holds a place in his nightmares, specifically the corner of town taken up by the Marsten House. It's doing its best impression of the Bates house from *Psycho* and, like Sukman's score, places us firmly in Hitchcock land. There's also the presence of not one, but two Hitchcock villains in the cast. We won't meet Reggie Nalder (he was the gunman in *The Man Who Knew Too Much*) until much later, but for now we get to know James Mason's (*North By Northwest's* feline Phillip Vandamm) Richard Straker. He makes walking down the stairs seem like the most complex, cool thing in the world. He sees Mears' gawking at him from the road and his face drops. But he quickly picks it up; taking the writer's rubbernecking in stride, tossing his keys in the air like a cartoon beatnik, and catches them. Nothing could spoil his mood, even this disconcerting interloper. Before he's said one word, this has completely defined his character. He stares daggers at Mears on his way out of the driveway. Mears eventually makes his way back to town and Hooper executes one of his new favorite tricks—panning with Mears' truck until it lands on a worried Petrie standing on a corner and letting Mears drive out of the frame, just like the bar intro in *Eaten Alive*.

Mason's body language and voice mimic the super smooth motion of Hooper's camera. Confident and velvety, he glides through the performance as if weightless. He's preparing his shop for the arrival of his partner, Kurt Barlow.

Across the street, Mears enquires about the Marsten house with a local realtor, Larry Crockett (comedy great Fred Willard). The walls are amazing: wood paneling behind the desk, tacky, cheap wallpaper in the front room. Perfect '70s suburbia. Hooper, Rabinowitz, and Adams did their homework when recreating the magnificently depressing rural paradise of Salem's Lot. Hooper's eye for the details of interiors is a consistent highlight in his films, from the commune in *Eggshells* to Leatherface's house to the many domains in *Salem's Lot* acting as fronts for imperfect marriages and childhoods in ruin. This was the first time Hooper took his despairing diagnosis of modern America out of the South, out of the fringes of polite society and into the heart of Waspy America. Now that he'd seen the ways in which the backwards political tide chewed up both the stubborn remnants of Eisenhower's America and the hippies who briefly threatened to dethrone them, he turned his eye to the main current of American life.

Salem's Lot may be in the ass end of Maine, but that just makes its ingrown routines all the more potently representative of the American way. Away from big cities, changing political landscapes, and left to their own devices, the people of Salem's Lot are an unchanging microcosm of suburban life just waiting to be prodded by agents of chaos like Straker and Barlow. Mears doesn't realize that the petri dish of Americana he was relying on for stability and boredom during his creative process would be in the midst of a bacterial infection. Nor could anyone have possibly predicted that this would become Hooper's raison d'être. *Salem's Lot* is the first of his studies of suburban malaise turned gangrenous. Of his seventeen feature-length films following *Salem's Lot*, ten deal with suburban life, families moving to new environments to escape the craziness of city life, or, more broadly, perverted American values.

Straker holds court splendidly when Crockett stops in for a round of hosannas for his help setting up a new base of operations for the wealthy out-of-towners. He has a series of delicious tells while dealing with the man, with whom he plainly loves toying. This town is obsessed and fascinated by the wealthy and the foreign. When Mears checks into the boarding house down the road owned by Eva Miller (Maria Windsor, whose career stretches back to noir staples *The Killing* and *The Sniper*), she seems deeply interested in his career as a writer and whether she knows any of his work. Naturally, the next woman he meets (Susan Norton, played by Bonnie Bedelia) is reading one of his books in the park. Susan is the art teacher at the elementary school and her father (Ed Flanders) is a doctor Mears knew when he was a kid. It takes Mears about eight seconds to ask her out and Mears being both a stranger and semi-famous makes him about the best proposition she's likely ever encountered.

That night, Mears is drawn once more to the Marsten house and comes face-to-face with Straker. Hooper captures him in a series of gorgeous tableaux, taking full advantage of the beautiful gothic architecture of the house to frame Straker in all his stately menace. There are almost too many lovely, gallery-ready portraits of Mason dwarfed by the decaying Marsten house to count.

Back on Main Street, we get a taste of just how *small* this particular small town is. Crockett and his secretary Bonnie are planning their next rendezvous under the unlinking gaze of town drunk Weasel (Elisha Cook, Jr. who played Windsor's cuckolded lover in Stanley Kubrick's *The Killing*, here playing roughly the same part many years later, their affair having long since fizzled). Constable Parkins (Kenneth MacMillan) walks by, wondering if he's being paid by Bonnie's husband (George Dzundza) to spy on them. He then asks Weasel to do some spying of his own, on Mears.

A word about some of these subplots. The few people who've managed to create compelling cinema out of Stephen King stories (Hooper, Kubrick, Carpenter, David Cronenberg) have done so by treating King's premise as a sounding board for their own aesthetic and moral fascinations. There's a reason King hates Kubrick's *The Shining*: it jettisons most of what makes it King's. The ideological underpinnings of Hooper's work align with King's in more than a few ways (both are old school lefties with broad senses of humor), but Hooper can't quite make King's baggy narrative sing.

The only satellite characters who wind up making much difference to the story are gravedigger Mike Ryerson (Geoffrey Lewis), Susan's ex-boyfriend Ned Tebbets (Barney McFadden), and Mears' old friend Jason Burke (Lew Ayres). The subplot involving Weasel and Eva having once been in love and now still stuck thinking about each other as they rattle around their hometown in their dotage seems mostly an excuse for Hooper to indulge himself and imagine an alternate ending to *The Killing*. The other subplots are largely in place to paint a broader portrait of the trap of white picket fences. It's worth pointing out that the Sawyer household actually has a white picket fence and Cully watches Crockett arrive to screw around with his wife with the fence between them. The framing, with the two men on different planes, cut off by accidental squares caused by the fence and Larry Crocket's car, is a favorite of Hooper's, and he'll use it again in *The Funhouse* when a young boy is waylaid by a truck driver.

Mears is met with a few possible endings to his stint in Salem's Lot. He could wind up like Susan's parents, who still remember when the young boys would watch Eva Miller "sashay" down the street. Or he could end up like Bonnie and Cully Sawyer, unhappily pursuing dangerous extramarital thrills. Hooper relishes recreating the dirty details of so many of these lives because he needs everyone to see that whether or not the vampires had arrived from Europe with, as we'll later see, their narcotic, sexual brainwashing, the people of Salem's Lot would have had their blood drained anyway. Hooper's highly detailed, almost romantic compositions of the town in its dormant state (caught in the box of Brenner's 4:3 framing) are all lies. They're just like the windows through which every character can't seem to stop spying on Mears. The windows keep everyone feeling superior for having decided their lives could end in Salem's Lot.

The promise of settling down with Susan Norton is, to Hooper, never anything worth celebrating or taking seriously. The hazy lighting during their romantic trip to the lake or their lunch at the malt shop looks like they were modeled after the covers of dime romance novels. The scenes of passion are just as fake as the play that Mark Petrie's school puts on. The stage lights over his head acting as a bitter mirror image of the soft-focus lighting at the lake, and just as sterile as the scenes in the hospital with their buzzing florescent bulbs and antiseptic atmosphere. It's only Mason's shark-like pragmatism as Straker that seems to earn Hooper's approval, which is why Hooper invests real romance in his images of the old Rennfield figure and his master. Like Hooper, Straker does what he has to in order to survive in a world of false promises and small minds.

Case in point, the box of earth in which Kurt Barlow arrives. It fits the confines of the frame beautifully, and Hooper and Brenner light it for optimal spookiness when Ryerson and Tebbets drop it off at the Marsten house. The cool blues of the work lights give it an otherworldly sheen. When they get to the basement, Hooper's attention to ghastly detail comes out to play. The animals, dead and alive, that litter the basement seem an extension of the monster in the box. Ryerson and Tebbets flee before it disgorges its malevolent contents. He'll kill Larry Crockett, Ryerson's dog, and one little boy walking home from Mark Petrie's house.

Mark Petrie is an important archetype in Hooper's cinema: the kid obsessed with horror movies who knows more than the adults around him. Hooper's postmodern, ironic suburban landscapes have their bubbles penetrated by the knowledge of kids like Petrie who've studied horror films throughout their childhoods. You'll see him again in *The Funhouse, Invaders From Mars, Mortuary,* and *The Mangler* under different names. He gets the fullest interrogation in *Salem's Lot* and answers a lot of Hooper's feelings regarding the people who kept hiring him to make horror films year after year. Petrie's dad (Joshua Bryant) finds him rehearsing for the school play in his bedroom, which is full of makeup effects, horror memorabilia, and tchotchkes (the *Frankenstein* poster on his wall will appear in Joey Harper's bedroom in *The Funhouse*).

"When you gonna outgrow this?" dad asks.

"Soon, I guess."

He's talking about his son's horror movie geekery, but the subtext couldn't be clearer. A few days later they'll repeat this interaction, except Mark pushes it by asking his father to tie him up with rope so he can Houdini himself to freedom. His father questions him a little more specifically about his interests in "monsters and magic."

"I always have been. I can't explain it, it's the way I am."

Petrie's creativity is what sets him apart from his friends (the doomed Glick boys are charmed by Mark's inventiveness, but can't identify with it) and family, and thus aligns him with Mears who, by coming to Salem's Lot in the first place, looks in danger of becoming one of the herd that Petrie doesn't fit into. The lack of creativity in the community is what enables Barlow to take over in the first place—no one suspects Straker except Mears, but even he's too late. When the constable comes to question Straker following the death of Crockett and the foul play involving the Glick boys, he's easily sweet-talked by the old fox:

"I'm always on duty," says Parkins.

"That makes me feel safe and snug," says Mason in his inimitable, frosty diction.

Straker sets the law off his scent by letting the cop think he and Barlow are lovers.

There is a continued investigation of the town's prejudices every step of the invasion. Parkins repulsion at the thought of two older men together makes it easier for him to operate without raising the cop's hackles about real violence. Vampirism has oft been used as a means of wrapping sexuality and fear of disease in a veil of mythology, and here it's the fear of one that allows for the spread of the other. Barlow and Straker's relationship will, maybe ironically, come to mirror that of Mears and Petrie, the older obsessive mentoring the younger one. Both pairs are coded as outsiders, which means that they'll be locked into conflict forever while the rest of a heterogenous society falls to chaos and death.

Mark Petrie is the only one who knows how to deal with the Glick boys rapping on his window because he's let monster movies become his bible. Maybe that's why his bedroom is sprawling and darkly colored like Straker's antique shop and *unlike* the other bedrooms and parlors of Salem's Lot: he's also an outsider, and the things on his wall are armor against the banality of the town. Interest in the arts is abnormal in a place like this. One suspects Hooper understands this only too well.

Hooper grants us our first look at a vampire when Mark's friend Ralphie Glick, dead after Barlow's first night in town, pays a visit to his brother Danny. He floats outside his brother's window surrounded by mist, scratching at the glass to be let in like a dog. Danny, in a trance, opens the window and his brother floats in like a rabid Peter Pan. It's a splendid sequence and also properly terrifying. Ralphie's eyes, dead and yellow, have a monstrous inhumanity in them. All of Barlow's victims will have eyes like this, gifts from their vampiric creator, who is the most horrifying of all of them.

We meet Kurt Barlow a few days later, when the town has already begun hemorrhaging. Mike Ryerson is attacked while burying Danny Glick. Burke and Mears try to help the gravedigger to little avail. Ned Tebbets finally decides he's had enough of Mears in town and coldcocks him outside of Straker's antique shop opening. Mears is laid up in bed when Ryerson attacks Burke, the shock of which gives him a heart attack. Tebbets is asleep in jail when he gets a visitor, announced by shadows and mist. Barlow, razor-sharp teeth bared, eyes aglow with brilliant psychedelic colors, pops into frame accompanied by a stab of Sukman's brass. No matter how times one sees this attack, it remains petrifying. It has the sucker punch effect of Leatherface with his hammer sneaking up on Kirk in the hallway.

Mears enlists the help of Father Callahan (James Gallery) in his crusade (his church has a big clock with a swinging, neon pendulum beneath it, one of the film's odder touches) and his first stop is Mark Petrie's house. He shows up in time for an attack that looks a lot like the goings on in *Poltergeist*. The table starts to shake, the lights flicker off, the cabinet vomits dishware onto the floor, and chairs start to race across the floor unprovoked. Then Barlow lets himself in through the window and kills Mark's parents. Straker appears to taunt both Mark and Father Callahan, having evidently let himself in through the front door. Mason seems to have a blast in this scene, shouting at Callahan while Barlow considers killing Mark. "Back, Holy Man! Back Shaman!" You can hear him smiling through his ultimatum. "Throw away your cross! Face the master! Faith against faith!" Their battle lasts as long as you'd expect.

Mears and Dr. Norton autopsy a recent victim looking for clues, trying to decide what to believe. When the body starts to move under the coroner's white sheet, Mears fashions a cross out of tongue depressors and burns a scar into the vampire woman's head. The crooked ritual feels of a whole with the psychedelic happenings, exploding paper airplanes, and one-sided sword fights of *Eggshells*. Fighting an ancient evil with a slapdash modern solution. When she vanishes, she knocks two carts full of medical equipment and blood on the floor like a little comedic afterthought, the kid who made *The Heisters* taking the floor.

The following day is a picture of inverted Rockwell. A tricycle overturned in a yard with a white picket fence. Everyone in town is tired, clutching neck wounds and telling strange stories. Susan is strangely drawn to the Marsten house, her trance only broken by the sight of Mark Petrie running onto the grounds with a pair of homemade stakes to drive into Barlow's heart.

The cellar of the Marsten house is still wonderfully wonky (a stuffed pelican is guarding the staircase), but it's got nothing on the gorgeous decay of the rest of the house. The furniture has been destroyed and its pulled stuffing looks like extra ornamentation. The air is full of dust and feathers. It's like Leatherface's living room designed by millionaires. This is the strongest portion of the film, the part where Hooper's design sense runs amok. It's a place unmoored from the tidiness of the homes in *Salem's Lot*. It isn't overly manicured or obsessively cleaned to mask the failed family units who reside there. The movie feels, finally, like the proper follow-up to *Texas Chain Saw*: the rats on the floor, torn curtains, the taxidermized animals, the green and orange mold, and water damage running down the walls. A disgusting extension of the self-painting walls in *Eggshells*, except the personalities have chosen a different color scheme. The free spirits went with a rainbow, the deathless evil went with vomit-stained collage. Hooper pulls the camera back, stranding Susan in a frame downstairs, while upstairs, Mark Petrie crosses the x-axis, over top of Susan herself. Mark discovers a room full of stuffed jungle cats and one dog stuck on a pair of impala horns—foreshadowing poor Dr. Norton's fate in a few minutes.

Hooper and Brenner lower their crane down to make Susan's journey up the stairs seem more terrifying. Susan, like Sally Hardesty and the women of *Eaten Alive*, is terrified but uncowed. Hooper's women, while repeatedly brutalized, are warriors fighting through their fear. His many heroines are driven by different impulses, frequently motherhood (surrogate motherhood included, as when Susan rushes into the Marsten house to rescue Mark) or, territoriality, to protect the things they believe in—their families, their homes, their accomplishments, and achievements. Hooper didn't invent the concept of the "Final Girl"—the last woman standing in a slasher film—but he always presented sterling examples. Compared to Susan, both Mark and Mears are cowardly and fumble with their many tasks during the final act. Mears freaks out being back in the house that haunted him as a kid, drops the holy water, doesn't save either of the Nortons, and nearly gets himself and Mark killed.

Mark and Mears finally stop Straker and find the resting place of Barlow's coffin, surrounded by bodies moving with the sluggishness of *Chain Saw's* grandpa looking out at the vampire hunters through dead eyes. While Mears hammers a stake into the feral vampire king's heart, Mark sits and watches, oblivious to the vampires creeping up behind him. It's a wonderful use of the negative space over his shoulder, taking advantage of the feeling of unease just being in the house. There are five cutaways before Mark notices Ned and Mark creeping up behind him, eyes aglow, hands outstretched, a nice bit of realistic action continuity. When Barlow dies, Hooper uses stop-motion time-lapse photography (first popularized in horror movies like George Waggner's 1941 *The* Wolf *Man* when Lon Chaney, Jr. has to transform into a werewolf on screen) to show his body's quick disintegration. Further underlining the ineffectual male in Hooper's cinema, Mears and Ben burn the Marsten house down, then flee, letting the world fall to the vampire plague. Susan follows them to the far reaches of the earth to take revenge on Mears for not saving her. Even dead, her will is stronger than Mears'. And Mark is destined to turn into him. They wind up in paradise, big German expressionist shadows on the wall during their confrontation, proving that their union would have been death to both of them.

"We'll always be together," says Vampire Susan, just before the stake goes in.

Salem's Lot is the bedrock of many of Hooper's thematic concerns in its nakedly tackling suburban hypocrisy and the stultifying wasp lifestyle. His direction would become more expressive, but *Salem* shows him spreading his wings, throwing his camera around to explore the impressive sets, a do-over for the cramped, cheaply appointed soundstage from *Eaten Alive*. Hooper was about to become the filmmaker he gestured towards being as far back as *The Heisters*. *The Funhouse* may want for some of the electric experimentation of his early work, but it's probably the purest expression of his ambitions as a filmmaker. He would evolve and make films with more resources and imagination, but *The Funhouse* feels like the perfect cross section of his artistic and thematic interests.

Productions like *Lifeforce* and *Invaders From Mars*, while fun and propelled by Hooper's unchained energy and enthusiasm, get away from him because he hadn't had much preparation for their scale. *The Funhouse* is the right size to ensure that Hooper's mix of grimy production design, bombastic lighting, and art direction would get his full attention.

The Funhouse (1981)

The Funhouse, which is about four kids who stay overnight in a carnival and get hunted and killed for their trouble, was released several years after Halloween and the slasher craze was in full effect. In *his* version of the teen body count movie, Hooper plays a game of bait and switch after a delectably upsetting opening sequence. To the sounds of John Beal's ornately creepy score (a mix of a carnival organ grinder and Bernard Herrmann), the opening credits unfold as we see images of disgusting little clown dolls and sideshow puppets. The introductory sequence ends on a cackling lady doll with ruddy cheeks and garish eye makeup, like the kind worn by Leatherface during dinner with grandpa.

Then there's a black-gloved man right out of a giallo (a popular genre of Italian proto-slasher movies made in the 60s and 70s replete with byzantine murders and named for the yellowing pages of the paperback books from which their plots were lifted), and we see everything he sees through a POV cam, which was slasher boilerplate by 1981. We cut to young Amy Harper (Elizabeth Berridge, who would play Constanze Mozart in *Amadeus* when she was next on movie screens) preparing to take a shower between bouts of POV-cam as the "killer" selects his weapon of choice from a wall of clown masks and torture implements. Hooper has him pick a mask like young Michael Myers in the start of *Halloween*, let himself into the bathroom during Amy's shower, then, like Mrs. Bates in Hitchcock's *Psycho*, pull the shower curtain away and start stabbing her with a plastic knife. There are many direct cribs from Hitch's compositions and edits in the *Psycho* shower sequence and Beal's score behaves much the same as Herrmann's: percussive stabbing to mock the action onscreen and busy strings when it's all over, recalling the opening movement of the *Psycho* suite.

The would-be killer, it turns out, is Amy's brother Joey (Shawn Carson of *Something Wicked This Way Comes*) and he's hiding in the closet with a Polaroid camera when Amy comes looking for him. He gets a picture off to startle her, like Audrey Hepburn in *Wait Until Dark*, but the purpose of the picture is for Amy to look at herself in the photograph, to see her own face when consumed by fear and anger—a horror movie looking at its audience. Hooper then pans up to the poster of Boris Karloff as Frankenstein's Monster on Joey's wall and cuts to Elsa Lanchester as the Bride of Frankenstein on the TV downstairs, showing the role that women in this film will be forced into by overbearing, violent men: Amy will be unwilling "bride" to both her boyfriend Buzz (Cooper Huckabee) and later to the villainous carny mutant (Wayne Doba) waiting for them in the Funhouse.

You won't find a more succinct deconstruction of the Freudian and grammatical underpinnings of the slasher movie (which Hooper helped create with *Texas Chain Saw* only to watch slip into cheaply, indifferently made gore delivery machines like *Friday The 13th* and *The Boogeyman,* both 1980). I don't think anyone else was interested in making it so early in the genre. The interesting young directors who were asked to make slasher films (Roger Spottiswoode on *Terror Train*, Paul Lynch with *Humongous*) just asked for the moon from their producers, making films that could stylistically stand on their own two feet with engrossing production design. No one could accuse *Terror Train* or *Humongous* of being brainless clones of *Friday the 13th*—they're too weird—and making sure that your movie *didn't* resemble the film for which your producers wanted competition would have taken up as much energy as thinking about the genre itself, which was still being formed. Hooper had a little distance from the subject and used it to his advantage.

The scene's genius is twofold: Hooper doesn't wink at his audience, which makes the idea of a brother spying on his naked sister as gross as it should be, and then after this amazing little pastiche of the history of the slasher film, *The Funhouse* then becomes something different. Sure it's about kids being stalked by a madman, but it's as much an update of the Universal monster romps from the '30s and '40s as it is a teen meat market. He *does* spell that out in black and white. It's in the poster for *The Wolfman* behind Amy in Joey's bedroom and the cut from the Boris Karloff to Elsa Lanchester, showing the complex sympathies the Universal films used to beg of their audience. Karloff's monster and *Funhouse*'s carny mutant (not to mention Leatherface) have a child's understanding of the world. If they're monstrous, they were made that way by their keepers and a society that rejected them.

Downstairs, we get another succinct lesson in suburban malaise. Cinematographer Andrew Laszlo, shooting in 2.35.1 (the first time Hooper had ever shot wide screen), expands the space of the Harper living room so that her parents and the couches they're nestled in seem huge and inescapable. Their zombie-like daze during their conversation with Amy about her plans for the evening are a short, sweet reiteration of the marriage as trap motif in *Salem's*. They don't want her seeing Buzz; it's implied he's not good breeding stock. Amy's uncertainty regarding her own future is all over her face for the entire first act. *Does* she want to end up with Buzz, the filling station employee? Would that make it more or less likely she'll end up like her parents? The fact that Franz Waxman's decadent theme for *Bride Of Frankenstein* leaks over from the TV during her conversation is a marvelous touch.

Little brother Joey has been listening from the staircase the whole time. Joey is the second iteration of Mark Petrie, the kid who's learned about the world from horror movies. That's perhaps what makes him feel savvy enough to sneak out and follow Amy to the carnival. Hooper frames Joey behind bars and in little boxes—the window through which he spies on Amy and Buzz, the railing on the stairs, the odd frame created by the side view mirror on a passing truck driven by a redneck—to show what it is about the carnival and its promise of escape he finds so appealing. This town, which could be any small American town, is depressing and small-minded even to a 10-year-old kid. No wonder Amy is so conflicted: she's had almost twice as long to think about it.

Which may explain why she wants to be with Buzz anyway. They'll sit in the front seat of his car in the carnival parking lot as he tries to get a fix on her dour mood. Laszlo's soft lighting and shallow focus (it could be a split diopter shot, but it's tough to say, as it's not obviously employed—there is one later in the film involving a gun pointed at Buzz and Amy) turns the car over Buzz's shoulders—the same color as his jacket—into a kind of heavenly glow. He looks like the romantic hero she wants in those moments, the sensitive rebel. The shot has the same function as the tableaux of Ben Mears and Susan Norton in the malt shop in *Salem's Lot*. The edit of the following scenes has a curious function. The intro montage of Amy and her friends

(Buzz, Largo Woodruff's Liz, and Miles Chapin's Richie) at the carnival, riding rides and playing games is too fast, too oppressive, and too woozy. Hooper piles on the Dutch tilts and layers action in single shots, like the dirty drunk (Reverend David "Goat" Carson, uncle of *Invaders from Mars* star Hunter Carson, brother of *Texas Chain Saw 2* scribe L. M. Kit Carson) walking past the spinning carousel, to dizzy the audience. This is a glimpse inside Amy's brain, drunk on her newly romantic idea of Buzz.

In the makeshift bathrooms, Amy and Liz talk about Amy's virginity until they're accosted by a dirty old woman shouting, "God is watching you!" The scene is similar to Pam reading Sally's horoscope: the audience will have forgotten it by the time the killing starts. Beal plays the old woman a spooky theme as she rushes over to the two girls, as if Hooper wants us to imagine she could be what winds up stalking our heroes. There's further foreshadowing in the "Freaks of Nature" tent. On top of the two-headed cow, there's a mutant fetus in a jar bathed in purple light (clearly the sibling to the mutant, who's hiding under a Frankenstein mask to make everything ring with iconographic and thematic symmetry). Adjust for milieu, and a case could be made that Hooper was the closest thing America had to Dario Argento. Both believed in the power of lovely yet garish lighting and folkloric imagery. Both also had long, interesting careers long after they stopped currying critical favor.

Speaking of symmetry, Kevin Conway (Weary in *Slaughterhouse-Five*, Smolka in *Portnoy's Complaint*, and Chillingworth in a made-for-TV *Scarlet Letter*) plays all three of the carnival barkers we meet. He's the flamboyantly sleazy animal sideshow announcer, and you can still hear his voice when we meet him again as the English strip show MC. And both of their nasal whines will be heard over Conway the Third beckoning Amy into the funhouse, a bit of lens flare over his shoulder: "There is no release...from the funhouse." Scared to death, Amy suggests the visiting the magician's tent instead.

Marco The Magnificent is *Eaten Alive's* William Finley, dressed up in corpse paint that brings to mind his most famous role in *Phantom of the Paradise*. His magic show is Hooper's aesthetic and career in a nutshell. Finley, looking a little stoned under all that makeup, offers a little curtsy to the woman who asks why he doesn't get a real job as he selects a helper from the audience.

"Comfy?" he asks his volunteer, pulled from the audience.

"No," she offers meekly.

"Good."

He's placed her in a coffin with a window like the one featured in Carl Dreyer's *Vampyr*. Doing his best Hunter Thompson impression, Finley tells the story of Dracula (one Hooper had just revised in *Salem's Lot*). He puts a stake inside a hole in the coffin and asks if his volunteer can feel it.

"Get a new profession," shouts another heckler.

He drives the stake in with a hammer and the girl spits up blood, and Finley panics as if he hadn't planned it that way. He opens the coffin and the girl emerges in a sequined leotard and bows. It was all part of the act. Hooper's precision and care frequently comes off as something beyond his control, as if the effect of horrifying the audience so majestically had happened by accident.

After a long pull from a joint, the gang heads to the fortuneteller (Sylvia Miles, made famous by Paul Morrissey's *Heat*). They're too high to keep it together and laugh as she reads Amy's palm. She gets fed up and drops the European accent when her crystal ball hits the floor: "Don't come back or I'll break every bone in your fuckin' bodies." When they leave, there's a plan-séquence, Hooper's favorite camera move, where the camera, in an unbroken take, follows a man through a tent as he walks past Amy and Buzz making out.

The mutant in the Frankenstein mask lets Joey Harper into the funhouse. It's filled with glowing neon lights like the Starlight in *Eaten Alive*. And just as in *Eaten Alive*, we see a little shadow play (like Judd's on the front door) when Buzz brings everyone around the back of the striptease tent to give them a free peak at the ladies in their tassels. The girls' shadows are thrown against the side of the tent. Buzz cuts a hole in the fabric so Amy can see the routine. She gets a better look at the perspiring oglers tossing their popcorn as the women writhe around for them, Amy once more on the receiving end of an unwelcome audience's adrenaline inebriation. The carnival is a tour of the delights offered to grindhouse audiences, the things polite moviegoers don't admit wanting to experience.

Right around this time, Rich has the brilliant idea to sneak into the funhouse and spend the night. Amy and Liz call their parents to lie about where they'll be sleeping and then they're off. Along with the barrage of insane colors and odd mannequins, there's a giant psychedelic eye inside, sort of like Reggie Nalder's in *Salem's Lot* or the orb in the basement of *Eggshells*. Joey, who spied his sister entering the funhouse, waits patiently for her to exit, but the carnival starts to close around him. Beal's score turns ominous and quiet as all the dolls and puppets stop dancing and giggling. Laszlo backs away on a crane as Joey stands in the shadow of the giant imposing funhouse before he finally decides to walk away, a truly wonderful camera move that gives us the whole picture of the carnival for the first time. He'll return moments later, worried about his sister, but the bag lady from the bathroom finds him and scares him off with a hearty "God is watching you!"

In the funhouse, the kids stop their make out session to eavesdrop on the fortuneteller giving the man in the Frankenstein mask an earful. He's trying to pay her for sex, drool coming out of the mask's mouth, and she relents when he agrees to pay more. Their dalliance ends prematurely, which sends the man in the mask into hysterics. He throws her into a circuit breaker, which turns the power and the lights back on in the funhouse. The power surge brings the puppets back to life as the mutant strangles the fortuneteller to death (more cutthroat economics). The lights are on in the Funhouse now, surrounding the kids with sickly primary colors. They try to find the exit, but all they find is the fortuneteller's body on a dirty mattress.

When the funhouse barker finds the mutant, he berates him loudly—not specifically for the murder or the prostitution, though he *is* mad he was going to drop a hundred bucks on the transaction. What bothers him is that he killed a member of the "family." The carnival is one more family unit trying to hang together in a country that doesn't take kindly to freaks like the kids from *Eggshells* or Leatherface's family. The killing spree that follows is a very American protection of property and the family unit. Hooper and screenwriter Larry Block know that people, no matter how morally compromised, never see themselves as villains. They're just doing what they need to so they might live to see another day. To protect their investment, just like the old man with his barbecue joint. (Conway has a strangely touching monologue about needing to take care of the mutant ever since his mother died, humanizing him in a way that never happens to Rich, Liz, or Buzz.) Thus, when the barker discovers that *more* of his money went missing, both he and the mutant go mad in a hurry. The mutant tears his mask off, revealing a face like the fetus in the jar and Conway realizes that someone else must be responsible for the missing cash.

At this point, we're an hour into *The Funhouse*'s one hour and 36 minute runtime, which should let viewers know that on the list of Hooper's interests, laying traps for his audience in the form of jump scares is very low on the list. What he's more interested in is contrasting the carny life from the point of view of outsiders with the slightly nostalgic look at the traveling attraction as a break from small town mundaneness. Just don't get too close. The world of entertainers and the entertained don't mix well (there's a contrast in the other carnival workers who find Joey later and return him to his parents, just so we don't think all carnies are bad people; it's circumstance and outside interference that turns the more libertarian strain of carnival folk into murderers). The kids learn this when Rich drops his lighter through the ceiling, getting the barker's attention. *He* took the barker's money, and they're all going to pay for it.

Like Leatherface, the barker and the mutant have the home field advantage inside the funhouse. To let the audience know how high the decks are stacked, Hooper treats us to a shot of Joey, back once more looking for his sister. The camera first dollies then pans across the giant face of the funhouse to show us its dimensions from the outside. That's a lot of space in which to get lost.

The funhouse is quickly used as a weapon of distraction and disorientation, with dolls and puppets mocking the kids and fake lightning surprising and confusing them. Neon pinks, greens, and oranges (the color scheme of *Eggshells'* freak-outs) flash crazily every time one of the kids is nabbed by the unseen barker and his mutant sidekick—Rich with a noose, Liz with a trapdoor, and Buzz when the mutant drops in on him from above. Every one of the kids dies twice. Rich returns as a dummy in a funhouse roller coaster seat and Buzz brains him with an axe stolen from one of the puppets. The mutant finds Liz in the guts of the funhouse's electronics (a lovely dolly-in finds her in front of a big fan—a beautiful shot possibly cribbed from *Alien*) after her fall through the trapdoor and does something to her we're not quite able to see. Buzz runs the barker through with a sword, but he wakes for one final attack before the mutant dispatches Buzz, then fixes him to a moving clown mannequin. Everyone becomes part of the funhouse's ghoulish upholstery.

Amy's journey through the funhouse involves repeated window and eye motifs. She and the gang stare at the sex and murder as if through a peephole, spying on a troubled world of adult psychosexuality. She sees her parents picking her brother up through the blades of a fan, but they can't hear her screams. And then, she travels through a giant mouth, green light spilling behind her, and that's when the freak-out begins. Editor Jack Hofstra, who has preserved Hooper's flow so admirably throughout, finally takes the gloves off. As Amy experiences her Sally Hardesty moment, screaming in terror at the sensory overload her captors use to terrorize her, Hofstra and Hooper bombard her with the best images from the funhouse (cobwebbed skeletons, the big eye, lots of menacing dolls, subliminal shots of the mutant's face), cutting between multiple angles of her experience. The camera wobbles with her, gently suggesting her grip on the situation loosening. Once more, her escape is into the room with the dead fortuneteller where the mutant finds her. All roads lead to dead ends for Amy Harper, unless she chooses to be resilient. She could become her mom or the fortuneteller, and she has no interest in either destiny.

The mutant dies twice as well—electrocuted like the fortuneteller, then ground up like hamburger. Beal's score turns into a heavy waltz as the mutant, strung up to spinning machine, is fed into grinding gears—a nod to the carnival's carousel—undone by the machinery he so relied upon. Amy watches in horror as the air fills with blue sparks and smoke. She'll stumble dazedly out of the funhouse, makeup running, dress torn, a horrific walk of shame, innocence sullied by the inevitability of adulthood's stranglehold. The bag lady is there waiting for her, reminding her that as long as she's in suburbia, god will be watching. To prove her point, Hooper's camera rises up to the sky to watch over her as she walks away. What Amy does next is up to her.

The carnival life is a funhouse mirror held up to the calcified suburban life the Harpers live, the extreme endgame of settling for what's comfortable instead of what's possible. Both hide from civilization, banded together against the outside world. But in so doing, they refuse to grow. The hermetic seal around communities suffocates their members, killing them inside. His next feature film would take a step even further inside the guts of the American household. The house opens its maw, wanting to be fed each of its complacent members.

Billy Idol, "Dancing With Myself" (1981)

In 1981 Hooper directed the music video for Billy Idol's fiendishly catchy "Dancing With Myself." It's got everything you'd expect from a horror director given free reign by a pop-punk sex symbol, and quite a bit more. First of all, Hooper reteamed with *Chain Saw's* cinematographer Daniel Pearl, who gives the video a marvelously sturdy look—post apocalyptic chic, trash everywhere, and a cool pinkish hue over everything. They would join forces again on *Invaders From Mars*, but in the meantime, Pearl had become something of a fixture on the video circuit. He'd get more work shooting music videos than features throughout the '80s and '90s (though he would shoot the Hooper-less sequel *Return To Salem's Lot* for Larry Cohen). You could almost mistake the video's dirty punk aesthetic for that of pioneer UK queer filmmaker Derek Jarman, if you didn't know who was behind it. Jarman was similarly disposed towards externalizing punk music in images.

The video has zombies (beating John Landis' *Thriller* video to the punch by a full year), ninjas, wife murdering bluebeards, puppets and skeletons from *The Funhouse*, demon barbers, etc. At one point, Hooper places Idol on an elevator so he can soar by countless comic horror tableaux. Hooper and Pearl uses scads of contrast and play with magnificent shadows and comedic cutaways. Idol is frequently imprisoned by shadows wrought by low-key lighting (he'd repeat the trick in *Poltergeist*). Hooper uses matte paintings to show the zombies climbing up the tower block Idol sings atop, the first time he'd ever employed the trick (look for them all throughout his next three films). Idol hooks himself up to a pair of electrodes like Frankenstein's monster, which blows the zombies off the roof of the building, which would also become a motif in Hooper's sci-fi: inexplicable forces coursing through bodies. Hooper evidently took much joy in imagining a London destroyed by horror movie conventions because he'd return in a few years to do it again in *Lifeforce*. But first, he had to make a fateful pit stop in Hollywood...

Poltergeist (1982)

> *There's some controversy about the individual contributions to the film made by Mr. Spielberg and Mr. Hooper, best known as director of The Texas Chainsaw [sic] Massacre. I've no way of telling who did what, though Poltergeist seems much closer in spirit and sensibility to Mr. Spielberg's best films than to Mr. Hooper's.*
>
> ~Vincent Canby, *The New York Times*, June 4th, 1982

To the sounds of a slightly gaudy version of "The National Anthem," the credits fade in and out in the unmistakable *Citizen Kane* font. Both it and *Poltergeist* are about the corrupting influence of money and media, and Hooper was about to become the Orson Welles of genre film. *Poltergeist* is less overly literal than *Kane*, but it's no less potent, though there's a slightly better allegory in Welles' body of work. In Welles' 1946 film *The Stranger*, a perfect suburban family is broken up when they realize that one of them is a Nazi out to steal their daughter. In *Poltergeist*, a perfect suburban family is broken up when a ghost invades their house and steals their daughter.

The connections between Welles and Hooper is everywhere once you notice it. There's the fact that both were judged their whole career against their iconic first success. Welles' work with cinematographer Greg Toland seems to define Hooper's relationship with the camera. *Salem's Lot* and *The Stranger* have the same story beats and New England setting. In 1951, Welles adapted *Othello*, which is about a man driven to kill by a manipulative puppet-master, not unlike Leatherface and the Carny Mutant working for their evil father figures. *The Trial's* persecuted Josef K and *The Funhouse's* Amy Harper both spend the third act fleeing malevolent forces in expressionistic lighting. The decaying family tree of Welles' *The Magnificent Ambersons* shed leaves all over Hooper's filmography, most notably in his *Texas Chain Saw* movies. *Texas Chain Saw Massacre 2* even has a deranged spin on the *Ambersons'* ball, that film's famous centerpiece.

Poltergeist starts by taking on the neuroses of filmmakers from the '50s: the emergence of TV. Film after film (*All That Heaven Allows*, *It Should Happen To You*, *Sunset Boulevard*, etc.) feared the small screen would usurp the silver screen, that people wouldn't leave their houses if they could stare at a hole in a box in the corner of the den. Having made *Salem's Lot* for CBS *and* having grown up in the '50s when the television first started making its way into American homes, Hooper understood the allure and drawbacks of TV. *Poltergeist's* first image is of the blurry lines of a TV screen in extreme close-up. Director of photography Matthew F. Leonetti, playing by the Amblin Entertainment guidebook, lights to pick up maximum dirt and dust, making the TV screen and the living room it's housed in seem pre-owned in that 1970s fashion (the look was *just* going out style, resurrected for nostalgic purposes by Douglas Slocombe for the *Indiana Jones* movies).

The national anthem playing while the family dog gives us a view of the house says that *this* is the new American dream under Ronald Reagan. The TV tucks everyone into bed. Leonetti follows the dog away from its sleeping owner, giving us a survey of *Funhouse's* start and endpoints, from the head of the family, Steve (Craig T. Nelson) ensconced in his easy chair like a gargoyle, the light from the TV like the sparks flying from the murder of the mutant and the fortuneteller. The dog finds wife/mother Diane (JoBeth Williams) asleep alone and a bag of potato chips under sleeping daughter #1 Dana (Dominique Dunne), then licks the hand of son Robbie (Oliver Robbins) and daughter #2 Carol Anne (Heather O'Rourke), which rouses her. With his dozens of movie posters and *Star Wars* toys, Robbie is almost one of Hooper's archetypal, precocious tykes. But his expertise in all things science fiction is never put to use (which says more about Spielberg's script than Hooper). Carol Anne walks to the television, drawn by some strange beckoning force, seeing patterns through the static like a junior Max Renn.

"Helloooo? What do you look like? Talk louder I can't hear you." As she yells at the television, Michael Kahn's edit takes us upstairs where Diane is woken up by Carol Anne's voice, the sound transition edit is identical to the ones Hooper used in *Texas Chain Saw, Eggshells,* and *The Funhouse,* maintaining continuity between the different areas of the set and linking them through character. The whole family comes down to watch her communing with the TV set, unsure what to do or say. Jerry Goldsmith is doing his best John Williams impression on the score. Carol Anne puts her hands up to the TV set, and then Kahn cuts to the beautiful countryside where the Freeling family lives. It's a bitter little comment—perfect houses and families are only on TV. *Poltergeist* will not be *Leave it to Beaver.* Leonetti's images make it seem like it might be at first, the picturesque suburban neighborhood looks right out of a sitcom. His depth of field is longer than Hooper had ever experimented with before, shooting real streets instead of sets. It doesn't feel like Hooper's framing, but Hooper had never filmed a cozy neighborhood before, let alone for an ironic counterpart. So naturally his grammar would have to expand to take stock of the changes. The image of a guy falling off a bike is straight up Spielberg, but the framing of the house and the crane shot that introduces us to the image are plainly Hooper's work.

The imperfections pile up like a traffic accident; the living room, with its hideous brown carpet and tacky furniture, is full of screaming football fans, friends of Steve's. There's a skirmish with a neighbor over a shared television signal, the two men using remotes like dueling pistols. Tweedy, Carol Anne's pet bird, has died. Fittingly, its shadow as it descends into the toilet is straight out of a Looney Tunes short (Dana munches on celery like Bugs Bunny when we see her next and the family share a last name with Isadore "Friz" Freleng, one of Warner Bros. top animation directors). The bathroom is even color-coordinated to match those of the dead bird. Carol Anne wants a proper burial for the bird, complete with cigar box casket and a flower for the dear departed. The dog starts digging up the bird's grave the minute he's been laid to rest, a morbid gag of a piece with the window washer from *Chain Saw*.

As Diane puts the family down for the night, Steve watches *A Guy Named Joe* on TV (another film about the supernatural which Spielberg would remake as *Always* in 1989) and rolls a joint for himself and Diane (suddenly, they seem like they could have been the couple who got married in the park at the end of *Eggshells*). The lighting in the bedroom feels very Hooper, all the lamps on to wash out the focus and make the scene a mix of mundane and romantic. Nelson's pothead baby boomer reads *Reagan The Man, The President*, all traces of his former lifestyle hidden from his children. The camera swivels around the bed while Diane tells a story about the police from her youth to which Steve barely listens—a slow dolly right out of *Chain Saw*. Steve stands up to demonstrate proper diving technique to assuage his wife's fear of their children falling into the new, planned swimming pool. The lighting is bare and awkward on him in the low angle from the bed, like the lights in Leatherface's house or the Sawyer home in

Salem's. Steve's big glasses and dorky nice guy routine say he could be *The Funhouse's* Rich all grown up (and not axed to death). The lighting is far uglier than anything in *Jaws, 1941,* or *Close Encounters of the Third Kind.*

Meanwhile, Robbie and Carol Anne (still adjusting to this new house) are terrified of everything in their room: the trees out the window, the goldfish, the spooky clown doll on the chair across from Robbie's bed (he looks like a refuge from *The Funhouse*). Everything looks like scary when lightning strikes. *Poltergeist* plays rough with the Freeling children. They're already scared of everything, so having all the normal objects in their room turn against them just confirms all their worst fears about life.

Hooper does a spectacular job of maintaining an even hand on everyone's perspective. No one is our POV character in the way that we're privy to Roy Scheider, Dennis Weaver, or Richard Dreyfuss' development in earlier Spielberg films. The character development in *Poltergeist* is communal, as in *Eggshells* and *Chain Saw*. We get a sense of the realistic behavior of each member of the Freeling family without ever being situated behind their eyes. When Carol Anne loses the parakeet, we get little sense during the scene that Hooper feels that this moment (a girl saying goodbye to a beloved pet) is a lynchpin in understanding her experience throughout the rest of the film. It's Diane's guilt at having botched the fish's funeral that gets the most attention, not Carol Anne's loss. No one experiences anything in the first act of *Poltergeist* that brings us exclusively to their point of view.

Hooper shoots the family in wides for the most part, favoring dollies to capture the ambling motion of the family unit through their day. Compare this to the shot-reverse-shot family scenes in early Spielberg, which serve to underline our lead's subjective experience of their family unit, and Hooper's design begins to stand out. Roy Neary's family watch him craft his mashed potato landing site from the alienating distance of a separate shot. They're outsiders to his journey. Here everyone is captured in the frame together. If someone is in the cutaway, it's typically for a joke, as in the parakeet flushing or Robbie in the tree during the bird's funeral. We're at a healthy remove from individuals because the story is the haunting of a *family*, just as *Texas Chain Saw* isn't really Sally Hardesty's story. It's the story of two groups of people whose fundamental beliefs place them at odds. *Poltergeist* is about a family recognizing that the evidence of their "happy" life is as much a threat to their happiness as the demon in their house. They were blinded by the swimming pool, the nice house, and the Reaganomic milestones of their wealth and success as people instead of paying more careful attention to each other. There's a lot of Spielberg in that scenario, but Hooper's films until this point in his career all say roughly the same thing and with more focus and aggression. Money, wealth, power, and position are all lies. Happiness is intangible and will not be bought or acquired.

The real joy of the film is in the way Hooper plays with the space of the house. After tucking Robbie into bed, Steve says goodnight to him and Carol Anne. Then, in the same shot, he walks down the hall to check in on Dana, who hides the phone she's not supposed to still be on, but not fast enough. He opens the door again and tells her to hang up. It's a Spielberg-style moment (redolent of the handwriting joke early in *Jaws*), but executed with Hooper's lighter touch with the camera and choreography. Steve's pep talk about the scary tree in the yard, like his phone talk with Dana, isn't particularly effective and, in a hilarious edit, the kids are suddenly sleeping beside their parents. The tree's spookiness has won over reason—the first of fear's many victories over the Freelings.

Carol Anne is roused by the TV (the national anthem appears again, heralding the static that comes with the shutting down of the signal for the night—something viewers under 35 will have to have explained to them) and welcomes a cartoonish hand made of smoke from out of the television signal and into the walls of the Freelings' home, which causes earthquake like tremors in the house. "They're here!" coos Carol Anne. The cut to the caterpillar digging equipment in the backyard is another not-so-subtle clue that the villain will wind up being the real estate company Steve works for. Also unsubtle—Carol Anne switches off pun-loving critic Gene Shalit in the next scene so she can watch static and communicate with "the TV people".

Little things start going wrong right away. Robbie's glass of milk breaks in half, dropping into his cereal bowl. Then his fork and spoon are bent out of shape. The dog barks at the spot in the bedroom wall where the spirits beamed in. The chairs in the kitchen are all moved away from the table at exactly the same distance (cameo by Lou Perryman as the worker sticking his head through the kitchen window, who we'll see again in *Texas Chain Saw 2*. That's Sonny Landham as his coworker, harassing Dana on her way to school). Diane rights the chairs, but a split-second later they're stacked up like trick acrobats on the table.

"TV people?" she asks Carol Anne, who nods slowly.

There's a lovely cut between the Freelings' kitchen and one of the houses Steve is trying to sell, playing up the identical blandness of perfection. The neighborhood they live in is called Cuesta Verde, in case we didn't get the point. Spielberg's storyboards are always apparent in the design and the spatial coordination of the shots. He mapped the locations pretty thoroughly. (It's interesting that for all the discussion about who did what, it's plain neither man felt entirely satisfied by *Poltergeist*. Spielberg would return to the supernatural with *Always*, a more thoroughly personal film combining his cinephilia and earnest, cornball religious investigation. Hooper's next film, *Lifeforce*, would pit a group of men against a woman who radiates all manner of psychic, telekinetic, and extraterrestrial power. Both wanted more out of the uncanny than *Poltergeist* gave them.)

"Reach back into our past when you used to have an open mind. Remember that?" asks Diane before showing Steve what the house has revealed to her since that afternoon.

Hooper's camera follows them inside, letting them vanish between the entryway and the kitchen—more Hooper over Spielberg, a more economical, straightforward image-maker. The kitchen has kept producing phenomena—place anything in a circle Diane has outlined and it slides across the floor as if by magnetic force. This scene, the awe, the staggered look on Steven's face are more purely Spielberg, but JoBeth William's excited response feels like the same energy that fueled Pam's horoscope readings in *Chain Saw*. Steven's stoned reaction is right out of Hooper's male rationalist playbook. Steven, like Buzz, Jerry, Kirk and Buck, is not just gonna believe what's handed to him. They head to the neighbors' house (there's a terrible edit thanks to a joke at Pizza Hut's expense that caused some corporate hand-wringing) and, bathed in yellow light (like guests at the Starlight Motel), try to ask if he's experienced anything similar. No dice. They're in this alone, together.

That night, Robbie's fears of the tree are confirmed in a terrifying display of power from Hooper and the effects team. Two tree branch arms burst through the window in a thunderstorm and try to pull Robbie out of his bed (Spielberg reuses this visual in his *BFG* adaptation)—a wonderful image that conjures up mountains of childhood dread, the flashing blue lights right out of *The Funhouse*. It's a diversion on the part of the angry demons of the house. While everyone bands together to rescue Robbie from the tree (it nearly eats him, a grisliness that one can't help but attribute to Hooper), Carol Anne is sucked into the closet. The demonic tree is whooshed into a kind of vortex over the house (the tableaux of the family outside watching the bizarre phenomena has the same depth of field as the shots of Susan Norton in the Marsten House, like they're standing in a painting). The Freelings look for their youngest daughter in the closet but find only Robbie's awful clown doll, which despite everything, makes them laugh a little. Robbie is paralyzed by what's just happened, coated in mud and blood, standing stock still, looking at what used to be his bedroom—we know the look on his face from the traumatized visages of Sally Hardesty and Amy Harper. Spielberg would use it again when filming Tim and Lex Murphy in *Jurassic Park*. It doesn't take them long to start hearing Carol Anne's voice coming from the TV. The box they rely on, fall asleep in front of, and fight over has taken their daughter.

The lighting in the parapsychology offices that Steven visits have four differently colored windows, a different light bulb behind each; Hooper's expressionist lighting from *The Funhouse* getting a quick, quirky showcase in a shot that feels like it was designed by the Spielberg of *Raiders*, with its slow movement around the conference table. Here and elsewhere, Hooper's lighting, nakedly expressionistic, will resemble the work of Dario Argento. His zooms and dollies feel very uniquely his. They're his way of drawing us inexorably into the horror. The first day in the house with the parapsychology team (Beatrice Straight, who'd taken on the evils of TV in *Network*, Martin Casella, and Richard Lawson) is a qualified success. They make contact with Carol Anne, and then her spiritual captor knocks everyone to the floor.

As the family settles down (Steve's framed with light through blinds on his face, his internal imprisonment writ large. Diane will have the same lighting on her face the following morning), when Straight's Dr. Lesh explains about the spirit world to a frightened Robbie.

"Some people believe that when people die...there's a wonderful light...as bright as the sun...but it doesn't hurt to look into."

It's Spielberg's dialogue, but it's weirdly applicable to Hooper's ethos. His camera stares into lights frequently during this period especially, as an obscuration device, but also to best highlight the contributions of every member of the creative team. It showcases the work of the rigging gaffers, the special effects crew, the cinematographer, the set decorators, production designers, art directors, and by reflecting his performer's eyes, they capture the deeply felt emotion of every character.

Marty, the nebbish on Dr. Lesh's crew, goes to the kitchen in the dead of night and is subjected to a nightmarish vision. His steak explodes with revolting decay and then he watches a version of himself tear his face apart to the bone. It's a more tactile and grotesque version of the melting Nazis at the end of *Raiders of the Lost Ark*, but with a little more of Hooper's fearlessness (and lighting—the scene changes lighting from one garish hue to another with each cut). Back in the living room, the cameras direct themselves towards an onslaught of ghosts—there's a smoothly propulsive dolly past Ryan, the third member of the parapsychology team, and his bank of monitors towards the stairs where the ghosts emerge. Dr. Lesh realizes she's outmatched by the sheer hugeness of the haunting and gets reinforcements.

In the meantime, we get a couple of upsetting vignettes. Diane goes to Carol Anne's bedroom door to talk to her and when she opens the door she's greeted by a loud roar, sending her into teary hysterics. Steven's boss, Teague (James Karen, whom Hooper would use again in *Invaders from Mars*), tries to talk his star seller back to work with the promise of a new house on a hill. There are two dollies in the scene, one past a white picket fence, and a second one that reveals that on the other side of the fence is a cemetery. Hooper's ethos in a cut. Teague explains that the whole of Cuesta Verde is built on a cemetery and Hooper gets to film the geometric design of the neighborhood with palpable dread and angst.

Dr. Lesh returns with a pint-sized southern bell psychic named Tangina (Zelda Rubinstein) who does her best to calm the frayed Freelings. Diane, looking in Hooper's close-ups like Amy Harper in her fear, excitement, and confusion, agrees to every one of the little woman's conditions. In a long take replete with focus shifts and ending on the door to the bedroom, the motley group begins their exorcism. Compare this to the opening of the Ark of the Covenant, the many scenes of shark hunting in *Jaws*, or the musical communication in *Close Encounters*, and the shot length alone make this feel more of a piece with Hooper's work. When they open the door, Hooper's psychedelic lighting makes a return and stays for the duration of the final act. The flashing blue from the closet, interrupted by yellows and purples when Tangina throws a tennis ball into it, is another version of the purple light in *Eggshells* that consumes the minds of the young communists. The houses, speaking for the land beneath them, full of angry history, want to eat their visiting owners alive. Steven kisses Diane and sends her into the closet with a rope he ties around her waist and Tangina starts her incantations.

When the void finally coughs up Dianne and Carol Anne (after sending a giant glowing skeleton head, like the cover of Texan psych band Josefus' album *Dead Man*, in the room to frighten Steve—there are a half-dozen edits of his reaction a la Sally in *Chain Saw*), the crew puts them in a bathtub as if they'd suffered an overdose instead of an inter-dimensional episode. The Freelings are packing their belongings into a moving van a cut later. Diane's hair has grayed thanks to the trip into the netherworld, making her look like Elsa Lanchester's Bride of Frankenstein. She vows to dye it, waiting for Steve to return from his last day at work.

Diane leaves the children unattended (Spielberg's screenwriting contrivance is the worst in the movie. On no planet would a mother who'd been through *that* leave her children alone in the room where it started) and takes a bath. She's bathed in red light like one of Judd's victims-to-be in *Eaten Alive*—code in Hooper's world for a nasty upset about to change her world. The children's bedroom is lit beautifully with bold pinks and yellows a la *Suspiria*—especially once the demon in the walls makes its move. The lighting here is way too weird to be Spielberg's doing. While Diane showers, the clown doll strangles Robbie (still one of the finest jump scares in Western Horror) and another figurative womb opens up in the wall, full of Hooper's signature oppressive colors, to suck the children back into the house. Their mother hears their screams, but a particularly handsy demon pulls up Diane's shirt then throws her up the wall to the ceiling, slowing down her rescue. She'll have to contend with an equine apparition and the swimming pool suddenly filling with skeletons before she can save her kids. Steve and Teague arrive just as the ground starts puking up skeletons and coffins. Teague's the only one left standing as the house crumples like a piece of paper and is warped into oblivion. The Freelings drive away while fire hydrants and gas mains explode into the air.

"Don't look back!" shouts Steve, making the attack feel biblical in nature.

The final shot finds the family walking to their motel room (they should have asked Clara Carter if that's the best place to rest). They walk inside and, just before going to bed, Steve pushes the TV out into the hall and the camera pulls back on a crane just like the finale shot of *The Funhouse*.

The trouble started when, according to a Los Angeles Times story at the time, advertising for *Poltergeist* featured Steven Spielberg's producer credit more prominently than Hooper's director credit and the Director's Guild of America sued the production. The lawsuit began an obsession with figuring out who was in control. In that story, as well as in interviews in Ain't It Cool News, at screenings, the Blumhouse Productions website, the *Post Mortem* podcast, and *Rue Morgue* magazine, dissenting takes on the role of Hooper and Spielberg have been collected through the years. Director Mick Garris, who was a publicist for the film, says Hooper was the driving creative force on set. Zelda Rubinstein and camera assistant John R. Leonetti said Spielberg. James Karen said he felt differently, that Hooper was his director. Spielberg published a letter to Hooper in The Hollywood Reporter that read:

> Regrettably, some of the press has misunderstood the rather unique, creative relationship which you and I shared throughout the making of Poltergeist.
>
> I enjoyed your openness in allowing me, as a writer and a producer, a wide berth for creative involvement, just as I know you were happy with the freedom you had to direct Poltergeist so wonderfully. Through the screenplay you accepted a vision of this very intense movie from the start, and as the director, you delivered the goods. You performed responsibly and professionally throughout, and I wish you great success on your next project.

Successful collaboration just isn't as fun a story as a secret feud. As I was writing this chapter, I was talking to a cinephile friend who expressed surprise that Hooper directed it. Everyone forgets or no one knows. That's how much history has closed the book on *Poltergeist's* director. Feels like Spielberg, must be Spielberg. For what it's worth, Hooper and Spielberg buried the hatchet—Hooper directed episodes of two different shows twenty years apart (*Amazing Stories* and *Taken*) produced by Spielberg, which doesn't sound like the kind of thing you do through gritted teeth. Whatever else is true of *Poltergeist*, it sent both Spielberg and Hooper on different, definitive paths. Hooper would become an independent, working for studios that would leave him to his own devices or for TV productions orchestrated by friends like John Carpenter and Mick Garris. Spielberg would try to produce more horror films for up and comers like Joe Dante without ever getting caught up in production debacles like this ever again. Hooper's choice left him without a mainstream ally to keep him in the public's good graces. *Poltergeist* grossed over a hundred million dollars internationally on a ten million dollar budget. The combined gross of the following nine films by Hooper that played in movie theatres wouldn't amount to half of that. The success of the film would not rub off on him in any way. He wasn't involved in any way in the production of the film's two sequels. To make things even more unbearably tragic, by the end of the '80s, stars Heather O'Rourke and Dominique Dunne had both died appallingly young. There was little silver lining in the making of *Poltergeist*, but as a testament to the talents of its director and dearly missed stars, it's invaluable.

Scout Tafoya

Chapter 3:
The Color Out of Space (1985–1986)

After a decade of increasing financial difficulty and watching his reputation become tarnished, Orson Welles went to poverty row production house Republic Studios when the majors wouldn't touch him to reclaim some of his independence as an artist. When the same thing happened to Hooper, he went to the Israeli-owned Cannon Group after he was burned by his experience working for a major studio on *Poltergeist*. Run by hands-off producer/director/cousins Menahem Golan and Yoram Globus, Cannon was famous for churning out both cheapie schlock like *Delta Force* and *Enter the Ninja* and art house outliers when directors like Jean-Luc Godard and John Cassavetes couldn't get major studio backing. Hooper was able to make the weird, thorny, outsized studio product he wanted under the less-than-watchful eye of the Cannon Group, which turned out to be some of his most low-rated, derided work—beneath the standards of the man who made *Texas Chain Saw*, or so popular opinion would have you believe.

Hooper took a long break after *Poltergeist*, as one would need to after the huge gut punch that accompanied its release. But when he came back, he was rejuvenated creatively, overflowing with ideas, and ready to reclaim control of his artistic destiny. If *The Funhouse* was Hooper elegantly, tightly, and confidently showcasing his strengths and interests and *Poltergeist* a compromise in the form of a restrictive collaboration that needed to take the will of producers into consideration, *Lifeforce* is Hooper unchained. He holds nothing back, moving at a breakneck pace to make sure he gets all of his ideas out before the credits roll and shows off a newly maximalist approach to art direction and visual storytelling. This film is replete with flashing neon colors, living mummies, buckets of blood, lightning bolts, hordes of zombie vampires, homosexual carnality, naked bodies, and all of it has an insouciant sexual keel.

Lifeforce was as far from Hooper's wheelhouse as he could get without making someone else's movie—out of the suburbs, out of Hollywood, and out of the tightly storyboarded world of *Poltergeist*. Hooper found himself by leaving everything with which he'd grown too cozy. The Hooper that worked for the Cannon Group over the next three years was a man letting his dreams run wild and, in some instances, get the better of him. But the one thing you can't say of him is that he seems compromised or restricted. *Lifeforce* may be too thoroughly insane for some, but it's the first time Hooper got to be the filmmaker he promised to be when he made *The Heisters*. It drips with love for Hammer films (screenwriters Dan O'Bannon and Don Jakoby retrofit Colin Wilson's source novel *The Space Vampires* into a patchwork of all three Hammer Quatermass films) and AIP schlock, and it *too* could use a title card warning the audience that the film they're about to see is ridiculous.

Lifeforce (1985)

Lifeforce would have perhaps been better served by keeping the title of the book on which it's based, *Space Vampires*. It's more pulpy and direct, and also pretty succinctly sums up the narrative: astronauts find vampires in space, bring them back to Earth, and then have to defeat them before they turn all of London's populace into vampires. Of course the film isn't nearly as simple as that makes it sound.

Even before the title soars at us like a cartoon spaceship, Henry Mancini's music has begun its proud march through our ears. Everything about *Lifeforce* is big and old fashioned. Mancini's theme has the pomp and excitement of many of the themes for Hammer films by Harry Robinson, Tristram Cary, or James Bernard. Our very serious narrator explains that we're aboard the spacecraft Churchill, which uses an experimental engine that creates gravity through "constant acceleration," which is also what'll be powering the film. Right away, Hooper's lighting is in effect (Alan Hume is our director of photography this time out). Each wall of the Churchill's control room is a different neon shade, reds and blues exploding from control panels onto crewmember's faces. We meet our crew, mostly British with the notable exception of Colonel Tom Carlsen (Steve Railsback, who played Charles Manson to Marilyn Burns' Linda Kasabian in *Helter Skelter*). The images of the spacecraft in flight are gorgeous, deliberately excessive paintings filled with unnatural color and light. The light from the comet's tail, where an object they plan to investigate is "hiding," is like a spun glass rendering of a 3D graph. Hooper's renders space travel by doubling down on the awe factor. He draws his objects and their atmosphere with a mix of boyish obviousness and sinister strangeness. The object of Churchill's investigation is some kind of craft, 150 miles long and perfectly alien in appearance, with a pointy, clawed base.

Carlsen leads an investigation inside the craft. He and the other spacemen are crudely, but charmingly, processed into the still images of space. The exterior of the craft has the same bulbous surface as the haunted closet from *Poltergeist* in its final iteration and the entrance looks just like the womb-shape it manifests when trying to suck the children inside in the final minutes.

"I almost have a feeling I've been here before," says Carlsen, submerged in by now trademark Hooperian red light.

The look of the spacecraft borrows from H.R. Giger and Moebius' designs for the planet in *Alien* (a poster of which hung on the walls of the Freeling kids' bedroom in *Poltergeist*), but with a flagrancy, a kind of Frank Frazetta pride in the lunacy on display (all of it would fit comfortably on the cover of a prog rock album cover—when Hooper goes sci-fi, he switches from Red Krayola to Yes). Hooper has prepared so much sheer spectacle that editor John Grover has a tough time showing all of it. Carlsen and his team discover that the craft is home to giant bats, all now apparently dead and stuck floating in gravity-free environments. It's a wonderfully uncanny image, the astronauts soaring past the freeze-dried, man-sized bats surrounded by what looks like intestines on the walls of the craft. They net one of the bats for further study, then the craft opens up for them to fly deeper inside the bowls of the ship, lens flares for miles.

Hume cranes around the astronaut's final stop on the craft: a holding room that looks like a beehive, containing three naked human beings (Matilda May, Chris Jagger, and Bill Malin) in glass tubes. He'll spin the camera around Carlsen, as he's entranced by the lone female among the perfectly preserved humans. Hooper understands the untapped sexual subtext in space exploration and makes it plainly about Tom Carlsen's sexual awakening—he travels through a rectum-shaped portal to find the object of his desire and will later kiss a man possessed by the female vampire's spirit. Hooper's *Lifeforce* wasn't the first film to hint at the colonialist, heterosexual attitudes of much of American sci-fi, but he was boldly unafraid of turning the subtext into text. *Alien, Demon Seed,* and others (few of them American movies) had explored these topics before, but never as bombastically. The crew bags the bodies and they're back on the Churchill.

Thirty days later, the Churchill has stopped broadcasting and, over a crudely rendered cartoon Earth, another shuttle comes to their rescue with a soft docking procedure that looks just enough like oral sex to kick off the film's vampiric fixation with the mouth, teeth, and sharing fluids. There's a little nod to *2001* as the rescue crew from the Colombia board the Churchill, all sterile whites in the spinning docking tunnel. The remnants of the Churchill are crispy and decayed like an interstellar version of the Marsten House—everyone on board is dead except the three pristine bodies recovered from the big vampire ship (Carlsen isn't on board any longer). The deep blues of *The Funhouse* are the film's dominant color, evinced by the cut from the bright blue light in the chamber where the bodies are held to the cool blue light reflecting on Big Ben, the florescent green of Halley's comet over its shoulder.

At the European Space Research Centre, a cadre of scientists under the direction of Dr. Bukovsky (Michael Gothard, so thrilling in Ken Russell's *The Devils*. Russell's films aren't a bad stylistic warm-up to Hooper's work in the '80s and '90s) discuss what to do next. Dr. Hans Fallada (Frank Finlay, like Gothard, a graduate of Richard Lester's *Musketeer* movies) is flippant on the subject of whether or not they should perform autopsies on the aliens they've recovered from the spacecraft, currently in a holding area at the centre.

One of his colleagues protests, "Well, you would agree that they're less alive than we are."

That, at least, makes Fallada smile.

Bukovski's office has the lived-in semi-coziness of the Freeling house. He's so outraged by a news report on the Churchill, that he misses something on one of the banks of monitors displaying CCTV footage of the rest of the centre. One of the security guards in charge of May's lady from space wanders into her holding room and is about to cop a feel, when she wakes up. Bukovsky notices far too late to save the guard from having his essence removed (the power in the room goes haywire, by now a favorite effect of Hooper's) in a cloud of blue electric smoke. Bukovsky's run to save the guard (who looks like he was carved from tree bark when May is done with him) is filled with wonderfully planned out movements through the corridors of the center. Hume still finds time to dolly amidst the confusion and momentum (recalling the first tour of the house in *Eggshells*). There's a sort of recall of the frames-in-frames device employed in *The Funhouse* (specifically, the shot of the truck driver's face when he pulls over next to Joey Harper) when the woman advances on Bukovsky. From left to right, we see his shadow, his body, her shadow on his chest, and then, finally, she emerges, the fourth figure in the frame. It's a little visual shorthand for the vampire's power—the way their shadows hang over their victims as in the final moments of FW Murnau's original vampire movie, 1922's *Nosferatu*. Fallada arrives with reinforcements too late.

"Don't worry, a naked girl is not going to get out of this complex." Finlay's voluptuous accent sells this ludicrous line with uncommon zeal.

Hooper shoots May in a series of low-key lighting set ups to best conceal her genitals. The same can't be said of the bawdy shot of her very naked shadow slowly passing the wall behind a bewildered night watchman, which, while probably the single perviest thing in Hooper's oeuvre, is also a warning to adjust expectations. Like the shadow of the bird hovering above the toilet in *Poltergeist*, it's a cartoonish tone calibration. Don't let the accents fool you; the man who made *Eaten Alive* is calling the shots.

The security guards' banter (flanked by red light) is almost Benny Hill-esque. One of the men tries to beckon her to him with a hand that happens to have a half-eaten cookie in it, making it look like he's enticing her with the promise of a treat like an animal—men believing women can be manipulated with rewards, themselves rewarded with psychic strangulation and electrocution. She shatters the windows of the centre's lobby and is off into the night. Colonel Colin Caine of the SAS (Peter Firth) is called in to investigate. Firth's intensity is greatly appreciated. Suddenly, his staunchness makes everything fall in line. *Lifeforce* can start acting like the Hammer film it's dressed as.

It's worth taking a second to quickly talk about the films from which the plot is patched together. Based on Nigel Kneale's BBC TV serial, Val Guest's film *The Quatermass Xperiment*, or *The Creeping Unknown* as it was called in the US, pits American no-nonsense scientist Bernard Quatermass (Brian Donlevy) against an alien life-form salvaged from a crashed spacecraft with the help of Scotland Yard Inspector Lomax (Jack Warner). *Quatermass 2*, also called *Enemy From Space* in some territories, revisits Donlevy's Professor Quatermass as he uncovers a conspiracy involving space slime that turns people into zombies. And finally, Roy Ward Baker's *Quatermass and The Pit, or Five Million Years to Earth*, has a newly British Quatermass (Andrew Keir) investigate a spacecraft under a tube station that causes mass hysteria—to pave the way for an invasion, of course.

Lifeforce's Quatermass figures are Colonel's Carlsen and Caine, his American and English interpretations split into two. Caine's discussions with Bukovsky and Fallada have Hammer's patented seriousness about a truly laughable subject. Keir, Peter Cushing, Christopher Lee, Michael Ripper, and many more used to sit around discussing vampires and mummies with the same sobriety once or twice a year during the company's heyday. Hooper frames the office with the same politely mannered spatial arrangement as Terence Fisher or Baker (whose queer horror masterpiece *Dr. Jekyll & Sister Hyde* sits in the back of *Lifeforce*'s influences). The images feel much more plainly Hooper's than the carefully storyboarded *Poltergeist*.

Caine furiously questions Bukovsky. "Tell me again how the girl overpowered you."

"She eh...was most the overwhelming feminine presence I've ever encountered. I was drawn to her on a level that..."

"Was it sexual?" interjects Caine.

"Yes, overwhelmingly so," says Bukovsky, voice an octave lower than we've heard it thus far, head shaking with imperceptible facetiousness, hitting the "H" in "overwhelming" like he was being judged on the Englishness of his diction.

Hooper's dollying and panning happens to synch up with the Hammer house style but we could well be in Frankenstein's laboratory as seen in James Whale's *Frankenstein* and *Bride of Frankenstein* movies thanks to the lighting and the array of scientific instruments on display. The rapport between Caine and Bukovsky has the familiar antagonism of Cushing and Lee from Hammer and Hammer adjacent work like 1972's *Horror Express* and 1967's *Island of the Burning Damned*.

Fallada explains that he believes that the girl sucked the life force out of the guard completely, and Bukovsky partially.

"Like a vampire?" asks Caine.

Hume dollies in on Fallada.

"...in a sense, we're all vampires."

Suddenly, Hooper's involvement makes more sense. He's dealt with vampirism (and cannibalism) in every one of his features thus far, most obviously in *Salem's Lot,* from predatory houses to ordinary people (think Grandpa sucking on Sally's bloody finger). The vampires are colonists, like Straker and Barlow from *Salem's,* and they want to suck the life out of the low-level bureaucrats working for the government—the woman from space is a perversely inverted Margaret Thatcher, using her wiles, looks, and sexual violence to dismantle a nation's working class through outright hysteria instead of prejudiced, inhumane policy. Is it any accident that one of her opponents in *Lifeforce,* Aubrey Morris' Sir Percy Heseltine, shares the surname of her famous conservative opponent?

"I'm not paid to believe nothing," says one of the guards looking after the still-slumbering male vampires. Be a good worker—have no beliefs. That's how oppressors win. The Vietnam-machinery hiding in the back of *Chain Saw* and *Eggshells* is repurposed to fit '80s England (*Lifeforce* works as an imagistic sequel to Hooper's video for "Dancing With Myself" with violence overflowing on the streets) and the anarchy has accidental echoes of Derek Jarman's *Jubilee*, The Sex Pistols, and *The Young Ones*. The male vampires wake in a sudden explosion of purple-hued flame and broken glass. Bullets don't stop them—you can't shoot insidious politics with deep historical roots.

When the smoke clears, we join the autopsy of the desiccated guard, already in progress. Our corpse is now a puppet right out of *The Funhouse*, who wakes up screaming and sucks the life out of the attending pathologist. The new life force puts sores and boils on the vampire's forehead on the way to restoring him to full vitality. Fallada coolly diagnoses the situation as an epidemic in waiting—the action in this shot is typically busy for Hooper. Caine listens to Fallada, gives orders and takes a phone call all while crime scene cleanup takes place in the reflection in the glass.

Hume's camera rides a crane down from a tree to the crime scene where the space lady has most lately struck. The body's been found thanks to two horny young men who were hoping the sight of a naked space vampire approaching a woman meant they could spy on some Sapphic goings-on in the park. Caine's interrogation of the two gloomy perverts is wonderful deadpan comedy.

One whiplash-inducing edit later, and we're watching the guard all but disintegrate in front of Fallada and Caine (Fallada pokes his stomach with a stick and watches it turn to cinders)—this is what happens when the vampires don't feed. The ad hoc vampire hunting committee (Percy Heseltine now in their ranks) will monitor the girl from the park as she comes to, in need of feeding, her pupils off-yellow spirals (similar to Barlow's), her skin is a mix of pinks and blues, her body, fingers, and teeth like one of the corpses unearthed by the hitchhiker in *Chain Saw*—she's a most Hooperian vampire, in other words. She explodes just as Bukovsky delivers news that the Churchill's escape pod has landed in Texas with a Manson-bearded Tom Carlsen inside. They fly him over to join the vampire hunt as soon as they fix him up.

Hooper dollies around Carlsen, seated in Bukovsky's office, to reveal Fallada and Caine waiting for him to begin his story, a move identical to the one he used to first introduce Ben Mears to Richard Straker in *Salem's Lot*. Hooper will swivel around Carlsen as he spins his yarn. Carlsen's story takes us back to the Churchill, which he boards in a pool of green light from the comet. Soon, the crew starts to die, Mancini's score turning to mournful horns and strings, while Hooper adds on the Dutch tilts and fish-eyed lenses to show the deteriorating condition aboard the spaceship. When Carlsen resolves to scuttle the ship and escape, Mancini's strings turn insistent and Hooper changes up his grammar, cutting quickly between the compartments he visits, choosing a new height and angle to give the rapid pace of the scene a sort of internal tension.

That night, Carlsen will have a bad dream where the bat creature will advance on him (arriving naturally in a burst of psychedelic light, explosion sounds, and Mancini's horns) then quickly turn into the space girl. They'll start mating in an oppressive orgy of neon reds and blues and he'll wake up screaming like Sally Hardesty tied to the armchair. Fallada hypnotizes him as Hooper spins out of his Dutch tilt and dollies forward, an old-school technique to show mental instability. We'll watch what he describes, his strained, sweaty recollection giving it the feeling of an erotic fantasy, especially when the woman he's watching (the space girl in the skin of another woman, played by Nancy Paul who looks like Julie Christie in *Don't Look Now*) cruise a passing motorist and seduce him while he's driving.

The spacecraft, all 150 miles of it, is approaching Earth, which sends Fallada, Bukovsky, and Caine into panic mode. Bukovsky suggests that the spaceship is the modern equivalent of a coffin filled with earth from the vampire's resting place. They track the seduced motorist and his companion to an asylum for the criminally insane run by one Dr. Armstrong (Patrick Stewart). The hitchhiker who seduced the motorist is Ellen Donaldson, and she has symbolic butterflies and David Bowie posters on her wall—we're about to see someone shed their skin. Carlsen can sense that the vampire wants him to beat the knowledge out of her. He offers Caine the chance to leave before it happens.

Firth, *Lifeforce's* secret comedic weapon, sits down and gets comfortable. "I'm a natural voyeur."

When Carlsen strips her blouse off, the vampire's shadow is tossed onto the ceiling, looking like the spreading of wings (she even has scratches where wings would fit on her body). He gets the information telepathically, and the vampire hunters are off—Hooper delights in framing the group, as he does the family in *Poltergeist* and the kids in *Chain Saw*.

The man Carlsen asks to see has a birthmark on his face just like *Chain Saw's* Hitchhiker's blood-colored blotch, but he's a decoy. Caine and Carlsen subdue Dr. Armstrong (flopping on the floor like one of Leatherface's victims) because he's the one who's been possessed by the woman from space. Hooper tries every conceivable angle while they start their metaphysical questioning in a brilliant green room. Spinning dollies, Dutch tilts, low angle establishing, a push-in through the z-axis while Carlsen, Caine, and Heseltine drape themselves over Armstrong, who forms the x-axis, interrupted by the attending nurse arriving with more drugs for the interrogation, changing the shape and dynamic of the composition. The lighting is harsh as in Leatherface's living room in the final act of *Chain Saw*.

Armstrong starts speaking in two voices: his and that of the space vampire. Caine can't settle on a gendered pronoun when asking Carlsen about his progress. Carlsen begins seeing the woman on the table instead of Armstrong, and she explains that she looks like his feminine ideal, culled together from all his deepest thoughts. This is a recurring motif in Hooper's cinema: everything is borrowed, our property, our homes, even our bodies. Carlsen begs the woman to release him from her grip to no avail. They kiss and it releases a torrent of psychic energy, every object in the room dancing into the air—Hooper's redo of the floating objects in *Poltergeist*. He'll get another shot at the exploding face trick from *Poltergeist* a few minutes later on their chopper ride back to London when the faces of Heseltine and Armstrong leak blood, becoming a gooey facsimile of the woman from space in front of Caine and Carlsen, which promptly explodes into a puddle on the floor.

Carlsen explains a little more about the bond between himself and space girl. There's a flashback to the ship with a compositional homage to another classic of psychedelic cinema: John Boorman's *Zardoz*. The trapezoidal box in which she was encased shoots reflections in every direction like the thought chamber Sean Connery's Zed is put through. There's an extreme fish-eyed close-up coupled with purple light as Carlsen first encounters the soul-sapping power of the vampires.

London quickly falls to pieces, blue light searing the sky, explosions rock a model of the town, and people scramble head over foot to get away from the vampire's zombie subjects (a callback to "Dancing with Myself"). Mancini's horns dance all over the soundtrack as clouds of Hooper's colors froth in the back of every shot. The prime minister, when they find him, is already a vampire, so it's back in the helicopter they go—there's a great aside involving a soldier hanging onto the landing gear, tearing his own skin off trying to stay attached. Mancini's score turns practically swashbuckling as Caine shoots a vampire off of the chopper with a flare gun. *Lifeforce* is a few different genres compressed into one, allowing Hooper to dabble in everything from sci-fi to action to romance, another reason *Lifeforce* is essential Hooper.

Carlsen and Caine take off into apocalyptic London, zombies flooding the streets, the lights from their cars illuminating new pockets of destruction at every turn—Hooper's imagination in overdrive. Carlsen gets attacked by one of the horde and pulls its arm off as he drives away, the fingers still twitching as he tosses it in the back seat. When Caine makes it to the research centre to check on Fallada, Hooper dollies with him as he runs down an expressionistically dark corridor. Fallada's lab is glowing orange from the destruction out the windows. Caine is framed with a mix of blue and orange behind him, strong shadows behind him, his face bright red. He's discovered that using an iron spike is the only way to kill the vampires.

Hooper's color here and during the rest of his tenure at Cannon is a mix of Michael Powell, Nicholas Ray, and Byron Haskin, all of them loud, confident stylists. Hooper may not have Powell's romance (they were both responsible for their share of commercial misfires) or Ray's incisively theoretical mise-en-scène, but he's at least as strong a craftsman as Haskin, who used to split his time between cutthroat noir like *Too Late For Tears* and big, boyish fantasies like *War of the Worlds* and *Tarzan's Peril*. The finale of *Lifeforce* is a carousel of rainbow-colored tableaux with too many wonderful compositions and contrasts to keep track of. Hooper has a ball turning Caine into an action hero, gallivanting around London with a gun in one hand and an iron stake in the other past barrages of harsh light, falling buildings, and bloodthirsty zombies. Fittingly, light becomes a malevolent character in this final act, sucking souls and blowing up subway corridors. Caine has only to catch up with Carlsen and the vampires and use Fallada's iron spike when they're in flagrante delicto. A Hooper film would never be this much *fun* again. Not that anyone noticed—it made back less than half of its 25 million budget and was maimed in postproduction with a new score thrust onto it and a lot of footage cut out. No one seemed happy with it at the time but when it was restored, *Lifeforce* was revealed to be earnestly thrilling cinema.

Scout Tafoya

The delirious excesses of *Lifeforce* are only atypically Hooper in their pace and they didn't take. The Boston Globe, The New York Times, and Leonard Maltin all found it too silly to take seriously. Audiences stayed away to the tune of a 14 million dollar box office loss. They failed to see or ignored that hiding behind the tightly constructed, carefully planned, and expertly executed camera movements in *Chain Saw* was a man with a million ideas garnered from watching horror and sci-fi from Hollywood's golden age. *Chain Saw* was Hooper at his most restrained, but the kid who made *The Heisters* had more ideas in him than one exercise in terror could contain. The Hooper who teamed with the Cannon Group was a man who got to spread his wings and make beautiful, weird, compelling genre jambalaya out of ideas culled from a lifetime of movie going. Hooper evolved and became an auteur right out of the paranoid, rainbow-colored fantasias of the 1950s, calling out the same foibles of governments ruled by fear as his predecessors, doing for film what The Sex Pistols did for music by combining modern angst with rock rhythms out of Chuck Berry. And what better way to announce the new phase in his career than by remaking a beloved sci-fi classic from the 1950s?

Invaders From Mars (1986)

William Cameron Menzies' *Invaders From Mars* is the platonic ideal of "gee-whiz" 1950s sci-fi. It's got a healthy dose of atomic paranoia, and Menzies' skill with matte paintings, bold lighting, and composition makes it a stunning dose of pop art eye candy even divorced from its subtext. But stronger than all that is its central conceit, one of the most potent in all of genre fiction—that people, your parents specifically, aren't who they claim to be. *Invaders From Mars*, three years before Don Siegel's *Invasion of the Body Snatchers*, imagined a world suddenly populated by shells shaped like the people we once knew and loved.

Tobe Hooper's interest in Menzies film plainly had as much to do with aesthetics as it did politics. Sure, Hooper's anti-Reagan streak would mean *Invaders* would veer even harder to the left than Menzies' original. But Menzies, he of *Things To Come*, the man who coined the term "production designer" and did it beautifully on *Gone With The Wind* and *For Whom The Bell Tolls,* among others, he was a man after Hooper's heart in that he made all of his work look gorgeous, even as it was terrifying, violent, and dreadful. All those matte paintings in *Poltergeist* and process shots in *Lifeforce* wouldn't have been possible without men like Menzies developing and perfecting them in films like *Things To Come.* Hooper's *Invaders From Mars* remake still works as a political allegory, but it's a tribute to Menzies' visual sense first and foremost, and to the filmmakers like him who weren't afraid of assaulting the viewer's corneas with too much light and color. The firework-heavy third act gets away from Hooper, but it has the benefit of being counterpoised by the ravishing design of the spacecraft we enter with our lead character.

Our hero is David Gardner and he's played by Hunter Carson (no relation to *The Funhouse's* Shawn Carson), who'd made his film debut acting in Wim Wenders' *Paris, TX,* which was based on a script by his father L. M. Kit Carson, one of the Texas' underground's favorite sons. Hunter Carson's mother was actress Karen Black, who plays the school nurse and Carson's protector in *Invaders.* The title flies at us (just as in *Lifeforce*) under the slightly less bombastic score by Christopher Young, which sounds like he's been cribbing notes from Jerry Goldsmith. The script is by *Lifeforce's* Dan O'Bannon and Don Jakoby and at first it emphasizes the realistic way a kid would see the world, talk with his parents, etc. We meet David hanging out with his father George (Timothy Bottoms, something of a cult fixture himself, appearing in Dalton Trumbo's *Johnny Got His Gun,* and *The Fantasist,* Robin Hardy's ill-fated follow up to *The Wicker Man*). Hooper, reunited with DoP Daniel Pearl from *Chain Saw* and "Dancing With Myself," spins the camera as it descends from the heavens to find the two cozily stargazing. The camera, like our villains, literally falls from the sky. When mom Ellen (the great Laraine Newman, who that year had starred in the short lived *Canned Film Festival,* a precursor to *Mystery Science Theatre 3000,* in which she played the lone usher at a theatre that only plays B movies) walks out, she steps into their field of view, standing tall in the y-axis against the side of the house, interrupting their lazy astronomy.

Our first good establishing shot of the house has some wonky geometry. The picket fence curving across the x-axis almost into the y, while the house sits on the x. The Gardner's family chemistry is perfect, exactly what you expect families to do augmented with a little overt cuteness. After Ellen tucks David in (Carson's adorable speech impediment adds to the film's cozy reality), Hooper pans around the bedroom to reveal George sitting at his son's desk, Hooper making expert use of the little space allotted.

David is woken up by a thunderstorm (those familiar flashes of blue), so he walks to the window to close it and the camera goes past him through the window to the lovingly crafted soundstage in his backyard, under the lightshow put on the by the landing gear of the Martian spaceship. The ship has a beautifully liquid design in flight (redolent of the blood doll version of Mathilda May in the helicopter in *Lifeforce*), surrounded by a flashing force field and sending a shower of primary and secondary colors all over David and his bedroom window. The window shuts on him as he watches the impressively tactile spaceship land just beyond the hill in his backyard, scaring him out of the room. Hooper and Pearl put the camera in the middle of the hallway so they can pan with David as he runs into his parent's room and then dolly into the room with him as he wakes them up.

"So glad you bought him a telescope," says Ellen groggily.

Hooper's intricate camera choreography is symptomatic of his return to the suburbs. He's built his idyllic small town on a back lot, which allows him full control over all of its dimensions. Pearl's camera can travel all over creation, maintaining just the right amount of continuity to preserve Hooper's illusions. He gets to dream up the perfect '50s environment, not just because he can relish in the designing, but because he can ironically appropriate the nostalgia inherent in '50s sci-fi, which itself was an accidental deconstruction of the televised *Leave it to Beaver* images of the '50s. The image of family life that Menzies' *Invaders from Mars* starts with is deliberately perfect so that when it falls prey to the Dr. Seuss inspired Martians, viewers will feel the weird imposition that much more. Hooper co-opts the broken perfection of '50s sci-fi with his crooked wryness, once again applying the logic of the Texan psych band covering rock songs. Hooper gets to try out the possessed suburbs of *Poltergeist* once more while building his vision of Eisenhower's America through the lens of Reagan's '80s. Perfection, even the fake perfection of '50s sci-fi, was now impossible.

Pearl's dolly shots have their own nostalgia about them as they hark back to his work with Hooper on *Texas Chain Saw*, the team's first dismantling of American values. Pearl's camera work is much smoother than on Hooper's last few films. Pearl's smoothness is the perfect mate for Hooper's quiet seething as he burns the outer layers of the American dream with a magnifying glass. Pearl moves in when George pulls David away from his window and puts him in bed, then backs off again, out the window when David leans up again and looks back out at the field (he did the same thing when the old man put Sally in his truck after straightjacketing her). Their collaboration, elegantly mapping the sets, feels like a band jamming again after years apart.

George comes back from over the hill a changed man—halting speech, no boundary perception, giant sore on the back of his neck—and David knows that something's up, even if Ellen doesn't. There's beautiful high-key lighting on David as he sits opposite his pod person dad, whose face is half in shadow as he stares the boy down at breakfast. Young's score has a little psychedelic edge, a high frequency humming underneath a soft flute melody; the oddness just underneath the ordinary. Bottoms plays the breakfast scene in a deadpan comic style that'd become a Hooper trademark since Craig T. Nelson in *Poltergeist*: people calmly ignoring the weird things they're doing or experiencing.

A portentous split diopter shot introduces us to David's classroom. He's staring at the class frog, hopping in its own slime up the side of a jar—Hooper letting us know it'll be playing a significant part in the story in just a short while.

"You know, this is Frog Week," says Mrs. McKeltch (Louise Fletcher).

Some antics with a dead frog leave David with a cut finger, so it's off to the school nurse, Linda Magnusson (Karen Black), who proves her cool bona fides by mispronouncing "McKeltch" in front of David. He'll remember this when things turn even weirder.

Back at home, Pearl waits with an off-kilter Steadicam shot (one of the first in Hooper's oeuvre—the handhelds back when the camera was light enough to lift with his bare hands don't count) following young David up the front door of his too-perfect house, only to discover that the door's been left open. Taking the camera off the tripod signals a sea change for the suburban life of David Gardner. The stability of the early scenes has been replaced with an uncertain, jittery, paranoid movement. The television plays static tinged with Hooper's usual yellows and purples (one of the many callbacks to *Poltergeist*—the film is a corrective in more than one way. Just traveling around the Gardner household feels like Hooper freed himself from the constraints of the set of the Freeling house) and when David changes the channel, he finds the end of *Lifeforce*, one of those in-jokes directors can't ever seem to resist. As David settles in, Hooper has him framed up close and to the far right of the frame while in the background, the shadow of the railing in the far upper left is obscured by his mother— Hooper and Pearl taking advantage of the spacious 2.35.1 aspect ratio— she's still normal, for the time being. Hooper will place David behind that same railing in the next cut, utilizing the prison bars provided by suburban houses wherever he can find them.

The police are called when George doesn't come home from work and they *too* vanish just over the hill. Hooper's fondness for gateways and portals is utilized for maximum mystery; rather than having his characters vanish *into* something, he just has them crest the hill and vanish. No one who walks over the hill will return intact and each time David watches them go, he'll lose a little more of his innocence. His apparently childish pleas that he saw a UFO are hushed by his mother, but soon he'll have to invert his understanding of the situation and be an adult to solve the childish problem of Martians and people snatching, one learned from a generation of cheesy sci-fi (he's another kid in the Mark Petrie mold).

Throughout *Invaders from Mars*, Hooper will play with his child hero's point of view. The deliberate falseness of the sets makes the film feel like something a child would imagine having been raised on sci-fi films and having been encouraged to look at the stars instead of at the world around him (the film will later be revealed to be a prophetic nightmare David is having). David is framed so he's dwarfed by both his surroundings and the replaced adults in his life. His father springs out of the bushes with another Martian plant just like George. David's tiny figure is small and brightly lit next to them, his expert side-eye making him look like he walked right out of a '50s sitcom.

"Ed works for the phone company," George offers of his new friend, still hilariously dry, "the switching division."

Ellen only wakes up to George's odd behavior when he asks her to do the dishes. The Martians believe in traditional gender roles; their plan is evidently to turn people into the spitting image of Ronald and Nancy

Reagan. That night, David pretends to be asleep when his father walks into his bedroom and looks ready to strangle the boy, but settles for stealing his goldfish bowl full of pennies instead. Pearl dollies in with gusto when David throws the covers off and then watches his father guide his mother over the hill into the misty night air—to the secret world of boredom and misogyny that claimed his dad. *Invaders From Mars* is slyly about the moral decay of baby boomers. The sitcom-pastiche of the production design makes more sense when you see that the aliens want to turn the '80s back into the '50s. Hooper must have started seeing that some of his once-radical friends were voting for Ronald Reagan, as so many did, and recognized that voting for the man was born of a strange, misplaced nostalgia for a time of racial and sexual disharmony, and for the president's movies. The Reagan critique must evidently be a little too subtle because *Invaders* is never mentioned in the same breath as *They Live* or *Nightmare on Elm Street* as an example of potent '80s political horror.

The following morning, Ellen's face (and George's when he arrives) will be in shadow as she cooks breakfast for her son. They'll both pound bacon and salted, uncooked hamburger meat in front of their horrified boy—what could be more American than red meat? At school, he'll hide in the jungle gym during recess, keeping himself distanced from everyone and everything and feel imprisoned all at once. Hooper does a wonderful job cultivating an atmosphere of fear and dread as only a child could understand, catching secret conversations between adults around shadowy corners. He indulges in noir lighting as David watches Mrs. McKeltch write on the chalkboard, noting the suspicious Band-Aid on the back of her neck. David follows Mrs. McKeltch into the back of the class and Pearl's camera is right behind him. She's up to something back there among the jars of fetal pigs and exotic beetles: she's eating a frog, a fabulously juvenile image to which Hooper and Louise Fletcher fully commit. David's escape is thwarted by Heather (Ed from the phone company's daughter, played by Virginya Keehne), her perfect pigtails a sign of regression/possession. He pushes past her to Linda Magnusson's office.

Linda doesn't believe his story until she notices the Band-Aid on the back of Mrs. McKeltch's neck. She lets David escape but, of course, the aliens notice. Heather knocks on Linda's door, her pigtails silhouetted against her window like Judd's shadow on the door of the *Starlight Motel*—

another silly image that nevertheless carries the necessary dread. When George and Ellen show up to retrieve him and she starts seeing firsthand that David might not be crazy, Hooper and Pearl engineer a *Vertigo* dolly-in-zoom-out to externalize Linda's perceptions exploding. It's one of the longest employments of the trick ever attempted, watching Linda react to the faces of the Martians only she can see. David flees right into Mrs. McKeltch's van—Leatherface's living room on wheels. It's full of taxidermy, which says something kind of funny about the kind of life David imagines she was living *before* the Martians invaded. On the soundtrack, David hears their screeches and squeals, his imagination working overtime. He won't need to imagine anything when he sees where Mrs. McKeltch is headed.

She pulls over in a park and David follows her into the woods. Once more, we see one of Hooper's womb-like gateways: an organic-looking tunnel, and the red light bath isn't far behind. It starts whenever anyone enters the tunnel system the Martians operate. This is the most literal of all of Hooper's womb caves because life is actively created, or recreated here. This is where the monsters toil and free will is drilled out of people. The womb more actively represents childhood here than in Hooper's other films, though it retroactively colors the others we've seen in his films—Hooper's Reagan Era-critiques pulled fuzzier points into sharper focus. What it represents here is the voting public's urge to follow the lead of someone who obfuscated free will. Ronald Reagan, and other fascistic rulers, wanted to impress upon the public that they'd be taking care of everything now. Show up and vote, then go home and don't worry about what the government gets up to. Irresponsible voting and no civil work ethic meant that the voters could be children again and only concern themselves with a juvenile conception of domesticity.

The problem of the tunnel system *could* have been solved with matte paintings, but Hooper plainly loves being able to have the real, defined tunnels extending for hundreds of feet behind his characters, making sure he earns the creeping zaniness of the images the old-fashioned way. Every penny of Golan and Globus' money is on screen, which is quite clear when we reach the Martian architecture, the most exciting piece of production design and art direction in the movie—possibly of Hooper's career. Hooper's Dario Argento influence is plain enough here in the baroque wall designs (directors like Guillermo Del Toro and Tim Burton would crib heavily from this and Argento's work). Pearl and Hooper frame it with maximum awe factor in mind (their camera hungrily prostrate before the magnificence). They crane around the spectacle of the set with the patience of Ridley Scott capturing the misty vistas of *Alien*, *Blade Runner*, and *Legend*.

The goopy aliens, designed by maverick monster maker Stan Winston, have oodles of grim personality. The foot soldiers are little more than mouths stuffed with jagged teeth on four legs with big bulbous protuberances on their backs. Their leader is a brain stuck to a big tongue-like conveyance with a sarcastic little face and two tentacles for arms. There are also tentacles (as in *Eggshells* and *Poltergeist*) emerging from the side of his throne, which hint at Hooper's Lovecraft-parallel.

Hooper's haunted residences, inbred families with big family trees, and hungry earth gobbling up new blood have a deep Lovecraftian feel. H.P. Lovecraft was afraid of many things, but especially of evil things kept secret, festering, and growing angry, suddenly unleashed on the unsuspecting and unprepared brains of the modern public. Stories like *The Lurking Fear* and *The Color Out of Space* unleashed horror on provincials, who are warped by their experience. *The Lurking Fear* is about a group of millionaires who, afraid of immigrants, secret themselves away from the rest of the world, turning into inbred white apes and occasionally venturing outside to feed on the poor (something of a favorite Hooper theme). You can see some of that fear and secrecy (and the consumption of the naïve lower class) in the carny mutant and his father, Leatherface's family and the aristocratic vampires in *Salem's Lot*. *The Color out of Space* concerns a meteor that crashes and poisons the local water and vegetation, driving the locals insane. There are *literal* colors flying out of space in *Lifeforce*, but the idea of a mind-altering alien intelligence is present in both that film and *Invaders*. And in both *Djinn* and *Night Terrors*, a woman runs afoul of a strange religion/cult like Wilbur Whately's Cthulhu-worshipping cult in *The Dunwich Horror*. Lovecraft isn't *quoted* per se, in the way Stuart Gordon or Del Toro quote him, but his interest in the secret, ugly American history is simpatico.

The aliens notice David's intrusion and chase him out of the tunnel—the nightmare logic and the childishness of the POV make it appropriate that the aliens would single him out as the biggest threat to their plan. He escapes the cathedral of intergalactic torment and runs to the woods; the overlapping trees suddenly look purposefully arranged to mock David, as if they're claws coming down over him. The world has turned against him, further proved by the police showing up at Linda's house and by the fact that the entrance to the spaceship is closed when he tries to show it to her. So it's to the pit over the hill they go. Pearl finds them hiding in the hills above David's house with a wonderful swoop of the crane. The crane also comes out to find the two public works officials who are sent into the pit and get eaten by the sandy ground—the composition and movement are similar to the shots of the Harper children at the carnival in *The Funhouse*. David and Linda watch in front of a painted sky, the color of dying London in *Lifeforce*. The earth consuming the workers is a natural extension of the Hooper ethos—the lower class has already been consumed by buildings, bloodthirsty old money, unchangeable families, and gators (as the manifestation of a country's forgotten veteran's PTSD). This just takes out the middlemen.

The police chase after David and Linda, finding them at school where they have to hide in the stylishly lit boiler room (a set that *almost* gives the Martian spaceship a run for its money on sheer color-coordinated beauty). There's a really touching moment where Linda starts panicking and David hugs her and says "It's ok to be afraid."

Knowing they're actually mother and child makes it even more adorable. Before the cops find the fugitives, they locate a toy of the original boss alien from Menzies' *Invaders* (oh, and the lead cop? That's Jimmy Hunt, the little boy hero in the original *Invaders*). Their demise looks imminent, but the aliens accidentally drill (with a very *phallic* drill) into the boiler room, giving them a chance to escape.

Their next stop is to involve the military, which is led by General Wilson (*Poltergeist*'s James Karen), an associate of David's father's with a big portrait of Eisenhower on the wall behind his desk and a bank of monitors in his office (three movies and three banks of monitors. CCTV: a tic of Hooper's Reagan Era filmmaking). The arrival of the military signals a shift towards louder, less carefully designed and choreographed action. The Martians blow up a rocket, so the men in fatigues launch a full-scale assault on the sand pit and the ship below. The images of the military rolling up on the Gardner house, tanks plowing down the white picket fence, and breaking into the school with assault rifles, are a nicely absurd view of Reagan Era military intervention. It's unwieldy cinema (and, once the shooting starts, monotonous), but it's perfect as a child's solution to the problem of aliens stealing his parents, if we take into account that this is all David's nightmare. The suburbs were the only place the military *weren't* deployed during Reagan's presidency. It's intended to make people uncomfortable and also imagine the absurdity of watching tanks roll down their streets, which has become a more or less common occurrence in American cities thanks to the militarized police forces in towns where the authorities itch to quell "race riots." At the very least, in all the shooting and explosions, Hooper and Pearl never forget to make everything as pretty as possible, lights flashing as if at a Moving Sidewalks or Pink Floyd concert. It's in the middle of one of those dazzling light displays that David wakes up from his dream. George and Ellen assure him he was just having a nightmare caused by the things he saw in his day (Hooper's films also made phantasmagoria out of very *real* fears of people everywhere in Reagan's America and the countries it invaded). Of course as soon as they close the door, down comes the flying saucer and the nightmare begins anew.

Invaders From Mars ends on a most bleak note, the bleakest since *Chain Saw*, but possibly even more downbeat. The aliens are real and there's no fighting them. David Gardner's world and his innocence are gone and the last thing we hear is him screaming into the void. The "gee-whiz" wonder and mystery of the original is suddenly and unforgivingly turned into the deafening, permanently echoing sound of defeat.

Scout Tafoya

Chapter 4:
The Body of An American (1986–1995)

Invaders From Mars is the last time Hooper's inner child was allowed to come out and play. The world became a darker place and Hooper went darker with it. He directed an episode of *The Equalizer* about the homeless population in New York, how quickly lives can be ruined and dignity lost thanks to the government's kill-or-be-killed economic practices. The episode was his treatise on Reaganomics, the proposed plan by which it the government threw money at the wealthiest Americans and told the poorest people that it would eventually trickle down to them. Like everything else Ronald Reagan proposed it was a lie to keep him and his base, other rich white people, at the top of the food chain. Hooper paints an incredibly vivid portrait of the dank, disgusting places that people are forced to sleep when they have no options and their pleas for understanding go unanswered (his craft is excellent throughout, relying on patient camera moves and grim production design). He turned down his giddy sense of humor as he got deeper into the Reagan years. The bombast and silliness of his Cannon group movies was just a phase, a response to a world embracing hopelessness. He too would embrace it.

During the Reagan and Bush years, Hooper envisioned the world ending a few different ways, but they got less madcap as the years progressed. During the Clinton years he was concerned with the evil hiding below calm surfaces, the scars of economic systems that had never fully been healed, his imagination nigh-permanently warped by watching Reagan and Bush on TV. He accidentally celebrated the election of George

W. Bush by killing a bunch of young, dumb party animals in *Crocodile*. He'd make dour films about families struggling to make ends meet or postapocalyptic carnivals throughout George W. Bush's presidency, but none of that was *overtly* critical of his horrible governance. His only film during Obama's presidency was about religious pressure placed on an expectant mother, and one senses that he only did that because it suddenly felt safe to dive headlong into political horror that specifically again. *Invaders* was the last time he'd make a film that young kids could conceivably enjoy, and the last time his flooring production design sense was allowed this much room to breathe. *Invaders* is Hooper's most visually splendid and easily digestible film. From here on out, his movies would sting going down. He was tired of being nice. American obsessions and prejudices were dragged kicking and screaming into Hooper's oppressive light to be poked, prodded, and caricatured.

This was also the start of his career as the creator of TV pilots, which makes up almost fully half of his body of work going forward. He recognized that the limited budgets for TV could be spent more judiciously on production design if he used whatever cameras and lighting setups were cheapest. His work for TV contained some of his richest and most expressionistically false work as a director, little micro-classes in his aesthetic obsessions. At his best during this period he seems to invent the concept of prestige TV by squeezing in as much florid postmodernism and disorienting compositional tricks into sci-fi stories of stolen identities. He would never stop trying to turn the middle-class American experience into the nightmare it looked like from the outside, like he was attempting to put the glasses from John Carpenter's *They Live* on everyone who tuned in for primetime viewing. Hooper never missed an opportunity to try and point out where the hate and callousness of the powers that be were hiding in plain sight. To the US government we the people were just meat in waiting, cattle, and Hooper was just trying to make us aware of it before the hammer fell.

The Texas Chainsaw Massacre Part 2 (1986)

The poster for *The Texas Chainsaw Massacre 2* is a parody of the one that sold the John Hughes movie *The Breakfast Club*, with Leatherface and his family posed like Molly Ringwald and her friends. This was the start of the film's troubles. Hooper didn't want to make another *Texas Chain Saw*, but if he was going to, he was going to combat the things that actually scared *him*. In this case, a burgeoning yuppie class and cinema eaten alive by cliché. The second *Chain Saw* movie is about predatory capitalism winning the war against the middle and lower classes. It starts with the murder of two Hughes-ian yuppies right out of *Ferris Bueller's Day Off* and ends with a woman killing her hippie stalker. Classes and generations were at war, and nobody was winning.

The too-portentous narration (and its smearing the details of the events of *Texas Chain Saw Massacre*, including the fusing of the words "chain" and "saw" in the title) and Hooper and Jerry Lambert's loud, tone-deaf synth score probably put too many viewers in the wrong mood. It's a bit of a bait and switch. It's huge, overdramatic, and stabs just like Bernard Herrmann's *Psycho* score. But the film has no interest in traditional horror beats. It'd pave the way (along with Charles & Albert Band, Stuart Gordon, and Brian Yuzna) for the wave of cartoony '90s horror like Peter Jackson's *Dead Alive*, Tony Randel's *Ticks*, Philip Brophy's *Body Melt*, and Ate de Jong's *Highway to Hell* by focusing more centrally on gross-out gags than on anything resembling a scare. The atmosphere is one of false calm penetrated by the absurd, the garrulous, and the macabre (that word appears in the opening crawl once more). This was the first time Hooper composed the music for one of his films since the original *Chain Saw*, and one senses he knew how far out on a limb, tonally, the film would walk and that he'd need the score to dance out there with him.

The first piece of found music we hear (many follow) is Timbuk 3's "Shame on You" (the band was most famous for their antinuclear proliferation anthem "Future's So Bright." The conservative authorities' insistence that nuclear war was just on the horizon informs *Chainsaw 2* and *Spontaneous Combustion*, not to mention every third sci-fi film of the era), which sets up the film's irreverent, hopeless, slightly industrial atmosphere better than Hooper's frantic synth piece under the opening credits.

Two preppy, young republicans are terrorizing a Texas highway. One of them, dressed in a tailored suit with holograph-eyed sunglasses, aims a shiny silver revolver at a rusty mailbox (the Texas of *Chain Saw* and *Eggshells* has aged to decrepitude and new money is bulldozing it). He looks like he could have escaped from Alex Cox's *Repo Man*, the punk analog to this new romantic, post-punk fever dream. The kid shoots up a sign showing the mileage to Dallas (they're not *quite* in the real world), and then another asking drivers to remember the Alamo; the history the right-wingers pretend to care about is one more thing to destroy during target practice.

The yuppies then decide to terrorize a radio DJ named Vanita "Stretch" Brock (Caroline Williams, who'd just been in Louis Malle's *Alamo Bay,* another film less obliquely about Vietnam vets) by holding up her phone line. It's how she'll become embroiled in the conflict—she's on the phone when Leatherface finds and butchers them (they run him off the road while gabbing on the phone to Stretch, he finds them, and takes bloody revenge). The steely DJ tries cutting the line, but neither she nor her station hand (Lou Perryman from *Poltergeist* looking more at home in his baroque button-down shirt) can get quit of them. Perryman, Eagle Pennell's favorite leading man, announces this film's Texas Indie bona fides. L. M. Kit Carson wrote the script with Hooper, who'd just finished working with Kit's wife and son on *Invaders*. Carson's leading man in the documentary *The American Dreamer*, Dennis Hopper, shows up to play our chain saw wielding antihero a few scenes later. Kinky Friedman has a cameo as an anchorman, and hillbilly cineaste Joe Bob Briggs was supposed to as well, but that didn't happen. On the soundtrack are Texas psych pioneer Roky Erickson, psychobilly stalwarts The Cramps, Stiv Bators' Lords of the New Church, and early indie pop bands like Oingo Boingo and Concrete Blonde. Quite the roster of peculiar elements, and yet people still seemed to view this as a failed horror film instead of as an experimental carnival of the grotesque. It made back twice its modest budget, but Roger Ebert's assessment of it as a "geek show" seems to have stuck with it over the years.

The light behind the heads of the two yuppies just before death rides up beside them is a classic Hooper cheat—one he'd been using since *The Funhouse*. Instead of using a rear projection screen or filming out in the world, he fixed big, static blue lights behind the car to simulate headlights. Here, the headlights hit the dirty back windows of the car and turn into a turquoise smear. It's still behind them when Leatherface's truck stops them on the bridge and rides alongside driving backwards, Oingo Boingo on the soundtrack (Tobe Hooper was one of the first directors to realize the spooky potential of Danny Elfman's rhythms). Leatherface jumps into the bed of the truck with a corpse puppet hanging from him like a baby in a bindle. It's such a bizarre, unforgettable sequence. The yuppies shoot at Leatherface's corpse, which just makes him madder. He cuts the top of the driver's head off and Tom Savini's nasty gore effects spurt to life. Stretch and her engineer are vexed, only able to hear the screams, uncertain if those are still part of the prank.

The following day, Lt. "Lefty" Enright (Hopper) is on the case, checking out the debris from the sawed up Mercedes, finding the holograph glasses staring back at him under the wreckage, a literal sight gag. And also a warning: you need to be able to see the world through crazier eyes to get on this film's wavelength. Lefty Enright is dressed like a cowboy and is as old fashioned and out of place as Leatherface's family—the authorities don't have time for his blood feud, his ancient sense of honor. The police have bigger fish to fry—like keeping the influx of yahoos in town for the big football game in check.

When Stretch shows up with her tape of the chain saw murders from the station, Lefty looks like he hasn't slept in days and he's chugging tequila in the middle of the day—he's cracked already, just hiding it behind his flinty gaze, as he tells her and us outright: "I got a perfect willingness to die. That gives me a moral on this bunch of mad dogs."

Stretch goes back to the lobby of the hotel Lefty's staying, where she left her engineer. He's eating barbecue when she comes in muttering to herself about Lefty being a hard-ass.

"Hard-ass? I got a soft heart...built ye a little fry house," Perryman says adorably as he puts the finishing touches on a stack of French Fries.

Stretch is a strong female character, acting out of both self-preservation and a desire for greater things. She doesn't want to be a DJ; she wants to do something meaningful with her life. And when her engineer calls her darling out of habit, she snaps back, "Don't call me darlin', damnit!"

The reason they've come to the hotel isn't Lefty at all. They're covering the Texas Oklahoma Chili Cook-Off. The winner: Drayton Sawyer (Jim Siedow, and the bad pun in his name fits *right* in this film's world). If he looks familiar, that's because he's the only returning cast member from the original *Chain Saw* and he's playing the same role. His barbecue business has thrived since Sally Hardesty escaped. Hooper has fun kitsching up the hotel lobby and all the cook-off guests. The film's design aesthetic is all *too much* all the time, Hooper's nightmare capitalist society ruled entirely by accessories. The car phone the yuppies use to call Stretch, the holo-glasses, the curly, classic American cars that look like they fell off the pages of a comic book, the scads of neon, the store that *only* sells chain saws; this is a world of whims and fetishes overruling need or convenience.

Lefty pays a call to Cut-Rite Chain Saws and drops a few hundred dollars on the showroom stump as he tries out models as if he were trying on a new suit. He plans to duel with them when he catches up to the Sawyer clan. An eye for an eye. First step in the plan—get Stretch to play the tape on her station.

"Figure out how to do it and do it," he says when she says the FCC won't let her.

Naturally, the Sawyer clan finds it, calling old man Drayton to alert him—and, just as naturally, he's got a car phone too. He wants a piece of the new wealth for himself, pretending he represents progress when all he's doing is literally chewing up other Americans. It's plain that Hooper and Carson have retrofitted the old man to resemble Reagan, even if he *looks* as Nixonian as ever. When Lefty finally comes face to face with him, Sawyer will fall back on empty platitudes and marketing slogans just like a political candidate stuck in a time warp. The world was a meaner place than it was a decade earlier and it needed more crooked and cruel villains to make an impression.

The studio at night is lit up with the signature Hooper color scheme—yellow, green, purple, red, and blue—coming out from the lights on Stretch's console and other smaller sources. She plays the national anthem (which brings to mind *Poltergeist's* TV going to static) as the engineer walks home, jilted after trying to get Stretch to go get food with her. Hooper always punishes the put-upon nice guy who thinks he's owed a night with the girl—Leatherface will try his luck with her, too. Before he exits the movie, the engineer walks up to a door with a burning pink light on the other side To be bathed in Hooper's intense lighting means a change is about to come over a character's perception of the world.

Stretch gets a no-answer phone call, checks the storage closet near the booth (there's a light-up neon clock like the one on the church in *Salem's Lot*), and then finally checks the break room. The break room has a cornucopia of psychedelic light jutting onto every surface of the room, including both sides of Stretch's profile, and sitting on the couch by a spinning novelty lamp is Paul "Choptop" Sawyer (Bill Moseley, the character actor equivalent of Adrian Belew—he'd come and solo in your film in impossible tones and registers, blending noise and harmonics). He keeps burning his skin with a hot coat hanger and talking endlessly about cosmic vibrations and Iron Butterfly (an overt reference to the psychedelic music of Hooper's youth). He's a Vietnam vet (the ironic pins on his overalls and metal plate on his skull say as much) and hasn't dealt with the combat shock terribly well. His burnt-out PTSD shtick is as kitschy as anything else in the film and he's the second example of an evil baby boomer turning against the ideals signified by those buttons and his tie-dye shirt. Like his dad, he has delusions of power—he wears a Sonny Bono wig, a symbol of conservative values and normalcy, wrapping himself in unearned morality. Their endless tête-à-tête is interrupted only when Leatherface comes flying out of the record closet with his chain saw.

While Choptop kills the engineer with a hammer, Leatherface corners Stretch and, in a bizarre courtship misfire, lustily drapes the phallic chain saw around her like men use roses in erotic scenes in bad romances and fashion advertisements. Stretch gains the upper hand easily, all too aware how dumb sex makes men, especially one with a child's intelligence like Leatherface, raised on his father's entitlement. Carson and Hooper paint with the broadest possible brushstrokes here. When he can't "perform" with the saw, failing to produce any kind of satisfied response from Stretch, he revs it up and destroys the studio.

The two assailants leave and Stretch gives chase, following them to Texas Battle Land, a large and flagrant Hooper womb cave. Lefty shows up just in time to watch her fall into a trap door and sink into the earth, swallowed by the womb like so many other Hooper heroes. The maze-like contraptions she falls through could be a parody of *The Goonies*. At this point, fifty-two minutes into the movie, the film becomes an extended riff on Sally Hardesty's imprisonment in Leatherface's house in the first *Chain Saw*, except there are fifty minutes left in the movie. In the original, Sally's imprisonment happens an hour into its eighty-two minutes. Narratively, *The Texas Chainsaw Massacre 2* will be little more the family tormenting Stretch, Stretch trying to escape, Lefty's attempts to destroy Texas Battle Land with his arsenal of chain saws, and Leatherface trying to get away without harming Stretch, on whom he's developed a crush. It's a fairly monotonous final act (especially considering that the second act was all that chaos in the studio), but there's a method to Carson and Hooper's madness. Hopper will be subjected to one bizarre, blackly comic tangent after another, in essence going down a rabbit hole to America's blood-soaked wonderland. The symbolism kicked up as he nears his victims—kicking open a stone stomach and watching piles of entrails spurt out, chain saw fighting with Leatherface as if they were knights, entering the inner sanctum of the family singing "Bringing In The Sheaves" (a tune favored by Robert Mitchum in the fairy-tale tinged *Night of the Hunter*)—will bring him one step closer to having all of the blood from America's foreign policy and domestic violence on his hands, becoming the thing he hates just in time to destroy it. Like Joseph Cotton entering the party at the Amberson manner (what is this act if not a big, festively weird ball?), he'll be rejected and ultimately destroy the family unwilling to accept his changes.

Stretch, on the other hand, will encounters a grim, gory version of the documentary *Grey Gardens* beneath the Earth's crust. Drayton Sawyer is a giggling, befuddled Edith Beale and Choptop his headgear-equipped Little Edie. This Sawyer family, like the Beales, was left to its own devices and allowed to let their brains decay inside their still-living heads, allowing themselves to believe that they're still a prosperous part of the American gentry. Another way to think of it: like a big budget remake of *The Heisters*, in which a gaggle of criminal lunatics duke it out in a cave.

In this giant meat locker the Sawyers call home, Stretch will be indoctrinated into their rituals as if in an arranged marriage (she's made to wear the skin of her previous suitor). The production design of the interior of battle land is beyond marvelous—a big industrial playground decorated to within an inch of its life, and Hooper and cinematographer Richard Kooris map the interior with an eye towards stranding us in the bottom of the frame, letting us gawk at the hardworking design team and the typically great job done by Hooper's lighting designers. Stretch will get away by using a piece of the set—a mummified woman with a chain saw in her lap (Choptop's grandmother) who bears more than a passing resemblance to Edith Beale—as a weapon. She'll fight Choptop off and use the saw against him, dancing like Leatherface at the end of the first *Chain Saw*.

Of course, it's not a victory by any traditional rubric. She's just as crazy as the men who kidnapped her and used her as bait, respectively (masculinity is the real villain here—its vision of men screaming at a captive woman for thirty minutes feels eerily accurate as a representation of the American woman's experience dealing with drunk, abusive, obsessed men). She escaped the earth that swallowed her up, but she seems a part of its sick design now. Hooper's proper follow-up feature would take an even dimmer view of surviving catastrophe when psychological scars linger. A spiritual sequel to *Texas Chainsaw 2*, *Spontaneous Combustion* would leave no one unscathed.

Amazing Stories, "Miss Stardust" (1987)

Hooper was no stranger to working for television at this point in his life, but he took to it with a vengeance after *Texas Chainsaw Massacre 2*. In the late '80s, he directed an episode of Steven Spielberg's *Amazing Stories* about an alien in a beauty pageant and the pilot episode of *Freddy's Nightmares*, an anthology series based around/introduced by Robert Englund in character as Freddy Krueger from Wes Craven's *Nightmare on Elm Street* movies. Craven appears to have had little to no involvement with the project, so Hooper was free to invent whatever he pleased. And he does fine work on a tiny budget, using editing trickery and expressionistic lighting. He'd direct an episode of *Tales From The Crypt* starring Whoopi Goldberg and Vanity, that cast alone about as weird as anything in his movies, and the pilot of a series dramatizing ghost stories called *Haunted Lives* hosted by Leonard Nimoy. His next two films after *Spontaneous Combustion* would both be for TV: *I'm Dangerous Tonight* for USA and the *Eye* segment of *Body Bags* for Showtime. After the commercial and critical failure of *The Mangler*, he'd work almost exclusively for TV for ten years, not unlike Byron Haskin after *The Power* or Orson Welles between his feature film projects, directing episodes of short-lived sci-fi and horror series like *The Others, Perversions of Science, Nowhere Man, Dark Skies, Night Visions,* and Spielberg's *Taken*.

The program that kick-started his work for TV in earnest was an episode in the back half of the second season of *Amazing Stories*. Unlike *Salem's Lot*, where he was obeying the darker dictates of Stephen King's prose, here he was more restrained by the show's established MO. Spielberg had brought on a murderer's row of directing talent to the show from Joe Dante to Martin Scorsese to Clint Eastwood, but they had to keep to a semi-uniform aesthetic and a story that could be wrapped up in a cute bow in under a half hour. Hooper's "Miss Stardust," from a story by the legendary horror author Richard Matheson (adapted by his son Richard Christian Matheson), is as interesting a tug of war between the Spielberg and Hooper identities as *Poltergeist* before it. Hooper brought from his rep company James Karen, Laraine Newman, and Jim Siedow, and worked for the first time with odd but endearing combination of Dick Shawn and "Weird Al" Yankovic. This would be Siedow's last screen acting gig. He died in 2003.

Shawn plays Joe Willloughby, a down-on-his-luck PR executive sick of his job and his life. He visits a bar to drown his sorrows, and it's both beautifully lit and ornate decorated. The rain and thunder outside is heard and the lightning flashes a pale, sickly green on Shawn's face. He tells the bartender a story about the last big job he had at work: he was approached by a firm (led by Karen, playing a suit for the second time for Hooper after *Poltergeist*) to create a beauty pageant called The Miss Stardust contest. Shawn's office is cluttered with tacky posters and trinkets, as dreary in its way as the Marston house. The whole episode is like something from a Vaudeville routine or an episode of *Looney Tunes*, though its one joke—grotesque aliens try to win a beauty pageant—never quite lands.

The action in the studio on the day of the pageant shoot is frenzied and cluttered. Hooper arranges many levels of extras and supporting players, like Newman, as his secretary, and Siedow as a contest judge in a tuxedo (an absurd and welcome sight) to surround Shawn before the guest of honor appears in a flash of green light from the ceiling. Yankovic shows up from a space ship, a living cabbage in a shimmering green suit from space to warn

Shawn that his Miss Universe pageant is invalid because it doesn't include any aliens in the competition. Yankovic and Shawn yelling at each other veers a little close to insupportably whacky (and Yankovic's every movement is scored by cartoon sound effects right out of *Looney Tunes*). This is the closest to outright comedy Hooper had come since *The Heisters*. Yankovic demands that Shawn accept interstellar entries to the pageant before leaving and absconding with Newman for good measure.

Regular *Amazing Stories* photographer Charles Minsky lights the set more like one of Spielberg's productions (Douglas Slocombe's work on *Raiders of the Lost Ark* is the obvious point of reference) with dust in the air and a more muted palette to render Hooper's lighting less pronounced. The neon and fluorescents are lost in a sea of grey, black, brown, and dark red. The tables at the Miss Stardust pageant are outfitted with blue lights, the stage is orbited by a big fake UFO, and multicolored spotlights shine on the stage, but none of the colors overwhelms the frame as they would in Hooper's other work. Siedow's judge doesn't know what to make of the thin green puppet Miss Mars who dances for her talent. Miss Venus arrives in a clamshell in a pink feather boa playing a harp with her tentacles and singing from behind wiggling catfish-like whiskers while bubbles float around her. Miss Jupiter sings opera from a snout that looks like it belongs to a horse or a pike that sits under a feathered crown. Taking its cues from the puppet designs and Shawn and Yankovic's chemistry, the episode has the vibe of a vaudeville sketch.

Hooper cuts from Yankovic describing the earth's rotation to a pool ball spinning across the green felt top of a table as Shawn finishes his story in the bar. The alien decided to spare Earth because he developed feelings for Newman's secretary. She drops Shawn a moving postcard from space and the bartender watches, stunned as the card plays on the pool table—a beautiful composition-within-a-composition. This is one of the few pure exercises in film comedy in Hooper's career and one of the only of his works absent left-leaning subtext, which is interesting given that he was working for Spielberg, which once again makes the radical politics of *Poltergeist* seem more like Hooper's doing than Spielberg's. Then again it's possible he was giving himself a vacation from his usual obsessions because the other episode of TV he directed that year was a dire and dour affair about the crisis of homelessness plaguing the US.

The Equalizer, "No Place Like Home" (1988)

The *Equalizer* was a series created by Michael Sloan and Richard Lindehim and followed a well-worn serial formula that can be traced at least as far back as the show *The Fugitive.* Like The Incredible Hulk or The A-Team, Robert McCall (Edward Woodward) would travel the country looking to help people in need, part of his atonement for working for a destructive US government intelligence agency. Hooper was brought on near the end of the third season, one of the few high-profile guest directors the show ever attracted. The show was better known for its guest stars than for its behind the camera talent despite hiring at various times writers like Mark Frost and Robert Crais. Hooper took the assignment because he wanted to be able to shine a light on the homelessness epidemic plaguing the country. It also afforded a rare opportunity for Hooper to do location shooting somewhere other than Texas or California.

After the Stewart Copeland–scored opening sequence (incidentally one of the most dynamic ever assembled, thanks in no small part to the progressive jazz from the former Police drummer) the episode begins with a montage of homeless people in New York set to a gospel version of "Uncloudy Day," which is heavy-handed on paper but quite striking and effecting in practice. The moneyed and uncaring Manhattan towers over the defeated itinerants on the streets huddled for warmth by burning trash cans and pushing shopping carts. Into the landscape of suffering walks McCall. In an unbroken dolly shot McCall is accosted by a homeless man and gives him twenty dollars, before the camera comes back to find Woodward's expression of pained resignation for the misery around him.

The folks in need of McCall's help are the Whitaker family, Bill (Michael Rooker), Paula (Kelly Curtis), and Billy (Matthew Stamm), lately evicted by their landlord despite Paula's pregnancy. We meet Bill and Paula on the front steps of their building and they discuss the minute practicalities of looking for a place to live that won't result in their freezing to death outside. Their decision to sleep in the van is undercut when someone steals it off the street. The cut from the visit to the cluttered, grey, and gross housing authority and McCall's luxurious apartment is quite stark. Hooper introduces the hotel where the Whitakers are placed by the city in a series of lengthy Steadicam shots passed the other despondent tenants. Bill has a meltdown when he sees what he's put his family through (he has to kill a rat with his suitcase mere seconds after they get inside). Rooker's method actor emotionality wasn't a style Hooper frequently worked with, so to see him bringing a real depressive core to the character seems a little at odds with the pulpy format. McCall shows up in time to rescue Bill from a would-be slumlord Jim Harding (Leo Burmeister) who wants to keep the family on the books while renting the apartment to someone else. He goes to regular sidekick Mickey Kostmayer (Keith Szarabajka) for help and he initially turns down the job. After all he was poor a lot of his life but he never ended up homeless.

Woodward shuts him down definitively. "Oh I am witnessing the natural superiority of the poor boy made good, am I? This country has changed somewhat! Just look around you!"

There's a splendid micro-vignette where a woman outside the Alexandria Hotel where the Whitaker's are staying sends her kid off to school, waits for him to walk away, then strips off her overcoat to reveal a leopard print top, short skirt, and high heels. That single shot conveys everything about the homeless situation in the city and how completely it's been subsumed and normalized by the city—an embarrassed woman waiting until her son can't see her to don her sex worker's uniform so she can make too little money to support her family. Every piece of the situation could be improved with universal basic income and less shame placed on a mother to keep and raise a child she can't support. Hooper films the drama with seriousness and an eye toward letting the grotesque trappings of the Alexandria speak from behind the actors (though there are flashes of his usual creative expressionism—venetian blinds throwing shadows on the wall of the Whitaker's room), but that one eight-second, slightly cartoonish shot scoops the entire episode in gorgeous Hooper fashion.

The script is full of very direct statements about what it's like to be on welfare in New York, so Hooper doesn't have much to do during the bulk of the episode but film shot-reverse-shot conversations and let the actors work. There's the odd memorable composition—the elder Whitakers sharing an embrace in front of a window, Billy sitting by himself by the front window of a tavern. The place is painted green with checkered green tablecloths (a touch of Deren).

McCall starts trying to help the residents escape from under Harding's thumb. He discovers that the Alexandria is owned by a man named Amar (Michael Lerner) and tries to do some investigating. Harding is killed off screen so McCall's got no one but Amar to investigate. He pits Amar's old business partner Robert Nichols (Ed Lauter) against him to put the hotel back in his more-charitable hands. Lauter is introduced in a shot that starts on the reflection of the Empire State Building out his window, hinting rather glaringly that the world is upside down and about to be righted in some small way. McCall convinces Nichols to let him empty out Amar's apartment, forcing the landlord to take violent retribution—he throws himself against his window after plotting his vengeance looking like Peter Lorre in *M*—wretched, sweaty, small, and desperate. McCall plans for a documentary crew to be waiting in the Whitakers' room in the Alexandria (film as deus ex machina) but Amar still manages to hit and wound Bill despite the sting operation taking the wind out of his sails. "Uncloudy Day" plays again as the Whitakers pile in the van toward their new home. Hooper ends the film with a close-up of a child still homeless who will still need help he won't get next week when McCall is on his next errand of mercy, Hooper's conscious shattering the fantasy. You can't fix a city's problems in an hour.

Freddie's Nightmares, "No More Mr. Nice Guy" (1988)

Hooper the Brechtian tended to emerge in the minor work, the TV episodes and movies like *Eaten Alive* and *Spontaneous Combustion* that feel like B sides to the bigger films. There was no more excellent alignment of his and another creator's sensibilities than when he directed the pilot episode of *Freddie's Nightmares*, an anthology show based on Wes Craven's runaway 1984 success *A Nightmare on Elm Street* about a murderer who attacks people in their dreams. After Craven's original movie became an international sensation, the sequels were given to disparate stylists Jack Sholder, Renny Harlin, Rachel Talalay, and Chuck Russell, and though

Hooper never got a chance to direct a sequel, his pilot episode for the TV series is a beautiful use of his talent. Unlike Talalay or Harlin, Hooper's visual vocabulary was like pop art and less specific to the time in which his movies were made. His *Looney Tunes*-inspired humor and luscious use of '50s Hollywood style has made his work age more gracefully without the arch artistic signifiers of the era. His work on the pilot is exactly what an hour of junk food television should be: fleet, funny, and fearless.

It opens with a news report being interrupted by the anchor vanishing into static and reappearing in front of the steps of the courthouse where Freddy Krueger (Robert Englund playing the same part he did in all five *Nightmare* movies, almost a decade after he first worked for Hooper in *Eaten Alive*) is being tried for his crimes. The anchor is shocked by the feat of bizarre magic that moves him in space—a joke that has a very specific media-savviness, like the work of *Looney Tunes* animator and later director of Jerry Lewis comedies Frank Tashlin. The skullduggery with the TV feels like subtext left over from *Poltergeist*. Freddy is in a glass box watching a slideshow of his victims being reflected and obscuring his face. Freddie's attorney (Steven Reisch) hilariously has a problem with the phrase "unholy aberration," so prosecutor Deeks (William Frankfather) rolls his eyes and corrects himself. "Excuse me...*alleged* unholy aberration..."

Freddy gets off on a technicality, and then we see in his mind's eye (literally, there's a close-up of his eye drowning in Hooper's red light) his dream of the courtroom filled with corpses. The arresting officer, Lt. Timothy Blocker (Ian Patrick Williams) now worries that his family, including his twin teenage daughters Lisa and Merit (Hill and Gry Park) are next in line to be killed by Freddy. Later the lieutenant's wife Sarah will place the film squarely in Hooper's haunted suburban milieu as she angrily folds laundry and scolds her impotent husband: "Here we are the land of white picket fences and PTA meetings...that maniac is still loose on the streets."

It takes about ten seconds before Deeks convinces the parents of the bereaved to take the law into their own hands and they all carpool over to Freddy's place with murder in their eyes. The swiftness of their judgment has something of the riot-ready tenor of the denizens of Springfield on *The Simpsons*. Everyone is very quick in this episode to decry that a murderer has rights—it's all delivered in hysterical, frenzied line readings from his cast that feel deliberately cartoonish.

Hooper films Freddy in his boiler room (in the red glow) in expressive obfuscation. We see his POV or the back of his head, but his face is hidden by the angle or by shadow, like a figure from film noir. Hooper films their search for Kruger with flashlights, placing them in another noir tradition—the criminal mob out for justice, introduced most potently in Fritz Lang's debut sound film *M* (1931), later remade by Joseph Losey in Los Angeles in 1951, which Hooper had just aped on his episode of *The Equalizer*. The noise of the steam in the boiler room also harks back to Lang's second sound film *The Testament of Dr. Mabuse* about a shadowy mastermind running a criminal enterprise that relies on mind control. "No More Mister Nice Guy" paints Freddy as supernatural in the same way Mabuse seems to be in Lang's telling. The police are helpless to stop him and he seems more than human. The funny thing about working for the more conservative broadcast content standards of TV is that Hooper has to rely on cutaways and innuendo when presenting violence, which also gives his film that kind of expressionistic feeling of noir. Kruger's clawed hand reaches into the frame or is visible in shadow and then blood will hit the ground in the reverse angle. Hooper frequently toyed with noir imagery (horror and noir were, in '40s Hollywood, largely the work of expats exorcising the lingering trauma still haunting their European homeland) but his use of shadow was rarely this potent or direct.

There's a lovely crane shot as Lt. Blocker arrives at Freddy's hideout to stop the lynch mob from exacting justice. The rust-colored, steam-filled hellhole that Freddy calls home is a beautiful piece of set decoration, and Hooper's later work would routinely be set in grotesque spaces like this. Blocker takes the onus of dirty justice on himself by killing Kruger on behalf of the enraged mob. The shots of Kruger burning are gorgeous, the flame lighting up the set and taking centrality in the composition and they hint at the more flagrant direction the rest of the episode will take. The next shot after Freddy's very brief resurrection—in Brechtian direct address—is of a boarded up house in a kind of nightmare shroud. Blocker is having his first nightmare of being visited at home. The colors are breathtaking. There are pools of blue-white, brilliant red, and neon green light pouring out from inside the house, from windows and behind frantically placed boards. Smoke rises from every corner of the set. Blocker receives a package from which Freddy's gloved hand emerges. When he wakes up he's got claw marks on his face from where he was attacked in his dream.

Blocker drops his twins off at school and has a genuinely disquieting encounter with them for his trouble. The more troubled of the two of them (in unsettling close-up) looks at him and sings at him "1, 2, Freddy's coming for you," scaring him half to death. Blocker has another vision of a letter from Freddy that ignites in his hand at the station, and another where he imagines Kruger's truck runs him off the road. Blocker returns to the scene of the burning that night and the set is lit by an eerie pink glow. They don't find Kruger but instead find Deeks, dead, with telltale claw marks across his chest. Blocker starts to crack up. He has a stress-induced daydream where his twins strap him to a chair (drenched in purple light) to execute him while Kruger's hand in shadow crawls up the wall behind them.

Blocker's daughter sings to him again and he snaps and shatters the coffee mug in his hand. A convoluted turn of events finally finds Blocker strapped to a doctor's chair being worked on by a nurse in her bra and underthings when Freddy arrives to finish him off, his glove outfitted with a series of painful drills. This was the start of the series' two-year run and its lovely encapsulation of Hooper's newly cemented aesthetic and color scheme—the pinks, purples, greens, and reds beamed in from a nightmare all Hooper's own.

Spontaneous Combustion (1990)

Hooper's cinephilia has been present in his work since *The Heisters*, but *Spontaneous Combustion* was the first time he made something resembling a traditional genre film outside of what was dictated by the material. *Salem's Lot* resembles previous film versions of the *Dracula* story because that's plainly what Stephen King was rewriting in his novel. Hooper's films had been horrific in nature but effective more so because he's relied on grammar learned from a generation of picture makers who had all either retired, died, or been ousted by the system. The directors Hooper references in *Spontaneous Combustion*, which is about the atomic spirit of the 1950s possessing a man's body like a ghost, were studio craftsman who'd run out of real estate on Hollywood's many backlots. In essence Hooper seems almost delightfully haunted himself by the history of studio filmmaking.

There are shades of Robert Aldrich's 1955 *Kiss Me Deadly* in the apocalyptic nature of hero David Bell's mystery. The structure, wherein he bounces from one person to another looking for clues, is identical and the explosions from his body mirror the one caused by the opening of a briefcase full of a mystery element at the end of the earlier film.

André De Toth, who appears in the film as a scientist, could have told Hooper a thing or two about being a great, ignored artist. Both Hooper and De Toth crafted beautiful studio films for a pittance and still haven't found mainstream critical appreciation. De Toth's final film was an uncredited pass at a low-budget horror film called *Terror Night* (not to be confused with Hooper's own *Night Terrors*) just a few years before *Spontaneous*, but his last official gig was the English production *Play Dirty*, a remarkably cynical delight about doing uncredited, unappreciated work for the war effort. Doesn't take a nuclear physicist to parse *that* metaphor.

Nicholas Ray (whose brilliant colors and disturbed noir heroes are all over Hooper's filmography, but who was forced out of Hollywood after one too many flare-ups) made two final features with help from college students, high-profile friends, and fans as he wasted away from lung cancer, which took him at age 67.

Michael Powell gave Hooper a prototypical antihero in *Peeping Tom*: a man who can't help but kill women with his camera (in 2011, Hooper would write his first novel, *Midnight Movie*, about a short film from his own past that causes people to go mad). The tormented agent of destruction (not to mention Powell's flooring color palette) is in *Lifeforce's* Carlsen, both *Texas Chain Saw* movies' Leatherface, *I'm Dangerous Tonight's* Amy, *Spontaneous Combustion's* David Bell/Sam Kramer, and especially *Eye's* Brent Matthews, a man who sees things that drive him mad. Powell's career was so tarnished after *Peeping Tom* he had to leave the UK to find work.

Byron Haskin (whose final film, the sci-fi noir *The Power*, also involves atomic age secret organizations and psychic pyrotechnics) was thrown out with the bathwater when MGM decided they'd had enough of his producing partner George Pal. He'd direct TV then nothing for the last decade of his life. He produced the same kind of overflowing, borderline sensual pulp that Hooper made during this period in his career.

Frank Perry, from whom Hooper borrows the names of his protagonists, David and Lisa, was also fascinated by nuclear/atomic panic, illustrated in his 1963 film *Ladybug Ladybug*. His debut, *David and Lisa*, is about pale, socially awkward paramours who've been institutionalized for different reasons and find order by opening up about their anxieties, which is also what ties together Hooper's David and Lisa. Perry and Hooper had the same suspicious attitude toward suburban families, seen in *Diary of a Mad Housewife* and *The Swimmer*, which, like much of Hooper's work, show men driven to madness by a belief in their own lithe self-righteousness and women suffering mightily at their hands when they try to assert their independence. Perry is, unfortunately, still remembered mostly for his ill-fated Joan Crawford biopic *Mommie Dearest*.

Fittingly, tragically, *Spontaneous Combustion* is a film noir about the terror of realizing that other people have decided that your life, your usefulness, your joy, and your growth have a half-life. It's a tribute to the directors who taught Hooper how great movies were crafted, but also an accidental look into his future. Hooper may have felt that he was being pigeonholed, that studios didn't have a place for a guy with an old-fashioned skill set. Or he may have just been channeling hopelessness without realizing he was riding the same wave as De Toth, Haskin, Powell, Ray, and a hundred other studio directors who died without realizing how important they would become. Hooper's legacy now stands as a kind of tribute to the other directors whose artistry was taken for granted during their lifetimes. His style was a walking museum of the rejected and neglected.

The opening credits roll over images of fire spreading across a void, the music by Graeme Revell—angry, moody synthesizers—mixing with loud bursts of industrial noise and screaming as the fire spews all over the screen. The prologue is set in 1955 (the same year *Kiss Me Deadly* was released) at a hydrogen bomb testing sight in Nevada. Brian and Peggy Bell, an angelic, pale couple (Brian Bremer and Stacy Edwards), are in a bunker preparing for a test, hooking themselves up to electrodes. Outside, on a beautiful little set, their minders prepare the atom bomb test, putting their goggles on while the missile, nicknamed Samson, prepares to go off (that's veteran-turned-actor and combat advisor Captain Dale Dye talking to them through the intercom—Hooper had given him his first onscreen role as an extra in *Invaders From Mars*. His superior is played by Chicago Bears star linebacker Dick Butkus, weirdly enough). The sun comes up over a nearby hill (viewed with a radio tower in the middle, cutting a lovely geometric figure on the false horizon) and Brian and Peggy start panicking, holding hands and crying in fear (perhaps realizing they're about to spend a month underground *if* they survive the blast).

When the missile goes off, it can be seen from space and in a bunch of amber-hued stock footage, which turns into a beautiful pastiche of patriotic industrial films. Hooper and editor David Kern get the tone and rhythm of these films to a T. It explains Brian and Peggy's preparation for the explosion test, including their bunker full of food to ride out the "nuclear storm." This is one of the best sequences in all of Hooper's filmography, harnessing his wit and precision to lie sweetly to his audience the way he was lied to watching TV and educational films as a child. Brian and Peggy are told there's no trace of harmful toxins or chemicals in their bodies and dance to "You Belong To Me." There's a slight snag, however. During all those weeks underground waiting for the fall out to go quiet, Brian knocks Peggy up.

When Peggy has the kid, Brian comes to her with a bunch of presents, including a little carousel toy.

"Isn't it amazing what they're doing with plastic?" he asks, stars in his eyes.

Turns out, the kid has two issues: a perfect circle birthmark on his hand and a birthday on the anniversary of the bombing of Hiroshima. A nurse puts a thermometer in Peggy's mouth and it shatters, her body temperature rising at an insane rate until finally she bursts into flame. Brian follows suit. Even the plastic carousel melts. The military is stumped by the event, so they bring in Dr. Vandenmeer (De Toth, in one of his few acting roles) who explains that what they're dealing with is spontaneous combustion—a natural phenomenon, the "fire from heaven." De Toth plainly has a ball talking it up and pulling Brian's ash-covered skull from his charred head.

Peggy and Brian's baby grows into high school teacher Sam Kramer. We meet him reading Shakespeare, poorly. Everyone agrees acting isn't his strong suit (there's a little irony in that he's played by Brad Dourif, who's never given a bad performance in his life. He fits into *Spontaneous Combustion*'s world of post-nuclear kitsch having appeared in anti-Americana touchstones like *One Flew Over The Cuckoo's Nest* and *Wise Blood*). The school Sam works for is emblazoned with antinuclear badges and posters. His girlfriend, Lisa (Cynthia Bain), walks him out to his car; neither sees the young woman leaving a gift wrapped box on the front seat of Sam's car. The mysterious woman leaves before Sam can question her. Inside the box is the watch Brian wore before the atom bomb test and other personal effects. Just as in *Kiss Me Deadly,* the mystery begins when a mysterious woman enters the hero's car.

A visit with his ex-wife Rachel (Dey Young) goes disastrously—the name of the restaurant? Café Kitsch, of course—but she insists he come say hello to her grandfather, Lew Orlander (William Prince), who's been watching Sam in secret all his life. He's about to expire, from the looks of him. Lew seems interested in Sam's migraines, but Sam himself is more interested by the news that a colleague has died in a tragic accident—smoking in bed. Sam walks back in to pay the bill Rachel left him with and then a small jet of flame shoots from his finger. When he sees a doctor about it, we realize the migraines aren't his only longtime ailment. He's had an internal temperature of 100 degrees his whole life.

Hooper puts Sam in a great old car, a 1951 Studebaker Champion Starlight, which makes it feel like he's driving into Haskin's *The Power*, in which pain researcher George Hamilton is pursued by a telekinetic killer. Both stories are about the human body as a site for atomic age destruction and torment, both are set in California, and both are ticking clock thrillers made by craftsman in love with studio lighting, color gels, and outlandish fantasy. *The Power* mixes the angst and paranoia of film noir with big, fantastical elements as well as a bold, proto-psychedelic color palette, something we see in earnest here. *Spontaneous* is dark film, Hooper's darkest and most hopeless since *Eaten Alive*, and he directs to ensure that we feel trapped. Lots of close-ups, a very slight art deco motif in some of the interiors (he was plainly taken with that choice as it reappears in some of *I'm Dangerous Tonight*), a reliance on shot-reverse-shot conversations, and very few long takes.

Sam switches to plot-specific radio, listening to a broadcast about spontaneous combustion. He takes a phone call with Lew Orlander, which overlaps with the audio from the radio broadcast as he finds the other bombshell in the package left on the front seat of his car—the letter his parents wrote to him just before they burst into flames. He starts a fire, receives a flash of memories (memories he couldn't possibly have), and then has another burning episode. Lisa has bad news for him too: another person they know has died of burning alive, but this one was in the shower. She makes him call a radio psychic and, as he starts regressing into memories from before he was born, the birthmark on his hand grows in size and he recalls his real name: David Bell. He's cut off and when he calls back, he gets a coarse station hand (director John Landis, who, along with Hooper's own tiny cameo in Café Kitsch's bathroom, makes three directors in this film). Sam/David sends static electricity over the phone line, causing fire to shoot out of the station hand's mouth and a hole in his leg. The studio is soon completely engulfed in flame. Sam/David's arm bursts like an oil well and fire starts streaming out of the wound. Lisa puts him the bathtub, but it seems to be making the fire worse—like the flames at Chernobyl, it's so hot it seems to be turning water back to its building block elements and hydrogen just feeds the fire. It's a magnificently grotesque sequence and prepares one for the almost comically hopeless second half of the film.

Lisa drives David to the hospital and accidentally reveals that his life has been a lie. She met him because Dr. Orlander got her a job at the school, and the story he's been told about his parents' death was also a lie. Everyone important in his life has been a plant. Orlander will also later reveal that he paid his dad to get his mom pregnant underground. The revelation causes an outburst of flame that almost makes Lisa lose control of the car. David's earnestness in these scenes makes him seem a bit too naïve, but that's just one more archetype on Hooper's part. David is like a Preston Sturges hero, his life spiraling miserably out of control. Like Eddie Bracken in *Hail The Conquering Hero* and *The Miracle of Morgan's Creek*, he tries to maintain his composure and good humor as he has his freedom and ideals stripped away.

At the hospital, he's quickly quarantined and checked for radiation (his doctor wearing neon green goggles and neon orange gloves, red flags that something out of the ordinary is transpiring). In a Dutch tilt, David watches his doctor make a phone call in another room—the world turning sideways as it makes less and less sense.

"Make yourself comfortable—maybe watch TV," offers one chipper doctor.

While Lisa is grilled by another doctor, Marsh (Jon Cypher), the shadow from some blinds is thrown on her face, placing her grammatically in the cold war noir milieu from which the film borrows. The doctor laughs at her hysterics, a perfect conservative undercutting of her personal pain. Meanwhile, David's physician fills a syringe with a glowing green liquid—a perfect pulpy symbol like *Kiss Me Deadly's* atomic briefcase and, maybe, a nod to fellow Lovecraftian Stuart Gordon and his *Reanimator* films. David reacts by burning the doctor alive with a burst of fire from his arm and he and Lisa independently escape the hospital.

David finds Nina (Melinda Dillon), who was present during the experiment that killed his parents. The crane shot that establishes her house is one of the few classically Hooper-esque flourishes in the film's grammar, as is the slow zoom/dolly-in to her front door. It's also redolent of the establishing shots from *Kiss Me Deadly*. Nina, finally, has a few answers for David in a trunk full of his parents' effects, including the melted carousel—memory games like this are *all over* classic film noir. As David watches the melted horses dance, the film reaches its emotional climax. That doesn't mean he's done suffering, of course. Nina sets up the projector and shows David footage of his parents. As he reaches for a handkerchief, we see just how big and ugly the birthmark on his hand has gotten. With a little help from Nina, David figures out that the architect of his doom is none other than Lew Orlander. He leaves in a hurry, which means he misses Dr. Marsh showing up to poison Nina. The film doesn't have much in the way of memorable dialogue, but his final words to Nina are bleakly marvelous: "Just close your eyes, a thousand years'll go by just like that."

David calls Lisa from a payphone and wheedles out of her that she's been taking orders from Lew Orlander. This makes him so furious, he loses control of himself momentarily, fire emerging from his face and singeing his eye shut. Across town, a hand made of flames emerges from Lisa's mirror and nearly scorches her face like the evil spirits entering the Freeling house in *Poltergeist*. It's boldly surreal—an improbable mix of the biological and spectral.

Two cops stop and question David, and he winds up burning them alive. Mr. Fitzpatrick, the kindly old security guard outside Orlander's house, meets a similarly sticky end. Hooper keeps David's face in darkness during his encounter with Fitzpatrick, signaling his change into outright violence and darkness.

The light inside Orlander's house, which looks like a mausoleum, is classic Hooper—the almost symmetrical framing, the foggy bright light bursting through open doors in the center of the shot. David walks inside, obscuring the light behind him, dragging himself across the tiled floors. The pattern resembles a chessboard (shades of Maya Deren's *At Land*), reinforcing his status as a pawn. The chandelier above David's head begins buzzing and flickering, and David starts smoldering like a human fog machine, making him his own lighting effect, merging him with the design of the film (Hooper would do this again in *The Mangler*, a film whose villain is literally a piece of production design).

Orlander arrives in a wheelchair, explaining that he's been looking out for poor David's best interests. "I gave you everything...you should thank me," the old man pleads.

The real kicker? Lisa's got the same disorder as David, which is why Orlander put them together: so they could control their abilities (like the heroes of Haskin's *The Power*) and become "clean killing systems." It sounds *very* much like something from the era of Star Wars missile defense system.

"You're America's atomic man," chirps old Lew, the weird humor right out of a Country Joe and The Fish lyric book. That's all David needs to hear. He ignites and takes his wheelchair bound "father" with him. It's a grotesque near-finish and it turns David into a beautiful lighting effect before destroying him, the smoke flowing from his body towards the light above.

To the strains of The Ink Spots' "I Don't Want To Set The World On Fire," Lisa frantically paces around her apartment. Hooper keeps a few neon objects visible in the blue moonlight and indulges in a little matte painting and processing when he shows lighting striking the nearby power plant. The plant going on line is constant white noise in the film meant to mock the progression of David's meltdown. It's also a further critique of the '80s climate of nuclear tests. Chernobyl and Three Mile Island still lingered in the culture's memory. Lisa draws lightning from the power plant through the power lines and into her apartment. She uses the blue lightning to off Dr. Marsh (dressed in archetypal noir trench coat) when he shows up to kill her with the same syringe of green liquid. We finally get a miniature version of the Hooper red light show when she races down her apartment staircase, the walls alternately green and blue around her neon-red skin. Hooper stages a fight between Marsh and Lisa on the stairs that's somewhere between *Kiss Me Deadly* and *Psycho*, all low angles and quick editing. She kills Marsh, but Rachel's waiting downstairs to finish the job. Thankfully, a thoroughly charred David shows up in the nick of time, killing his ex-wife. He melts into a pile of blue light right out of *Lifeforce* and takes Lisa's fire with him, saving the day. What little of it there is to be saved.

Spontaneous Combustion takes place in a world without good, and just a little cushion when you fall, if you're lucky. After eight years of Reagan and a few of Bush, Hooper saw no easy way out of the life that the architects of America's future crafted in the years he was growing up. *Spontaneous Combustion* is a metaphorical investigation into how a country could possibly have led itself down the path on which it was still blindly stumbling in the late '80s. It's a deeply angry film, as broad and kitschy as it is, furious and burning for answers like its hero. There were none, of course, except that, as always, everyone thought they knew what was best.

I'm Dangerous Tonight (1990)

I'm Dangerous Tonight is loosely based on a 1937 Cornell Woolrich novella about a French dressmaker who stitches a garment from cloth gifted to her by the devil. Everyone who wears it is compelled to lust and murder. Hooper and writer Bruce Lansbury reset the story in an American college town and cut the devil, but retain the malicious essence of the story. This was Hooper's first TV movie after *Salem's Lot* and it's one of his strongest works, if also, unfortunately, one of his least personal visually— aptly televisual in composition, shot length, and lens choice. It becomes even tougher to parse out Hooper's typically pristine visuals, as the film is only available on patchy VHS rips.

It opens on a beautiful image of a crooked road outside the fictitious Tiverton College. As in *Salem's*, a delivery truck brings evil to town. An Aztec sacrificial alter (its big snake heads are the predominant aspect of its ornate, overblown design) is dropped off at the college's museum. Nicholas Pike's music is like a trick plane diving, rolling, and weaving all over the place. It's one of the better scores from Hooper's synth era, which lasted from *Texas Chainsaw 2* until *Crocodile*. Dr. Jonas Wilson (William Berger) is beside himself. He's so anxious about its appearance that he doesn't wait more than five minutes before he's hammering away at its seal to see what's inside. He uses an industrial lift to get the lid off and finds a skeleton draped in a perfectly preserved red cloth. As Wilson pulls it from the body, the sound of moaning and screaming fills the air. A security guard comes to check on the noise and Wilson, draped in the cloak like a Klansman, murders the poor sap with a sword, and then kills himself off screen.

On hand to explain the event in the next cut is Professor Buchanan (Norman Bates himself, Anthony Perkins—finally, a direct link to Hitchcock's *Psycho* after boosting technique from it all these years), in mid-lecture.

"The primitive mind believes that certain inanimate objects are quite literally alive. That they possess sentience, feelings, a will of their own... we call this belief or doctrine animism."

He breaks a mirror on his desk to prove the point that we, civilized people, are above animistic superstition. Buchanan will be teaching the late Dr. Wilson's book on the subject for this particular course. In the lecture hall, young Amy O'Neil (Mädchen Amick, *Twin Peaks*' siren Shelly Johnson, who also worked with fellow "masters of horror" Mick Garris and John McNaughton) groans along with everyone else when they hear they have to study the giant tome. Her study partner, Eddie (Corey Parker), is cute enough to her that she agrees to shoulder the brunt of learning Jonas' book. She even agrees to help find props for Eddie's production of *Romeo and Juliet*—the film's none too subtle way of commenting on the divide that will arise between the lovers, and the soon-to-flower subject of female agency.

Amy is living in a fairy-tale-esque home: under the thumb of her wicked aunt (Mary Frann, from *Newhart,* who died weeks before her planned marriage in 1998) following the death of her parents, making clothes, and feeding her infirmed grandmother (Natalie Schafer, perhaps best known as Lovey Howell from *Gilligan's Island,* but she'd worked with Anatole Litvak, Fritz Lang, and Max Ophüls in her youth. This was her last film, something of an unfortunate trend in Hooper's work) while her cousin Gloria (Daisy

Hall) frolics with her boyfriend Mason (Jason Brooke). Her personality shift into a modern vamp will be her way of breaking the antiquated mold of feminine suffering in which she's trapped.

The following day, Amy goes to Dr. Wilson's estate sale and buys an old trunk for Eddie's play. Inside is the red cloak. She touches it and has flashes of the horrific murders that Dr. Wilson committed before killing himself. The flashes are lovely little fright tableaux: an axe ripping into an easy chair, blood on the pages of a book, Jonas' wife screaming. Even so, Amy buys the trunk and not a minute too soon. *Someone* calls asking after the trunk as she drives away, the audio from the estate agent's phone call bleeding into the sound of swords clanging during the rehearsals for *Romeo and Juliet* as the trunk is being carried backstage. Eddie tries on the red cloak and immediately wants another crack at the sword fight, attacking everyone in sight remorselessly, possessed by the same spirit that provoked Jonas to commit murder, the one hiding in the red silk. Amy promptly steals it back when it slips off his shoulders.

That night, all it takes is Amy touching it with her fingers and she's hitting on her cousin Mason right in front of Gloria. When the two lovebirds leave, Amy tries explaining the day's events to her grandmother. "Scary to think what's bottled up inside of us just waiting to get out."

Grandma doesn't appear to be listening until she sees the red cloth hanging on Amy's bedpost. That scares her.

When Gloria comes home from her date (something always draws Hooper to film dialogue scenes in the front seat of cars, something so archetypically American; this one ends with Mason frustrated as hell that Gloria won't put out), Hooper and cinematographer Levie Isaacks frame her in the blue moonlight pouring in through the windows on the staircase behind her. She's about to go to bed, when she hears Amy sewing a gown out of the red silk. Her progress frightens both Gloria and their grandma.

"Get the old lady out of here!" barks Amy, Pike's synths cooing ominously in the bottom of the mix.

The next day, Eddie throws rocks at Amy's window and quotes Shakespeare at her. He can't explain his actions with the sword, but he'd still like to take her dancing. She decides against watching her grandmother as she's supposed to, throws on the red dress, and goes out with him, to the chagrin of her aunt and cousin. Pike does his best impression of a New

Romantic dance anthem as Hooper and Isaacks glide across the dance floor—the tiles the same black and white chessboard pattern as those on the floor of Lew Orlander's house in *Spontaneous Combustion* and the ones that compel Maya Deren in *At Land,* all the better to mesh with everyone wearing the same shades of black and white. They're all pawns about to be moved by an expert player—this subtly evokes Deren's manipulation of two chess players on a beach at the end of *At Land* as Amy, who cuts a Deren-like figure in the dress, gets in the heads of both the women and men around her. Gloria and Jason look into the corner of a room and see Amy, a vision in her red dress and red shoes, taking up the perfect amount of space in the left third of the screen. Hooper trades his typical flood of red light for the red dress hugging Amick's body like a bunch of electrical tape. It signifies the same thing—the end of innocence and the beginning of the pain of adulthood. It stands in stark contrast to Gloria's muted blue cocktail dress, which, while plenty revealing, looks almost like a nun's habit compared to the way Amy's red dress seems to writhe around on her, as if it has a mind of its own. While she beckons to Mason from the dance floor, behind the big lug is latticework whose shadow forms another chessboard design on the wall to his left and square holes in the walls, which produces a similar effect. Isaacks orchestrates the conflicting geometry sublimely: it's checkmate for Amy. As Pike turns the music to something approximating Donna Summer or New Order, Professor Buchanan enters the party and is stunned to see the brilliant red fabric on his student.

Amy leaves with Mason, and makes out with him in the back of his car. Blinding white light splashes on the top half of her face when she throws off the dress in the throes of passion and suddenly loses her possession. Hooper is plainly restricted by the budget and time to come up with an elaborate use of his camera, but he and Isaacks do wonders with the lighting all the same. Back at home, they throw a half-dozen different shades of light on every bare wall, hinting at the roiling tension in the house and in Amy's mind. Grandma tries to pull the offending dress from Amy's mitts and the ensuing struggle ends with her dead at the bottom of the stairs. Hooper shoots Amy from low-angles during her dance and seduction but during the confrontation between the two cousins afterwards he will shoot Amy from above and Gloria from below. Without the dress, she has no power. She contemplates cutting it up but can't quite bring herself to do it, stashing it in her closet instead.

Gloria apologizes the next day in a pale purple silk robe, in contrast to the red silk of lust and murder. She asks for the red dress to wear to her makeup date with Mason, and Amy lies and says she threw it away because it was "bad luck." As soon as Amy leaves, Gloria rifles through her closet and finds it. Hooper drops the camera to her knees to film her admiring her own reflection in the mirror, power changing hands once again.

Meanwhile, Eddie and Amy have their own makeup session. He too asks about the dress, equally enthralled by the sight of it at the dance. He's deeply upset that she threw it away. That's nothing compared to Gloria's upset across town. Dress on, she finally sleeps with Mason under the impression he's going to propose to her. The "big secret" he was going to share was that he'd been drafted by the 49ers. So she waits until he's in the shower, puts the dress on, destroys his apartment and gleefully strangles him, another riff on the *Psycho* shower sequence, ending with her slitting his wrists with a razor to make it look like suicide.

There's a truck chase (a la *Texas Chainsaw 2*) when Gloria comes home in Mason's truck and finds Eddie and Amy kissing in the driveway. She runs the lovers off the road, they escape on foot, and Gloria swerves off the road and crashes (Hooper stages this confidently despite clear budgetary constraints). The car blows up and then, unfortunately for the pace and tone of the movie, there's a commercial break. This means we cut right from Amy screaming as her cousin blows up to Amy jogging an indeterminate amount of time later. With mist hanging heavily in the air, she runs into Professor Buchanan walking his Doberman. As Buchanan tries to pry some info on the red dress out of her while obliquely explaining its supposedly mystic properties, Hooper and Isaacks dolly with them. Buchanan compliments Amy on the way she looked in the red dress (Perkins' eyebrows leap into the air, a little James Mason in his performance), but lets her leave without making it *too* clear that he wants it.

A detective named Ackman (R. Lee Ermey, like Dale Dye, a veteran— he'd later turn up in *The Apartment Complex* as well as in Michael Bay's remakes of *Texas Chain Saw* in the 2000s) also questions Amy. Hooper introduces him with a languid, lateral tracking shot on a lunch line—a classic Hooper move, going back to the bones obscuring the action during a dolly through Leatherface's living room in *Chain Saw*. Ackman, investigating Mason's death, wants to know about the red dress, too. Every man in the movie is obsessed with it. Sex obscures the issue of murder and accidental death. Gloria, Mason, and her grandmother all die within days of each other and the lead detective can't quite let go of the red dress.

Meanwhile, the coroner who looked into Gloria's remains, Wanda Thatcher (Dee Wallace, the genre director's best friend. Look for her in *Critters, E.T., The Howling, Cujo,* and the thematically simpatico *Lords of Salem*) has been running around town murdering people after taking the dress from Gloria's body. Hooper gets in a truncated dolly-to-zoom reveal (the ones all over the first act of *The Funhouse*) as Amy leaves the library after researching animism and passes a newspaper whose front page is about Wanda's latest victim. But the more interesting part comes next.

The librarian who kicked Amy out (Felicia Lansbury, niece of the great Angela Lansbury and daughter of producer/writer Bruce, who wrote the script for *I'm Dangerous Tonight*) runs up behind Amy on her walk across campus to the parking lot. They share an awkward second of silence before the Librarian asks, "I hate this walk, don't you?"

And just like that, so much of the film comes into sharper focus. The world is terrified of a woman in a red dress killing with impunity, seducing whomever she pleases. But the men in this film are all only *not* terrifying because they have the phantom killer as a counterpoint.

It may not be a Take Back The Night powerhouse like *Ms. 45, Foxy Brown,* or *Rape Squad,* but it's also more sensitive to the way in which sexuality can be frightening and empowering in equal measure. It lets Amy consider the killer a person because she too was at the mercy of the Aztec garment. She knows how tempting and terrible having access to that power can be.

Even Aunt Martha, who at first seems callous and uncaring, is revealed to have three dimensions. She has to deal with the death of her mother and daughter, even if only on the periphery of Amy's story. The scene we get of Martha grieving—subdued thanks to inebriation, falling asleep on the couch, and breaking a glass—is the most heartbreaking scene in the movie and Hooper could easily have just skipped it—she's dead the next time we see her and her grief isn't a narrative necessity. But it *is* a thematic one. This is the window we get into what drives Wanda once she's possessed by the red dress. She, like Martha, is a single woman in her 40s and her boss talks about her compassion as if it's a hindrance.

It's telling that what winds up scaring Amy in the park is Professor Buchanan, not any knife-wielding woman. The men in *I'm Dangerous Tonight* are a constant, condescending threat to Amy, always hitting on her, scaring her, taking advantage of her meekness, and invading her personal space. It's her taciturn femininity that makes her seem like less of a threat to Wanda's landlord when she stops by, trying to search her apartment. She narrowly escapes and heads right to Ackman's office, who immediately makes it known that he won't be taking her seriously as anything but a suspect. As soon as *that* ordeal is over, who is waiting for her at home but Eddie, who wants to tell Amy he loves her (this is a ploy to get her in bed, as we'll see in a moment). She is a pinball between masculine registers. Even so, she doesn't yield to his romantic declaration, even if she does ask a little too politely to be allowed to go inside her own home rather than stand there and talk to him. There's a fake split diopter shot with her keys in the door on the left hand side of the frame while Amy answers a phone call on the right—a ceding to fetishism and a hint that things are about to change, as is frequently the case with Hooper's doorways—she's crossing a threshold into new depths of violence. Wanda's inside, and she's killed Martha.

After a mighty struggle, Amy wakes up in her bed wearing the dress. The catch is that *Eddie* put it on her. He wore the cape for a minute and wanted to kill his scene partner, so he knows how powerful it is. But she fights the power of the dress and Eddie's advances when he throws himself on top of her and starts trying to have his way with her. His sex drive is evidently supposed to outweigh her panic and grief at having lost her last living relative. Eddie is her last obstacle—the supposed nice guy with an axe to grind. Amy escapes and flees to the garden shed and finds Wanda's body where Eddie left it. He committed murder under its spell and she only barely convinces him to destroy the dress with her before Ackman shows up, gun drawn. She has to convince Eddie *not* to succumb to his ugly masculine urges, to dominate her, to commit violence. All that remains is to feed the dress into a wood chipper, which spits it out in tiny pieces like viscera (a motif picked up in *The Mangler*). She drops the fragments on Wanda's grave like rose pedals the following morning. Not that it stops Professor Buchanan. No man can resist the urge to possess *more* power.

This is a film with a terrifyingly accurate depiction of male power dynamics. It would seem outlandish, thanks to Hooper's usually excessive style, but it all registers as truthful, that for instance, Mason is so furious that Gloria won't put out he just about kills her driving away. And she's expected to put up with his leaving her to pursue a football scholarship after having dogged her for weeks about sex? A woman having power and agency terrifies every man in the film. They believe they deserve whatever they want, and thanks to the film essentially confining its drama to male/female domestic and social scenes, the film doesn't cloak its intentions in metaphor; it's all right out in the open, as bold as the red dress. And what the terrified and frustrated men don't like is that for once "their" women think twice about giving in to man's every desire. The women who wear the dress are essentially granted the power of masculine confidence and agency—superheroes with a cape killing the men who've made their lives more difficult and sleeping with whomever they please. The film treats them as villainous, inasmuch as they all become murderous, but there's zero sense that men need the red fabric because they already behave like this.

I'm Dangerous Tonight proved that Hooper could not only bring the full weight of his thematic and political bent to the small screen, but he could do it without fully compromising his aesthetic vision. *Dangerous* may not look as rapturous as *Invaders From Mars* or *Lifeforce*, but it still has enough of his stylistic touchstones to remain thoroughly *his* while exploring storytelling with the daytime TV audience in mind. *I'm Dangerous Tonight* is one of Hooper's best films, righteously angry, flamboyantly stylish despite the limited means used to make it, and possessed only of characters interesting enough to nearly sideline the thriller plot. Naturally it's been all but forgotten. His work for TV was never given the same consideration as his film work, even his most neglected entries. But at least that spared it the derision that greeted *Spontaneous Combustion, Chainsaw 2,* and *The Mangler*. As a TV director, Hooper killed his darlings until the day finally came when his name was enough to guarantee him the freedom he chased his entire career.

Haunted Lives: True Ghost Stories, "Ghosts R Us" (1991)

Haunted Lives: True Ghost Stories, "The Legend of Katie Morgan" (1991)

Haunted Lives: True Ghost Stories, "School Spirit" (1991)

Bruce Nash and Allan Zullo created the short miniseries *Haunted Lives: True Ghost Stories* in the early '90s for CBS. There was a third installment for UPN three years later and the ratings weren't nearly as good and so the project was allowed to vanish. Hooper directed the first episode, narrated by Leonard Nimoy, no doubt intended to conjure memories of *In Search Of...* the mystery anthology show Nimoy inherited from Rod Serling after his death in 1975. Nimoy hosted *In Search Of* for five seasons between 1977 and 1982 and it became a phenomenon akin to Serling's *The Twilight Zone* or *The Outer Limits*. *Haunted Lives*, like *In Search Of...* blended fact and fiction by juxtaposing Hooper-directed reenactments of hauntings with interviews with the people who claim to have been haunted, though they were also just actors directed by Hooper. Largely this was a chance for Hooper to pay homage to himself on a tighter budget for a prime time audience, who likely didn't know he was involved. Cinematographer Levie Isaacks came with Hooper from *Spontaneous Combustion* and would also shoot his *Tales from the Crypt* episode the same year, and later would photograph Kim Henkel's *Texas Chainsaw Massacre: The Next Generation*, a project with which Hooper had nothing to do, in 1994.

The first segment, "Ghosts R Us," takes place in a Toys "R" Us in California that kept losing managers to fear of ghosts, before a medium named Sylvia Browne (Marianne Muellerleile) was called in. She discovered a ghost story that begins in 1881. Farmhand Yonny Yonson (John Hammil) is in love with his boss' betrothed daughter Elizabeth (Shawn Kristy). It's funny to see Hooper shooting a kind of would-be bodice ripping frontier romance (a Vaseline-lensed tableaux of a man hard at work and a woman rushing to his side) before it gives way to woozy Steadicam and quick zooms as Yonny starts menacingly chopping wood to let out his aggression.

"Time passes, as time will," says Nimoy helpfully.

Hooper's quick shots of the Toys "R" Us are a scream: employees juggling basketballs and being knocked over by unhelpful kiddie customers. Needless to say the performances are all huge and pronounced like the primary colors in the set design. There's a shot of a haunted storeroom that calls back to the shot of the levitating objects in the Freeling children's bedroom in *Poltergeist,* and an unnatural stack of skateboards that bring the kitchen chairs to mind. Staging *Poltergeist* in a toy store is plainly beneath Hooper's talent but he appears to be having fun. There's a mini-*Shining* riff involving blood coming in through the automatic doors instead of the elevators and they repeat the "go towards the light" séance from *Poltergeist,* complete with bright light behind the ghostly apparition from the other plain of existence, though in a much more relaxed register. Hooper could have done this in his sleep.

"The Legend of Katie Morgan" is about a haunted room (3312) at the Hotel del Coronado in San Diego. Alvin Silver plays investigator Alan May, who heard about the legend of a woman named Kate Morgan (Sarah Carson) who is supposed to have died in the room and wants to see it for himself. He narrates the whole thing like a noir protagonist. He sees her one night in his television, in what looks like a cross between the poster for Irvin Kershner's *The Eyes of Laura Mars* and the living TV in David Cronenberg's *Videodrome.* Turns out Kate was in love with a conman named Tom (Robert Lee Jacobs) and together they fleeced businessmen, but that ended when Kate got pregnant. They parted, she lost the baby, he remarried, and she killed herself—or did she? Kate comes to visit Alan through the television (more *Poltergeist*) and she takes him back in time to the scene of the crime. The crudeness of the ghost effects don't seem to faze Hooper, who for the most part favors functional compositions in this segment, though there is the odd tracking and dolly shot that looks lovely in the auburn lighting of the antique hotel.

"School Spirit" is set in Austin and starts with a tracking shot meant to evoke the traveling camera outside Leatherface's house in *Texas Chain Saw Massacre.* Construction workers are in the process of tearing down a school when they start to hear ghostly children singing and playing. The school is nicely roughed up, covered in graffiti and lit through boarded up windows. The haunted school hallways will later make an appearance in Marcus Nispel's Remake of *Texas Chain Saw* in 2003, who similarly shines stadium lights through cracks in old hallways. Hooper mostly keeps the camera fleet here, following workers in unbroken tracking shots around the construction site and keeping low angles. A priest is brought on to perform an exorcism, which requires him dousing tractors with holy water, an image so delightfully absurd it makes the entire toothless enterprise worth it. Hooper getting to play with a camera is almost always good value, though it's tough to escape the utter banality and silliness of a show like this. Hooper on a budget selling ghosts like snake oil is still Hooper.

Tales From The Crypt, "Dead Wait" (1991)

Tales From the Crypt was a phenomenon unlike nearly anything else in genre. Hosted by a skeletal puppet with the voice of John Kassir, known as the "Crypt Keeper," the anthology series ran for almost a hundred episodes, and were written and produced by heavy hitters Richard Donner, Walter Hill, David Giler, Joel Silver, and Robert Zemeckis, who between them had racked up an enormous collection of hits in the 1980s. Like Spielberg's *Amazing Stories*, it was meant to turn a brand of genre storytelling into a household commodity—and thanks to its home being the liberal pay channel HBO, they could get away with blood, gore, and nudity. The producers recruited every single hot genre director they could find, from people as disparate as Fred Dekker, Mary Lambert, Arnold Schwarzenegger, Bob Hoskins, and one-time English genre stalwart and ace cameraman Freddie Francis just before he retired. Hooper was naturally called in. As he would be when a sci-fi spin-off called *Perversions of Science* was ordered to series a few years later.

Hooper's episode "Dead Wait" was in the third season when the show was already a hit, allowing him room to do something more adventurous. He got David Mansfield (*Heaven's Gate*) to do the music, and the cast includes Jamer Remar, Vanity, Whoopi Goldberg, and John Rhys-Davies. We meet Remar's thug in a mosquito net lit with signature pink and purple gels and playing chess on his bed. Remar wants to steal a precious stone from Rhys-Davies, a plantation owner. The general air of perverse decay is very Hooper, while also not belonging to any particular era—it's redolent of *Eaten Alive*'s brothels and psychopath-run hotels. Remar meets a white suit-clad Rhys-Davies (doing a Cajun-flavored Orson Welles impression) while he's out with girlfriend/plaything Vanity at a bar. Their conversation about hiring Remar to work his plantation is framed by the silhouette of a slowly spinning fan's shadow dancing on their faces, the frame alive with action at all times.

The floor of Rhys-Davies' porch is a chessboard design, and his house is ruled by his pet priestess Peligre (Goldberg), who takes an instant dislike to the new surveyor. The sweltering conflict is already at a fever pitch, between Vanity making eyes at Remar behind Rhys-Davies' back and the voodoo practitioner sniffing out his ill intentions. When Remar discovers a severed goat head on the wall of his apartment, Goldberg gives him a warning he won't heed about respecting her culture even though he doesn't understand it. His room and nearly every room on the property are, naturally, overcome with venetian blind shadows. The stone he wants to steal glows purple from below like the lit-up tables in "Miss Stardust." Hooper shoots as much of the episode in long takes as possible, emphasizing the distance between his actors and the dead space on the set. The episode seems to directly hark to the similarly sweltering horror parable found in the Val Lewton–produced *I Walked With A Zombie*, even though the plot has more in common with Welles' *The Lady From Shanghai* (hence Rhys-Davies' impression). Which of course means that Remar has Vanity in bed by the midway point, though the line "Red King takes Black Queen," hasn't aged as well as either of those films. Vanity, with her mess of black hair, is another of Hooper's Deren stand-ins, and along with Goldberg one of his few Black leads.

Remar wakes with a dead chicken flapping in his bed and a lurking Goldberg, who warns him again not to sleep with the boss's wife. Rhys-Davies insists everyone leaves when rebels come to overrun the estate and Remar makes a fatal miscalculation when he decides the pearl he wants to steal is worth more than Vanity. Rhys-Davies swallowed the pearl and Remar now has to cut it out of his worm-infested body. It's suitably disgusting. Red looks home free, but this is a *Tales From The Crypt* episode, so a happy ending just isn't the cards and Peligre's got an ace up her sleeve.

Hooper was gifted at short-form storytelling like this; it allowed him to throw out visual shorthand in the form of homage to his favorite films. His willingness to take nastier turns in the story plays as clever rather than bleak, and his ability to choreograph elaborate tracking shots favors storytelling in ten-minute bursts between commercials. He may have done better work for theatres but he was no slouch on the small screen where he could have more resources than a typical low budget film could afford him.

Body Bags, "Eye" (1993)

The man in the corpse paint is director John Carpenter, who orchestrated this project. He and his producers worked out a deal with Showtime for a one-off horror anthology called Body Bags in which Carpenter would play a horror host like Vampira, Count Gore De Vol, or Sir Graves Ghastly (lovingly parodied by Joe Flaherty's Count Floyd on SCTV). Body Bags was apparently never supposed to be a series when it was conceived, though the idea was floated later on. This was just a way for Carpenter and co-director Hooper to pay homage to The Twilight Zone, The Outer Limits, and other horror/sci-fi TV series from their youth, the modern iterations of which Hooper would be employed by in the '80s and '90s. Carpenter's two segments are more in keeping with the spirit of those old TV shows. Hooper's sole entry for Body Bags, entitled "Eye," feels much more like the natural step in his exploration of political horror with TV considerations. Like Hitchcock directing Psycho, Hooper seemed to welcome the challenge inherent in making an original horrific work with the space and budget of one of the TV shows he'd directed. Since the show would be running on Showtime, he wouldn't have to worry about the gore quotient as he did in I'm Dangerous Tonight or any of his network TV outings. Eye showcased a purer Hooper deliberately running more efficiently.

The opening is certainly peppy. A close-up of Brent Matthews' (Mark Hamill) eyeball zooms out to reveal him at bat. He swings and we cut to the aftermath on a television in the locker room where his manager (legendary character actor Charles Napier) congratulates him on a job well done. In one take, Brent talks to his manager about his future prospects, then calls his wife on a payphone—Hooper dollies with him the whole time. Cinematographer Gary Kibbe (Carpenter's go-to at the time) liked whites and high-key lighting more than Hooper typically worked with, but they compromise. The shot that introduces Brent's wife Cathy (Twiggy) is a good example. She fixes a card to a present addressed to her husband ("To:

Dad From: Mom"), and there's a light approximation of the Hooper psychedelic color scheme: the paper card is tinted purple and there's a faded yellow bow and green trim on the white wrapping paper on the present, but we only get a glimpse of it before we follow Cathy to the couch to answer the phone, lightning and thunder exploding just outside her window. It's Hooper all right, just slightly domesticated.

Brent makes the mistake of reaching for a cassette to play during his ride home in the stormy weather, unbuckling his seatbelt to extend his reach. He doesn't see the deer until it's too late and crashes his muscle car into a telephone poll. Hooper dollies past the car to the road and back again (the technique from the gas station in *Chain Saw* once more) when a passing car stops and the passengers disgorge to check on Brent. He's got a piece of glass from the windshield in his eye.

Brent wakes in the care of Dr. Bregman (legendary B movie producer Roger Corman), who informs him his eye is history. His colleague, Dr. Lang (John Agar of *Journey To The Seventh Planet*, another relic from Hooper's youth), on the other hand has a crazy idea that just might work.

"When can we do it?" asks Brent.

Hamill is hilarious in his sweaty, exhausted desperation. The next scene, where he explains it to Cathy, he's back to aw-shucks God-fearing baseball hero, goading her into seeing things his way by making the surgery seem perfectly harmless and natural.

"Is this God's will?" she asks.

"Isn't it?" he offers lazily. "He gave us the ability to think and make discoveries, you know what I mean, ya know science and everything."

Hooper's contempt for athletes is obvious, but very funny. Hooper and Kibbe shoot this, like many of *Eye*'s dialogue scenes, in a single traveling take. They rhyme the opening shot of Brent's eye with that of the donor sitting on a pile of ice—a close-up that zooms out to reveal the operating theatre; both are games. These are Hooper's version of mad scientists; and like the villains of *Spontaneous Combustion* and *Poltergeist*, they ruin lives *officially*.

The surgery is cartoony and gross—the eye itself is so plainly a *prop* and Hooper loves filming it out in the air, just taking up screen space. The final shot and reverse shot of the surgery is a classic low-angle POV from the eye itself looking up at his doctors (almost an unspoken requirement for surgery scenes). And then we zoom back in on the eye, which hasn't yet been properly sewn up, the skin flaps folded back over Brent's face. Post-surgery, bruised and bloodshot, he slowly gets his focus back as he looks at Cathy with his new eye, but, except for her face, the shot is blurred. Even after something grotesque like the surgery, Hooper can still find his romantic streak.

Brent starts having flashes, throbbing pains in his head, represented by white flashes briefly obscuring the screen. When Cathy visits, he finds himself grabbing her hair but can't explain why—the eye, like the dress from *I'm Dangerous Tonight*, is giving him a will not his own. In keeping with the animism in *Dangerous*, what it brings out in Brent is what was buried in him all along—the violence and mania seem like they're barely contained by his religious, all-American athlete persona. It took so little for him to agree to dangerous surgery because without baseball, he'd lose his purpose and all his potential to stay rich. What's a wife and happiness without money and fame? When Cathy refuses to sleep with him a few minutes later, he reacts with predictable frustration. He's a man who needs to consume everything all the time, religion be damned. *Eye*, like *Poltergeist* (the neighborhood in which Brent and Cathy live looks exactly like Cuesta Verde), is about deciding whether your soul is worth your family and your life. This is one more in Hooper's playing with the elements of *Poltergeist* in a way more uniquely his. American values seemed to increasingly preclude the ability to live with yourself. So of course, as soon as Brent gets home, Cathy tells him about her pregnancy—the gift from the opening was a crib. They try to celebrate by being intimate but they no longer gel romantically and Brent's sudden brute lustiness scares Cathy.

Stinging from his wife's rejection of his hybrid body, he looks into the backyard (they're having a pool put in—*Poltergeist* again) and sees a zombie unearth itself from the disturbed earth below, the mystery of his new eye becoming clearer. The following day, Brent goes to investigate the earth by the pool, and Hooper and Kibbe follow him out with a crane starting over his head, then flattening out as if spying on him. At breakfast, he snaps at Cathy after one of the flashes, looking perplexed the next moment. There's another *Poltergeist* crib when he puts his breakfast into the garbage disposal and a bloody arm jumps out of it. His reaction shots are just like those of Marty looking at the steak in the Freelings' kitchen.

Brent returns to the backyard to start looking for the corpses he now thinks are buried there, tying neon green twine around posts to make it look legit—appearances are still everything to this American. He digs up a pair of feet and runs back inside to read his bible. The Matthews' household is stultifyingly perfect. The carpet looks so thick, you could get stuck in it and every picture looks like it came with the frame. It could be a show room at a department store. Thus, the intrusions by the undead feel perverse, but necessary—the mangy, cigarette-stained menace of imperfection.

When Cathy comes home, she finds Brent has finished building the crib. But just as he puts on the finishing touches, he looks through the crib bars (Hooper loves finding prison bars in suburban homes) and becomes a child in a waking nightmare. His "mother" is a woman in a yellow dress with a cocktail in her hand, the purple shadow of the bars splashed against her. She scolds him and puts a cigarette out in his eye. That night, he imagines Cathy dead while he's having sex with her, his hand wielding a knife appearing in a low-key tableaux (more Robert Aldrich—it looks like the opening of his Clifford Odetts adaptation *The Big Knife*) and then he'll kill her all over again in his imagination.

In the next cut, Hooper cranes his camera from the dirt in the backyard to Brent's bedroom window, where the troubled fellow paces back and forth reading scripture. Cathy walks upstairs to check on him and the camera starts on her feet, traveling up with her as she ascends the stairs, the railing creating a contrapuntal momentum—the best shot in the film, short though it may be. She wants to help, but doesn't know how. Brent takes the car to go find Dr. Lang, using the same choreography Hooper's utilized since *Salem's Lot* for car-side confrontations: a C-shape dolly from our first subject (Lang) around to face the second (Brent) as he runs to the car and places himself in front of the first. Brent demands answers and when Lang gives up the name of the donor—John Randall—it's off to the library's microfiche department. His eye now black having foregone the corrective contact lenses, Brent looks crazed staring into the newspaper articles, reading back the nature of John Randall's crimes. Hamill's voice is a never-ceasing joy—it's little wonder he spent most of his life doing voice over.

The next morning, Cathy sees Brent digging in the yard again and asks him to talk. "I have to finish digging your grave..." he says as he cocks his head to the side and swings the shovel. He chases her inside, garden shears in his pocket, and ties her hair to the dining room table. He starts talking to himself as Randall takes over his psyche, but Cathy convinces him to look in the bible at the inscription he once wrote in it for her—family and religion working together to exorcise Brent. He plunges the shears into his eyes and his blood winds up all over the pages of the bible. "And if thy right eye offend thee, pluck it out, and cast it away from thee…"

Eye is a bite sized look at Hooper's view of American hypocrisy and the cages we build for ourselves, to happily only ask for *this* much because we've been conditioned to believe it's the end of a man's journey: family, sex, material goods, a career, fame, fortune. When Randall takes over, Brent he sees that pleasure for pleasure's sake exists. He starts to become dissatisfied with his suburban existence, which Hooper renders as comfortable, plush, boring, and depressing as he can by shooting it in the broadest, brightest light imaginable. You can't escape the lie of suburban living when you can see every "perfect" inch and corner.

Night Terrors (1993)

Hooper maintained his relationship with the Cannon group's Yoram Globus and Boaz Davidson even after the group dissolved in the early '90s. A Rom Globus is co-credited with the screenplay of *Night Terrors*, about whom almost no information exists online. The other writer, Daniel Matmor, would appear in *The Mangler* and later had a small part on Guillermo Del Toro's *The Strain*, a TV show with no small debt to Hooper's *Salem's Lot*. Yoram Globus produced *Night Terrors* with his new outfit Global Pictures, a film evidently very close to *someone's* heart. Gerry O'Hara, a director with one of the *strangest* track records, was apparently attached to make *Night Terrors*, but when one of the writers added the subplot involving the Marquis De Sade's prison stay in flashback, O'Hara left the project to direct *The Mummy Lives*, then promptly retired when that turned out to be a colossal mistake.

Hooper had no problem with the subplot, probably because he knew that Globus would give him the respect and space he evidently missed working for television. And even though the film's budget might not have been *Poltergeist* high, Hooper was plainly given just enough to make every image and idea as vivid as he could. *Night Terrors* looks and feels whole, a complete statement from Hooper, every inch of it is committed and confident, his first film to incorporate all of his stylistic tendencies from every era of his career, every itch he ever needed scratched. It has the mythic sexuality of *Lifeforce*, the colors of *Eggshells* (not to mention flashes of its honest study of social groups and their habits) delivered with the boldness of *Invaders From Mars*, the fear of men from *I'm Dangerous Tonight*, the gonzo production design of *Texas Chain Saw* and its sequel, and it features Hooper's typical finesse with the camera (here operated by Amnon Salomon, a Cannon Group holdover). Rounding out the cast were William Finley from *Eaten Alive* and *The Funhouse* and Robert Englund from *Eaten Alive* and *Freddy's Nightmares*. Unfortunately, after a few festival dates, the film landed on VHS with no fanfare six years after its completion. Try to find someone who's seen it, let alone who might defend it, and I wager you'll come up empty-handed.

Night Terrors may look silly on paper, but being able to shoot in Israel seemed to embolden Hooper to dream big, selling the ridiculousness through sheer excess. He goes hog wild with his sleazy, dreamy imagery. This is his most fun grindhouse film after *Lifeforce*, especially when you're looking for Hooper in every composition and see how thoroughly in command of these bawdy ideas he was. If *Eye* was Hooper contained and coiled, doling out a little bit of himself where he could make room in his efficient storytelling, *Night Terrors* is Hooper unbound. Or, as the Marquis De Sade (Englund) says after a thorough lashing in the first scene, with "Such enthusiasm!"

Night Terrors has two stories, one in Alexandria in the present and the other about the Marquis de Sade in prison, tormented while he slowly dies—this is of course ahistorical, but our writers were more concerned with the metaphor of the tormented intellectual getting pleasure from pain and bucking the establishment. In Hooper's telling, the Marquis thrived on criticism (a touch of autobiography?) and laughs in the face of religion and conformity with his last breath, spitting blood on a priest to prove his point. Better to be alone than be wrong. We can forgive Hooper his indulgence with the facts for the thematic resonance with his own life.

The Marquis' story (which pops up intermittently throughout the present) is also used as a counterpoint to his modern day relative, Paul Chevalier (also Englund). Hooper knows that Chevalier's commitment to his ancestor's ways of life is mere dilettantism. He gestures towards a lifestyle in opposition to the Christianity of protagonist Genie (Zoe Trilling), but he's just as rigid in his dogma as Genie and her father, the hypocritical Dr. Matteson (Finley), which is why they're both punished. Hooper uses their myths against them and Chevalier can't begin to measure up to the Sadomasochistic ancestry he gestures towards. It's a story he's told himself, like the ones used to determine who is and isn't a part of polite society in this film's world. Everyone is a little too comforted by myths until Hooper makes them own up to what they're pretending to be. Every man who wants to be indoctrinated into Chevalier's life of debauchery is killed and Genie is punished with sadistic torture because her Christianity is a put on—she's just as taken with the wild nightlife of Chevalier and his minion Sabina (Alona Kimhi) as her father is, but both keep it secret in favor of the myth of their Christian beliefs. And Hooper uses this as an excuse to exoticize their exoticism—he gives into every hoary cliché of silly, orientalist sensuality, but only because he knows that this is the extent of his hero's imagination. The same way that *Invaders From Mars* is young David Gardner's dream of a sci-fi movie world come to life, *Night Terrors* is the id of a repressed Christian girl in a foreign land run amok.

But before all that can get started, a little of the Marquis... The Marquis de Sade sequences don't have a plot, really, they more exist like a Greek Chorus, commenting on the action in the present through images of torture. When we meet him in the opening minutes of the movie, it's to watch him sashay across the tiny, well-designed torture chamber where he's imprisoned. Hooper strolls with the aristocrat as he travels the length of his prison in a few detailed tracking shots, checking in with every inmate along the way. Englund's decadent performance as de Sade is some of his most lovable work. The prison has been coated with every possible sign of rot and the business of anguish, with prisoners in every corner of the frame, like a disgusting play on Max Ophüls' *Lola Montès*, about the famed dancer and her courtesan reflecting on her life during an elaborate stage production. The Marquis delights in their anguish being as flamboyant as his, taking particular pleasure in forcing a prisoner chained up across from his cell to look at his eye, white after having been blinded by his jailers (a little call back to *Eye*).

Just before archeologist Dr. Paul Matteson picks up his daughter Genie from the airport in Alexandria, he runs into Sabina, who tries to make friendly conversation with him. He brushes her off.

"Been tied up."

"Oh...I thought that's the way you like it?"

"...uh...not right now."

Just like that the film's Sadean B story has caught up with its main narrative. Finley is as fine as ever as Matteson, one of his final screen performances before his death in 2012. He worked almost exclusively for Hooper and Brian De Palma throughout his life, closing out his career with the latter's *Black Dahlia* in 2006.

The three-story building where Paul stays with his daughter is like a dollhouse: coral pink with ornate, multicolored windows, a white picket fence, and balconies.

"This is our first meal together in six months...it's real special," he says just before asking Fatima, the maid (Irit Sheleg), for more potatoes—both Hooper and Finley detest this man. He's bummed out that his fellow archeologists don't take Christianity as seriously as he does and he's even more scandalized by their belief that the devil and god might be one being (cue symbolic flashback to the Marquis).

The following morning, Paul brings over Genie's childhood friend, Beth (Chandra West)—their reunion is realistically joyous, letting their body language and facial tics guide the conversation. Beth's boyfriend Chuck (Niv Cohen) is a typical Hooper alpha male a la Buzz and Mason, and he honks at her to wrap up their reunion. Female agency will repeatedly by undercut by male desire throughout the film.

Genie hits the bazaar in a very American outfit—Sabina sees her and shakes her head as she pulls off her jean jacket revealing a midriff bearing polka-dotted top. She predicts the sexual assault that almost takes place in an alley a moment later. Apparently they happen like clockwork here and she's got enough practice stopping these things from happening that she finishes her cigarette before stepping in to do anything. Genie believes the place to be harmless thanks to her American conception of the world, so she's an easy target and needs reeducation. Sabina only enhances her exoticized understanding of the foreign land.

Sabina takes Genie to her apartment, filled with exotic statuary and artifacts. Hooper dollies in front of her until she reaches the balcony, then he's just as full of wonder as she is—he's never filmed a landscape like this before and his thrill at capturing it without the aid of matte paintings is palpable. Dollying in on the ladies in conversation on the balcony, letting the cool browns, grays, and greens of the Israeli vistas wash calm over the scene (the movie was quite obviously not shot in Alexandria) as Sabina offers Genie a permanent shelter from her troubles as long as she lives in this city.

When she's driven home, the Matteson house and the walls surrounding it from adjacent buildings are lovely shades of pink, blue, and yellow. Paul sees Sabina drop his daughter off (a sort of filigree just behind his head) and warns Genie off spending time with the other woman—she has a bad reputation. "Everyone is not what they seem."

She promises not to hang with Sabina while Paul is off at the dig, so of course it's a cut later until they're together at a party. Hooper loves the satisfaction of catching people in lies with his edits—people can't help themselves. The party is flooded with Hooper's psychedelic colors, starting with Genie's rainbow dress. He goes overboard lighting every free surface in *Night Terrors* and it's easy to marvel at his glee. Every frame has a new combination of shades. The drugs Sabina gives the American girl, the sight of topless women nearly eating live snakes while dancing, all of it intoxicates Genie. Genie succumbs to visions of sexual decadence in what's the first full-on free-form freak-out we've seen from Hooper in many years. The rapid cutting puts us back in *Eggshells* territory, along with the misty den, the jittery push-in on Genie's face, and the arrangement of bodies. Just as it all seems too much, Paul walks in quoting the bible and waving a cross, which may or may not be fantasy (cue symbolic visit with de Sade).

Genie's nursing an incredible hangover when Beth and Chuck come to pick her up to take her to a desert race. Their conversation has the easy, sarcastic rapport of the kids from *Eggshells* and *Chain Saw*. Genie is immediately taken by a champion horsemen, Mahmoud (Juliano Mer-Khamis, an activist who was assassinated outside his own theatre in 2011), but her lust is interrupted by another freak-out, this one from behind a

Plexiglas bubble right out of *Eggshells*, her father diving into the bubble shouting, "You will be damned!" between visions of snake-eaters and horses legs pumping. Her champion sees her distress and comes to her aid. He finds her the next day at the bazaar while shopping with Fatima and is *very* insistent that they spend time together—just as pushy as Chuck, if more charming. He too is in on the plan against Genie. Hooper films the two riding in slow motion like they were in a commercial paid for by a tourism board. He loves how easy it is to idealize the landscape—in the era of pay channel erotic thrillers, *Night Terrors* flirts with territory covered by the *Emmanuelle* series, seeming to be about a woman's sexual awakening in a foreign country thanks to a strapping alpha male. Hooper films a lot of topless women in *Night Terrors*, but has a good look at Mahmoud's penis during a later dream sequence, so at least he's an equal opportunity voyeur (like Colonel Caine). His excesses here have the fun, shamelessness of Ken Russell, who had also fallen on hard times by the '90s. Films like *Valentino*, *Lisztomania*, *Crimes of Passion*, *Lair of the White Worm*, and *Gothic* have the same gleeful derangement of *Night Terrors*. Both arise from a postwar tradition exemplified by Robert Aldrich and Max Ophüls—flagrant, profane, loud, and byzantine. Russell similarly eschewed subtlety for outsized symbolism, nude and lusty vampires, men reverting to primordial ape form, nazi robots, and gigantic phalluses swallowed by enormous vagina dentata. The idea of the Marquis De Sade providing running commentary on a story is something Russell would have approved, taking as he did figures as deliberately antisocial and incongruous as Adolf Hitler, Lord Byron, Dante Gabriel Rossetti, Richard Wagner, and Richard Strauss as his subjects.

Hooper takes us back to the Matteson's house with a dolly through a trellis and a pan to Genie reading de Sade on a swing in her front yard, prompting both a flashback and a freak-out/fantasy where Genie sees Mahmoud naked on his horse. She's also, alternately, in a tent filled with red/purple light (symbolic, as ever, of loss of innocence in Hooper's world) and eats the head of a snake, a visual metaphor that probably would have made De Sade roll his eyes. But it fits right in with the woman dressed as Little Red Riding Hood at the costume party to which Sabina takes Genie. That party too is overflowing with color and wonderful design, odd paintings, balloons (*Eggshells* again), and party decorations mingling with the costumes to create a wacky, uncertain aesthetic.

Across town, Fatima emerges from a misty blue alley to enter a kind of cult worship session. A bunch of penitents kneel and pray while red smoke billows and blue lightning flashes from an altar thanks to chemical reactions caused by the "priests."

Back at the party, Hooper pushes in on a puppet show detailing some portion of the Marquis' story, hinting that the cult and the Marquis will play a part in things to come. The scales on the wall of the cult's chamber of worship will be what tips Chevalier over into insanity as he loses any sense of his own identity versus that of de Sade's.

Paul Chevalier, the party's host, shows up at the end of the puppet show and introduces himself to Genie. She's not impressed—if he throws the kind of party where men hit a woman dressed like Little Red Riding Hood with balloons in some weird sexual ritual, she doesn't want to get to know him.

"I do have an *alternative* sense of humor," he says.

You can almost hear Hooper giggling off camera in agreement.

From behind a green door outfitted with shiny fabric, Sabina joins their conversation, trying to smooth their introduction. Englund's white-collar sadism is pitch-perfect, as he fancies himself so much more depraved than he actually is.

As a direct counterpoint, Beth interrupts her conversation with the two old lechers so she can complain that Chuck wants some weird sexual favor she won't indulge. "I think being a pervert is hereditary...if you ask me, it's some kind of cult. They're into some weird shit," cautions Beth.

Hooper routinely films his lovely empty sets and streets in this film with a kind of dreamy purpose that recalls Edgar Ulmer's *The Black Cat* (it contains a famous shot of empty stairs, which Ulmer dollies across while the 2nd movement of Beethoven's 7th symphony plays on the soundtrack). Both films concern legacies of brutality, per *The Misfits*, and the ways in which locations can be infected by death. Hooper suddenly finds Beth running for her life, but her figure, framed by blue mist and shadows, which seems like an afterthought to the staircase she runs upon (which is also true of the many shots of the Matteson house, a building with which Hooper plainly fell in love). She's pursued by a man with a phallic retractable knife, who catches up with her right as Genie wakes from another restless sleep.

Paul's archeological team finds the crypt they're after, which opens slowly into a secret chamber containing ancient artifacts—another womb space. As in *Invaders From Mars*, the womb space claims parents and sends children into nightmarish paths of self-discovery. Paul will be killed for his find at the dig—a box containing scales. Of course, Chevalier doesn't wait to hear Matteson describe the contents of the box before he cuts the archeologists' throat, replacing him as Genie's father figure (they already share a first name). Fatima, sensing something is definitely not right with her charges, casts a charm on Genie's room. It will prove useless but Hooper still puts more store in outright magic than in religion.

That night, as Genie stalks the empty house, Hooper and Salomon follow her and eventually frame her with a pastel-colored window over her head as she answers a phone call from no one—the lighting in her den is nearly identical to the Freeling house just before Marty's visitation in *Poltergeist*. She finds Beth's head in the fridge and Fatima hanging from the ceiling, her eyes gouged like Brent in *Eye*. She flees down psychedelic alleys, corridors, and streets looking for help, brilliant yellows and reds all around her. Hooper has an ace little trick in store when Genie reaches Sabina's house: she knocks on the door and when Sabina turns her lights on, the two surfaces that look like garage doors on either side of Genie light up as well. It says very subtly that Sabina was expecting her, as it traps Genie in a tableaux of suffering and hysteria. She comforts Genie with a mix of drink and sex—knowing that what Genie wants is to experience the world her father kept secret from her.

Genie has a sort of a freak-out after kissing Sabina, imagining herself in bed with blood on her face and a lapful of snakes, capped off by the appearance of a nude, green snake woman (Tamar Shamir). A magnificently cheesy apparition, but the image of the two women on a bed enshrouded in mist feels right at home in a film this hysterical and overripe. The image could easily be album art circa 1976. The Marquis appears to Genie in a vision, nailed to a cross. He throws her a rose and then leaves her to her Sapphic vision just as Chevalier arrives to spy on Genie and Sabina's real dalliance. Big things are about to happen. Meanwhile, Fatima's cult chant loudly in their candlelit chamber, praying over her dead body. An identical scale to the one from the dig sits in a corner of their chamber.

The best of Hooper's Ulmer-cribbing shots passes an archway, which splits the frame into uneven halves before finding Chevalier and Sabina in their parlor drinking and smoking casually, while Gioachino Rossini's "The Thieving Magpie" plays on a phonograph. To cover Genie's screams for help, Chevalier stands and turns the volume up, conducting it a little for good measure. Only Hooper, among his American horror peers, had any nose for real decadence. Stuart Gordon, William Friedkin, Sam Raimi, John Landis, Wes Craven, Mick Garris, John Carpenter... everyone who had ever let aesthetics overwhelm story had retreated by '93 to the other end of the pool. By this point, even Argento had abandoned voluptuousness in favor a more grim, psychological horror. Hooper still believed in the power of too much, and Genie, handcuffed in her underwear to a skull-faced ornament in a room filled with candles and erotic art, the walls a sickly turquoise and orange mixture, Rossini blaring behind her screams, is just enough of "too much."

Mahmoud shows up and taunts Genie by threatening to release her before revealing he too is in on it. He's even brought her father's head in a bag. Chevalier kills him too after a little too much celebration on his part. Genie faints into one more dream—the best part of which is when a heavy gate closes behind her with a dead body stuck to it, its awkward jiggling motion like the corpse puppet from *Chainsaw 2*. When she wakes, Chevalier has gotten into a De Sade costume. He hears his ancestor in his head and becomes so frustrated, he breaks a mirror—all the better to look at his crooked reflection as his mental state deteriorates. Genie tries seducing Sabina into helping her escape, but they only get as far as making out before Paul comes back, ready to roll play. He wants what was in Matteson's box—he thinks that it's going to contain an ancient text that re-explains God as an old testament hard-ass, more in keeping with what De Sade would have wanted people to worship (he plainly doesn't see how ludicrous it is to affix this particular desire to his ancestor). Of course, all the box has are those scales, which send Chevalier into a torture-happy frenzy, at which point Sabina loses her stomach for the ritual. She dies fighting Chevalier and freeing Genie, who escapes into a tunnel filled with gorgeous psychedelic fog. Chevalier catches up to her, but Fatima's cult send a spectral mob to warp his brain, allowing Genie to just gently shove him over and escape. Back in flashback, it's De Sade who gets the last laugh, coughing up blood on the priest sent to hear his confession—he knows so few people will ever *truly* understand him. Even his own descendants can't get it right, but perhaps that's for the best. The world wouldn't know what to do with two of him.

Night Terrors is thematically perfect as an exploration of Hooper's obsessions and as a showcase of his favored visual tricks and fetishes. As an extension of *I'm Dangerous Tonight*'s sexual politics, it says rather boldly that you needn't find a man to discover yourself (sexually or otherwise), especially considering how deeply untrustworthy and power hungry men can be. It doesn't punish Genie explicitly for her sexual behavior and it turns out her gambit to seduce Sabina was the right savvy thing to do. She ends the film in control of her sexuality, having vanquished her enemies and having been freed from the religious dogma that's flanked her the whole movie (and, it's implied, her whole life). At times, *Night Terrors* looks like the perfect Tobe Hooper film, even as it opens up into a new tonal register: a mix of the huge, odd, high-pitched mania of *Chainsaw 2* and *Spontaneous Combustion* and the jagged Americana of *Eye* and *I'm Dangerous Tonight*. It's also excellent trash cinema, unafraid of its most obscene absurdities and knowingly, flagrantly beautiful in spite of the sins it commits. There's a celebratory aspect to the production design, art direction, and grammar—like George Bush left office and Hooper produced a greatest hits album for himself, a tribute to every stage of his artistic life. *Night Terrors* is a feast for the eyes and a rousing exercise in sex and torture which meant that when it was finally seen and reviewed years later, it was called a new low for the director by critics who had failed to take notice of his evolution since the 1970s.

Chapter 5:
Body Snatchers (1995–2002)

Most rubrics for success would have to write off this period of Tobe Hooper's career. His film work reached a widely accepted nadir, and he worked for TV for most of the time. *The Mangler* remains one of his most despised works and a film like *Crocodile*—made for TV and released straight to VHS—seemed to hint that his best days were behind him, and he was now a hired gun. Of course with his TV work during this period he writes an alternative history of the '40s–'60s that ends with the government ready and able to ruin and co-opt our lives for the sake of a cosmic vendetta. Humans are moved like pawns as untouchable, infallible agencies run rampant with our freedom, with our bodies, specifically. Humans are chewed up and spit out by machinery too great to be combated.

His trilogy of pilots for *Nowhere Man, Dark Skies,* and *Taken* venture back in time to the foundation of the radicalism and paranoia that guide the political left that Hooper eagerly joined up and are also a biographical sketch of his own development.

Nowhere Man is about a man who suddenly finds himself without allies and a job in the mid-'90s after having proved himself a worthy and necessary artist. It's a picture he took in his past that proves his undoing—it's a mirror of Hooper's own life, bereft of the connection to the horror movie paradigm he helped coin. Working for television was not necessarily a step down, but the idea that he couldn't get funding for anything more expensive and sturdier than *Crocodile* after having changed film history must have felt a little like he was being erased.

Dark Skies is a show about idealistic liberals going to work for the Kennedy administration only to discover that there are greater forces at work, and they'll have no trouble killing you to make way for their version of progress. It's set right when he started making films on his own terms. The heroes are basically as old as he would have been at the time and have the same awakening he was having but from the inside, rather than from without. He would have seen the start of the Vietnam war and JFK's assassination from his TV (a scene he stages in *Dark Skies*) as planes landed with the war dead and wounded. His father died in 1961, right as the show's timeline starts.

And finally *Taken* goes back to the time of his birth, with a WWII fighter returning home scarred in more ways than normal from his time overseas. The show starts in 1944, a year after Hooper's birth. It's also the last time he worked with Steven Spielberg, whose presence was the sight of his pivotal brush with limelight and trauma: the making of *Poltergeist*. Reteaming with Spielberg was a way to seize and recontextualize his past, to prove beyond a shadow of a doubt that the two men were not in competition and worked together in something like harmony. It didn't work. People still dispute who directed *Poltergeist* and almost no one talks about the beautiful work Hooper did on *Taken*.

Hooper slowly eases up with his grammatical ticks and obsessions as he goes, starting with his eccentric and singular work on *The Mangler* and *Nowhere Man* and flattening his aesthetic until it starts to resemble the burgeoning style of prestige TV later typified by programs like *Mad Men, The Sopranos* and *The West Wing*. *Taken* treats the era of his birth with "seriousness," indulging in honest nostalgia, even as he picks apart every lie about the lives people lived in the postwar South, the way the idylls were always at the mercy of controlling and violent forces. All the bright-eyed heroes of his TV shows are all slowly making their way toward a hungry mouth built by capitalism and militarism, a mouth he made literal (not flesh but steel) in *The Mangler*. The past, his past, becomes the last embodiment of the carnivorous womb that has haunted his work from the beginning, the last cave he would ever explore.

The Mangler (1995)

It never ceases to astound me what qualities are singled out when people decide they're watching one of the worst films ever made. If you hate the script or the performances, what about the set design, the cinematography, the art direction, or the sound editing? What about everything that goes into your ears and eyes that bypasses the logical mind? Sure, that takes concentration and calling something terrible is fun, but it does show a startling antipathy in the viewing public towards artists when they pick a film like *The Mangler* and hang it out to dry. "Perhaps it's time for Tobe Hooper to hang up his light meter," wrote Marc Savlov at the time of its release (a tiny run on 800 screens, which saw it earn just over a million dollars). The *Baltimore Sun*, the *New York Times*, the *Washington Post*, the *Philadelphia Enquirer*, *Variety*, and the *Los Angeles Times* echoed Savlov's statement.

I accept many of its sins are unforgivable through a certain lens—its central performance has one register, its villain is a living cartoon character who uses a laundry press to commit murder, it isn't scary, and it has a hopeless, unhappy denouement. But those are all logical concerns from an artist who deals in paintings over scripts, who will tailor light before he'd tell an actor to rein it in. The image comes first for Hooper, and on that front, there is nothing wrong with *The Mangler* that can't be explained by a lack of money.

We open in media res, Hooper selecting a suitably odd angle with which to begin his thoroughly odd tale. We're looking up at the foreman (Demetre Phillips) at an industrial laundry on a catwalk, the grimy purple and blue ceiling over him *just* industrial and busy enough to draw our eyes past the man in his black and white suit as he shouts down at his workers. Hooper then lowers the camera on a crane (cinematography by Amnon Salomon again) and finds the dank factory floor, green and purple light staining the walls like oil—probably the most appropriate use of his stained glass color palette to date. Yes, it's marvelously artificial (as always), but it's motivated to match the aged colors of industry and machinery rather than merely unique to Hooper's hungry world. As furnaces billow in the background and workers mill about, the laundry press ominously slams two big plates together as Hooper cranes by the rumbling guts of the contraption, all rusty chains and churning gears, its material old and weathered like scales, surrounded by bags of clothes hung in flesh-colored sacks being carted around, moving past the camera in the opposite direction creating compositional tension through momentum (he's been using the tactic with his plan séquences since *Chain Saw*).

It's the perfect introduction to *The Mangler*, giving us Hooper's ethos on industrial capitalism in one lovely, sustained shot. His colors are in full flower, his movement as careful and supple as ever, and the frame bustles with carefully chosen detail. The people in this laundry are no different to its owner than the maelstrom of whirring, steaming parts—they make the machine run. That's all that matters; their humanity is a detriment to progress. The music by Barrington Pheloung releases a chorus of low cooing as we see the front of the machine, like a blunted, angry typewriter with no keys.

"You wanna watch yourself here. Take care of number one. Don't let the pressure get to you," says Adelle Frawley (Vera Blacker), a kindly old worker, to the new gal on the floor, plainly riddled with the promise of economic gain, taking pills to stay upright, and worked to the bone. She's unaware (or simply ignores) that looking out for yourself in a capitalist society still means having no control of your destiny.

A woman (Vanessa Pike) cuts herself on the machine and throws the blood off her hand right into its mouth, which slaps its metallic plates together in response. Some workers accidentally knock into the poor girl, causing a reaction between the icebox they're carrying and the big press. Some of Hooper's blue lightning sparks between the two, causing an explosion. Up on a catwalk by his office, the boss walks out to inspect the commotion. Bill Gartley (Robert Englund as pinched and unpleasant here as he was luxuriously twisted in *Night Terrors*) seems turned on by her pain.

"Work 'em like there's no tomorrow," he bellows to the foreman after he regains himself.

Englund is like a steampunk Mr. Moneybags walking on two Lofstrand crutches, his legs encased in ornate metal casts, a cigar in his mouth, one eye of his sunglasses blacked out, his hair a white widow's peak, his office doors adorned with frosted art deco design. He's Hooper's ultimate bad capitalist: a crotchety monster with no nuance or humanity whose soul is trapped by the demands of the press (the extreme end of the line started by Drayton Sawyer, the Carnival Barker, and Mr. Teague). It'll later be revealed that his soul is tied to the machine and that it captures the spirit of one person to be its minder forever, instantly rendering them into a grotesque parody of a greedy boss. Hooper filming people trapped in desolate locations that are now like burial grounds for progress, coupled with the never ending sound of destruction and progress (mingling and interchangeable), reminds me a little of the work of Pedro Costa, though obviously they have nothing in common as image makers beyond a love of decaying opulence, of crumbling kingdoms. Costa's Fontainhas and the hermetic worlds of *The Funhouse, Texas Chainsaw 2,* and *The Mangler* share a sick, faded glory, an all-encompassing depression that's seeped into the ground and the walls. The denizens of both refuse to leave because it's their home, but also because they have nowhere else to go.

It's a shame *The Mangler* was made when it was because at the time (relative economic prosperity, no war on TV), it didn't have an obvious allegorical equal in reality. Released in the '80s or during George W. Bush's presidency, and viewers would have immediately seen the cartoony dictator and his sarcophagus machine as stand-ins for the most powerful men in the world and the corporate criminals allowed to exist under their lax policing. Republican governance has become synonymous with corporations running wild because more than ever high-profile politicians on the right side of the aisle are all lousy with business ties. That wasn't untrue in the Clinton years, but it wasn't the story the same way it was during the 2008 collapse, the Madoff and Abramoff scandals, or the Worldcom/Tyco/Enron years when it seemed like every day brought more bad news for every poor person in the US. *The Mangler* wasn't released when people were looking for scapegoats for their woes, so it's possible no one felt the urge to forgive its over-the-top theatrics. *The Mangler* is elementally always going to be relevant—its tone and images are more a matter of taste.

This being a nominal Stephen King adaptation, we're in a fictitious Maine town, Rikers Valley, meant to put images of prison cells in the viewer's mind. After we meet our hero, cantankerous cop John Hunton (Ted Levine), the delivery truck (by this point a Hooper motif) taking the icebox away nearly flattens his jeep. Levine, a great actor, is all wrong for this part: jittery, nervous, and unsuited to the heightened dialogue. The delivery guys accidentally drop the icebox on him, and it's tough to tell whether this should be a comic beat or not. Levine wears a trench coat (so will his sidekick), which codes him as a noir hero a la David Bell in *Spontaneous Combustion*. He can't really do comedy as anything but the straight man (he's sort of a human Droopy Dog) and he's not even especially useful in that regard.

Back at Blue Ribbon, Mrs. Frawley puts her hands a little too close to the laundry, which opens its maw expectantly like a snake eying a rodent. Sherry, the woman with the cut hand, notices blood seeping into her bandage at an unnatural rate right as the machine looks ready to swallow Mrs. Frawley. The foreman surprises her and the old woman drops her pills onto the press' conveyor belt. Seconds later, she's being eaten by the machine, her legs kicking, blood spraying all over her coworkers. Sherry hits the kill switch, but it does no good.

The machine being the film's chief antagonist—it, after all, pulls Gartley's strings—is a fascinating alignment of Hooper's concerns as a filmmaker. His liberal streak meets his love for the work of his designers and the result is that the villain of *The Mangler* is literally a piece of the set, the logical cap to his hyperactive and loving appreciation of the chambers of horrors conjured for him.

Gartley, green light jumping all over him, comes to inspect once more, muttering to himself about his meddlesome employees (something of a *Scooby-Doo* villain quality to him). Hunton is called to investigate—the classic cars in the parking lot put this in a kind of nebulous time period, as if entering the Blue Ribbon Laundry puts you out of step with modernity, perpetually enslaved to an industrial age working method. A gust of steam hits Hunton in the face as he enters—Hooper plays with atmospherics like David Fincher with a joy buzzer.

"Can you show me what happened, Mr. Stanner?" Hunton asks of the foreman.

"Do I have to?" he replies queasily.

That's about as funny as the movie gets. Hunton pukes when he sees the old woman's remains, and steals her pills to steady himself as they carry her out in buckets. Safety inspectors show up with the sheriff (character actor Larry Taylor in the last role of a career that started in 1946) and deem it an accident.

That night, Hunton visits his friend Mark Jackson (independent filmmaker Daniel Matmor), whose yard is a little Eden of art direction, the air filled with heavenly dust right out of Ridley Scott's *Legend* or *Kingdom of Heaven*, colorful glass hanging from trees, and orange light from weird lamps littering the yard. These are the trappings of Mark's boho lifestyle. The blue stadium lights over their heads are all Hooper. There are (unsubstantiated) rumors that Hooper walked off the set at some point during production, leaving producer Anant Singh in charge, but the film's style bible is in Hooper's handwriting. It's plainly the gothic cousin to *Night Terrors* and the swampy atmosphere in Jackson's backyard would be used again in the better parts of *Crocodile* and *The Damned Thing* a few years later. There's a minor freak-out as the machine runs once more in Hunton's imagination after he looks too long at a waterwheel, all impressionistic greens and reds over images of progress smashed together with grinding sound effects. The effect nearly recalls the work of pioneering communist silent filmmaker Sergei Eisenstein, obsessed by machinery and the camera as a reflection of progress through technology. "A woman's dead and that machine is running right now. Like nothing happened!" cries Hunton.

At the laundry, a hose bursts open, shooting burning hot steam all over the floor. Sherry retreats to Gartley's office where he paces around her, giving a mumbled lecture (he's her uncle and legal guardian). The office is gorgeous—full of taxidermy (no Hooper villain is complete without some), expressionistic designs, and shadows. Their conversation ends as queasily as possible, with him following her into the bathroom.

Hunton is called to the hospital to check on one of the other women from the laundry (Ashley Hayden) who was burned by the steam. Her skin is yellowing from her burns and she has some crazy ideas about the machine having gotten a taste of blood. The machine is eating the working class like the sand pit from *Invaders*, the closet and pool in *Poltergeist*, and the basement in *Eggshells*. Back at Mark's place (flooded with blue, green, and red light), he tries explaining about haunted objects (an extension of the animism from *I'm Dangerous Tonight*), but Hunton doesn't want to hear it.

Sherry leaves Gartley's office and is nearly crushed by the machine—the sequences involving the machine are all jaw-dropping, some of the most wonderful, mesmerizing stuff Hooper ever directed. She's still plainly shaken when Hunton and Mark pay her a visit that night. Hunton's sensitive questioning is derailed when Mark starts trying to see if she fits the bill for his mystical take on the press. Asking a woman who just saw a violent death if she's a virgin is a great way to freak her out. While scolding Mark in the car, all the light that passes by Hunton's car is the same neon green shade. They're interrupted by yet *another* crime—the icebox killed a little girl. The crime scene photographer (Jeremy Crutchley) who's been dogging Hunton this whole time takes a picture of the body, sending birds scattering. He knows something. Mark thinks that the bloody handprint on the icebox has transferred the hunger of the laundry press. It tries to bite off Mark's arm, so Hunton attacks it with an axe, sending a tornado of blue light into the sky.

Hunton stops by the mortician's office for a little more investigation, but largely winds up talking to himself between two corpses. The photographer snaps a surprise photo, catching him at his lowest. They're kindred spirits—the photographer is dying. "The doc says I'm going fast. Being eaten up inside," he tells Hunton. The fate of many Hooper characters. They have their conversation on a brick stairwell swimming in blue light, the diametric opposition to the red light—rather than transformation and loss of innocence, it hints at a missed opportunity. Hunton and the photographer want their innocence *back*.

Hunton breaks into Blue Ribbon and the machine tries to eat him, but it only gets his coat tails. He wrestles his way past the foreman and into Gartley's office, and the old man gives Hunton a lecture on power. "We are the lifeblood of this town." Hunton leaves, once more enshrouded in steam from the press, his body language huge, legs shot out in front of him with every step, drunken momentum trying to put his torso ahead of him. Sherry watches from the back of the office as Gartley calls to have Hunton fired.

The enormous elemental/metaphor-heavy fiction, mixed with the enormity of Hooper's atmosphere, and the odd body language of Englund's mechanical man juxtaposed against the drunken modern dance of Levine's bull-in-a-china shop mannerisms has the effect of turning *The Mangler* into a sort of opera or ballet. Hooper's debt to Michael Powell has been on display as early as *Eaten Alive*, with its carefully chosen odd faces swathed in fierce light, but *The Mangler* feels like a deliberate Powell homage. Powell's films of *The Red Shoes, Bluebeard's Castle*, and especially *Tales of Hoffmann* (which also has a man tormented by the creation of a mechanical woman—Gartley's ultimate plan for Sherry is to make her into his replacement, leg braces and all) are beautifully externalizations of the complex psychological underpinnings of the humans singing and dancing where words fail them. *Hoffmann* has Powell's typically exuberant style and rejection of reality—the bright color and boldly hyperactive set and production design, compositions perfectly chosen to accentuate the work done by the decorators, and artists working behind the scenes (all true of Hooper as well). There are also touches in common beyond the usual flare. The destruction of Coppélius' mechanical woman is a little horror show unto itself—the legs of the dancer emerging from behind a curtain to appear like they're dancing cut off from the rest of the body. Frawley's legs, when she's sucked into the Mangler, are similarly macabre.

Lin Sue (Lisa Morris), Gartley's consort who shows up in the final act, looks like Hoffmann's second lost love Giulietta. The design of the photographer, the corpse paint, and old age makeup make him look like on the men in the theater audience watching the mechanical woman dance in *Hoffmann*. The design of Gartley (silver widow's peak especially) is very close to that of both of Hoffmann's romantic rivals Councilor Lindorf and Dapertutto (both played by Robert Helpmann), who conspire against him in similarly dastardly ways. And in the end, Hoffmann and Hunton are both left alone, defeated by monomaniacal industrialists in high places. When the Mangler takes the foreman in its jaws, Sherry asks for help.

Gartley responds, "Do something...I'll dance, that's what I'll do."

(There's also a *Peeping Tom* connection in a man's spiritual connection to the machine he uses to commit murder.)

Hunton and Gartley arrive to exorcise the machine of its demons and catch Gartley trying to sacrifice Sherry to its spinning, industrial mouth, but turn the tables on him. It folds Gartley like a sheet, crushing his legs and killing him. The machine doesn't take kindly to the religious ceremony, explodes, changes shape, lifts itself up off the floor, and chases the three amateur exorcists into the basement of Blue Ribbon Laundry, which is where the film really looks operatic. After making it through a long corridor, Hunton and Sherry reach a hellish subbasement, a spiral staircase green like mold or oxidized copper. Hooper introduces it in a series of swooping crane shots to highlight its meticulous design. After they vanquish the Mangler in the basement Hunton passes an American flag being raised—the ironic shoe drops when he sees that Sherry's become Gartley's replacement, having lost a finger to the machine during their struggle. This is the American dream—a never-ending cycle of blood sacrifices to the capitalist machine. As in *Hoffmann* and *Salem's Lot*, a romantic idea of the world will only end with you alone and disappointed. King and Hooper both agree that, though they play with the language of fables, they owe their audience an ending that doesn't shortchange the political reality undergirding the narrative. Things must be just as bleak in fantasy as in reality.

Nowhere Man, "Absolute Zero" (1995)
Nowhere Man, "Turnabout" (1995)

Nowhere Man only lasted one season, which was nothing new for creator and producer Lawrence Hertzog. Hertzog had written for dozens of shows that wound up cult items and footnotes, including *La Femme Nikita, Seaquest 2032, Hardcastle And McCormick, Mrs. Columbo, and Stingray. Nowhere Man* was well-liked but it was still cancelled young, and the closest thing Hertzog had to a hit afterwards was his stint on *Painkiller Jane* a decade later. *Nowhere Man* was a sci-fi tinged show like a lot of Hertzog's TV, about a photojournalist named Thomas Veil played by Bruce Greenwood who wakes up one day having been forgotten by his family and friends. Hooper directed the first two episodes, "Absolute Zero" and "Turnabout," which aired on UPN in the autumn of 1995.

Hooper begins the pilot with eerie sounds—cracking wood and crying children—playing over a slow zoom out from a photograph of men being executed somewhere in a warzone. It's a bloodcurdling opener and places it thoroughly in the mind of the hero, who has to forget the horrors he photographed and be a public artist (foreshadowing his own supernatural fate). Veil has to play nice with art critics who view his factual recording of trauma and tragedy as objects to be admired and judged aesthetically rather than for their content. He chafes at the attention and makes his wife Alyson (Megan Gallagher) let him leave. Hooper cuts to the black and white images of warfare as husband and wife have a conversation about the dinner they're going to get when they leave the gala. The disorienting whirlwind of incongruous talk and stark images of murder and suffering never relents. Hooper is clearly in his element throwing real world horror in the face of aesthetes. Dinner with the wife is cut short first by a dropped plate (the sound design is some of his sharpest and most off-putting since *Texas Chain Saw*, overwhelming the audience with percussive and grating sounds leaping out to cut short conversations. Veil is never at peace and neither are we), and then by what happens to him when he goes into the men's room.

Veil leaves the bathroom, his wife is gone, the pianist isn't playing "La Vie En Rose" anymore, the maître d' doesn't recognize him, and asks him to leave when he insists another couple took his table. He goes to a phone booth to call home but the number isn't in service. Hooper introduces this shot on a crane looking down at the booth and then dropping to the ground, where the booth, between a fire hydrant and a tree, is covered in pale green light. Veil gets a cab home and home is flanked by stadium lights. His wife doesn't recognize him and her husband (Greg Wrangler) threatens him with a shotgun. He gets a cab to an ATM and it eats his card. He breaks into his studio and his self-portraits have been replaced with pictures of another man. There is one, of an execution, that's missing, and he'll later connect the missing photograph to his being replaced. He's been replaced in all aspects of his life.

Hooper had never made an out-and-out conspiracy thriller like this before (*Spontaneous Combustion* came close but the conspiracy and its players are clear from the word go, and it doesn't go very high up) and though the TV cameras render the images a little thin and a little flat, he and director of photography Ric Waite make a meal out of the premise. If anything the banality of most of the set makes the reveals more unsettling. Take the dream sequence that waits for Veil when he dozes off in the studio. He wakes up back in his apartment, which is lit in naturalistic light, runs to throw water on his face in the bathroom and then returns to his wife. When she turns to face him, her face has no features, but then eyes emerge from the blank mass and blink. It's all the more upsetting for how simple the effect is and how ordinary the setups are.

He breaks into Alyson's car and she tells him he's being watched by some shadowy organization, but it's a ruse. They're pulled over by a cop and she rats him out and the cop beats him up and hauls him to a psychiatric hospital. The first shot of Veil in the asylum is perfect Hooper maximalist expressionism. Veil sits in a chair bisecting the middle and right thirds of the frame. Over his left shoulder is a huge beam of blue sunlight coming from outside and a marble bust of a man, and on the wall to the left is a black and white squiggle pattern. It's not the first time Hooper has cribbed from the German Expressionist movement of the early 1920s, but this is a near perfect recreation of the kind of set decoration-as-externalized-mania that started with Robert Weine's *The Cabinet of Dr. Caligari* and continued through to late Fritz Lang silent like 1928's *Metropolis* and 1929's *The Woman in the Moon*. Veil's attending doctor Bellamy (Michael Tucker) ostentatiously lights a cigar, also flanked by the black and white pattern, sitting in a puffy armchair while a buff orderly sits over his shoulder ready to stop Veil when he gets too excited. Hooper's mid-career turn toward the arch reaches its apotheosis here, a reworking of something like John Frankenheimer's *The Manchurian Candidate* or Hitchcock's *North By Northwest*, which gets a direct quotation later, as a kind of live-action pop-up book. It's exactly the kind of thing that wouldn't be taken seriously, and yet demands it retroactive respect for its specificity and commitment to the kitsch-adjacent aesthetic.

Veil has no luck convincing his doctor he's sane, and when next we meet him he's being introduced to his roommate in the sanitarium—Dave "Eddie" Powers, played by *The Mangler's* Ted Levine. He claims to be a paranoid schizophrenic but he also seems more with it than Veil. Bellamy organizes a trip back to Veil's old life to have everyone tell him in black and white that he isn't the man he says he is and nobody remembers him. The studio has a new receptionist who doesn't know him and who claims the photographer responsible for the work all around them is overseas. He can't find his negatives, so it's back to the asylum.

The break room is flooded with more shafts of blue light and beset by ornate latticework. Eddie plays ping-pong with an inmate (Jay Arlen Jones) who sings every word he says like it's a blues song. Eddie further presses Veil. Levine is a swaggering marvel here, far more at home as the wise fool than as a private dick. Veil does some snooping around that night, and Hooper lets Waite pan the camera to show most of the action and cuts infrequently. Veil sees Bellamy and Alyson laughing together but the guards find and drug Veil before he can find out what's happening. When next he wakes up, Eddie's been operated on and no longer seems aware of anything. Recognizing he may be next, he kidnaps Bellamy at syringe-point and they head to the doctor's car. It may or may not mean something that the exterior of the asylum looks like a film studio.

Veil breaks back into his studio to make himself a fake ID that'll give him access to Bellamy's credit cards. The doctor finally admits there's some kind of conspiracy afoot, that he and his wife are in on it. He locates the previously missing negatives, proving his identity conclusively. Veil can't try to torture any information out of Bellamy because men in white arrive with machine guns and he has to blow the lab, killing everybody inside, to escape. His next stop is his friend Larry's (Murray Rubinstein) postmodern apartment, outfitted with tall glass banisters, see-through telephones, kooky sculptures, and bad paintings. Larry's not in the still-running shower (but an eerie hanging robe is—another simple shock effect that has no business being as effective as it is) but rather dead and stuffed in the closet.

Veil heads to his mother next, whose dusty country house is emanating "La Vie En Rose" when he arrives. A series of clocks start chiming when he enters, the table is set for two, and a kettle is boiling on the stove. The place is believably jammed with too much stuff. He doesn't find his mother (Mary Gregory) at first but rather her nurse (Mariah O'Brien), installed in the place after a stroke the old lady suffered at the precise time everything went cockeyed for Tom. Mom's hooked up to a giant chugging breathing apparatus right out of *The Mangler*. A cop (John Hillard) arrives on the scene with suspicious speed, but he can't arrest him in time. A priest (Bernie McInerney) arrives and his presence scares mom into pretending not to know him. Tom disarms the cop and flees, Hooper shoots most of the chaos at mom's house functionally, letting the action breathe and behave normally.

Tom drives down a desert road, and Hooper shoots it with the same long lens with which he captured the motion of the kids' van at the start of *Texas Chain Saw*. It breaks down and comes to a halt in focus right in front of the camera. When Veil gets out of the car the road is completely different than the one we were just staring at—a neat and easy trick for further disorientation. Tom takes off walking on foot. He finds himself at a crossroads and the composition is meant to evoke Cary Grant in *North By Northwest* before the famous plane sequence. Tom flags a man in a truck

(David Brisbin) who cuts his cigar the same way Dr. Bellamy did, alerting him that the conspiracy will follow him everywhere.

"Turnabout" starts by reiterating the most important points of the pilot episode. Veil lost everything because of the photo of the execution, and he's still got the negative. Hooper finds him on a ferryboat and stays on him as the camera slowly drifts away from him—typically showy camera work that is nevertheless effective in placing Veil in compositional isolation. He checks into a motel and Hooper films him as the smallest object in his room, lit from below to highlight his paranoid state. A van pulls up outside the motel in the misty night and the game is afoot. Men carrying flashlights (like the lynch mob in "No More Mr. Nice Guy") enter his room and he flees out the window. The credits roll and we find him in a well-upholstered office of another sanitarium run by a tightly wound supervisor (George DelHoyo). Since Bellamy's dead, Haynes thinks Veil is him, and lets him kick up his heels, even letting him smoke a cigar and lighting it the way the dead doctor used to. There's a collection of monks on the campus and Hooper will film them magnificently throughout the episode. Veil takes to the order of the shadowy organization with quickness and the episode feels very much in the tradition of the ITV series *The Prisoner* created by Patrick McGoohan and George Markstein. Though it only ran for seventeen episodes, it had a monumental impact on televised storytelling, introducing the idea of a protagonist who loses his identity and is imprisoned by shadowy forces. Everything from *Lost* to *The Simpsons* bore its influence and a show like *Nowhere Man* took many cues from its format.

Veil sees in his tour as the false Bellamy a woman named Ellen Combs (Mimi Craven) who hasn't been successfully brainwashed. She lost her family when they were abducted during a carwash—a scene of magnificent claustrophobia and co-opting of familial fun. The arrival of an empty van absent a husband and child send Ellen around the bend. She had a similar event to Tom's, having her life erased in the blink of an eye. She almost runs through the car wash looking for them. Tom now has to prove his identity by convincing Ellen Combs she never had a family, as Bellamy tried to do to him. Veil has a voiceover track now that aligns more perfectly with the tradition of paranoid noir heroes. When he can't open his bedroom door he freaks out and one of the monks has to open the door for him—his voice is twice as loud and imposing as Greenwood's on the soundtrack.

Ellen is reintroduced rocking in place with a fire roaring behind her and prison bars obscuring her face—her imprisonment literalized by Hooper's blocking. She's in a cage in the middle of a room lit by floodlights. The strangeness of the set—the cage on a blonde wooden floor with lights everywhere—is like a mock-up/reversal of the set piece at the third act break in Jonathan Demme's *Silence of the Lambs*. Combs walks around the perimeter of the cage while Veil sits inside watching her, and the camera follows suit. It paces around Veil and stays put watching Combs. The supervisor is nonplussed by Veil's approach, and we know it by the Dutch tilt and the placement of him in the center of dark yet cluttered frame in the control room, but hasn't much choice but to put up with him.

The next day Veil takes Ellen to her kid's school to do what Bellamy tried to do to him—show him the world has moved on, that her life is not her own. He can't handle the sight of her kids not fleeing from her and breaks from the program, saving her from the electroconvulsive therapy that fried Eddie Powers. Hooper films most of this in a straightforward manner; the individual horrors speak for themselves. The supervisor reports him in a lovely medium close-up that places him in a spin with an orange-brown blurred background behind him—like his office is in hell. Combs explains to him the following day—recorded on the facility's CCTV while the supervisor observes—that it's just Veil's kindness that has convinced her she's crazy. Hooper's distrust of the "powers that be" is more evident here than it is even in *The Mangler*. The supervisor congratulates Veil-as-Bellamy on his methods, with the same marble bust from the interrogation in the pilot over his right shoulder. Veil spends the next little while surreptitiously photographing the monks around the grounds before being informed that they're getting ready to once again zap Combs to clear her memory. The doctors present during Veil's rescue apologize to him but the supervisor stops them, saying they would have been "less convincing in their performance. It was theater at its best." Hooper the Brechtian at play once more.

There is a machine dropped over Combs' face that places her in the Hooper red light as the doctors grill her before the procedure. She stares into the row of red coils meant to hypnotize her and Hooper gets within spitting distance of *2001: A Space Odyssey* or anyway the interrogation scene from *Conquest of the Planet of the Apes* reimagined as the opening of *Looney*

Tunes. Veil frees her and disarms the supervisor and his cohorts and sneaks into a station wagon. Veil tries to wake her up by putting her in the shower of their safe house and Combs responds as if she's being seduced—Hooper films them through the shower curtain. He tries to explain the situation to her when she wakes up in a robe that matches the bed spread in the motel in which they're staying. Again Hooper films the conversation normally, letting the performances do their work.

Tom has to go retrieve the negatives that prove his story to Ellen's satisfactions—he's locked them in a bowling alley locker, allowing Hooper to briefly indulge his '50s fetishism, from the antique car parked outside to tiled checked floors. When he returns, Ellen says more than she's supposed to and Tom catches on that she's just as much part of the program as the supervisor. He tries to flee but they head him off in the lobby. He jumps through a window into a pool, runs across the lawn, and steals a truck to the relative freedom of next week's episode. Turns out Combs was the one trying to break Veil all along—that's all folks.

Dark Skies, "The Awakening" (1996)

Brent V. Friedman and Bryce Zabel created *Dark Skies* in the thick of a culture-wide love of the unknown. Movies like Robert Lieberman's *Fire in The Sky* and TV shows like Chris Carter's *The X-Files* and *Millennium* had blown up to the point that TV stations everywhere wanted their own supernatural, UFO-laced programming—the mania would lead back to Steven Spielberg, whose own *Close Encounters of the Third Kind* and *E.T. The Extra-Terrestrial* had helped normalize the search for alien life, and who would once again provide the public with a UFO show of his own in *Taken*, which Hooper would direct an episode of in 2002. In the meantime, NBC had bought Zabel and Friedman's idea—an alternative history of the Kennedy administration and the space race that involved alien life—and Hooper was brought in to direct the pilot. Unlike much of his work on the small screen, he seems to have been gesturing towards the future of prestige TV. Everything from the White House setting to the beautiful smart people at the center of a government conspiracy hint at the later emergence of shows like *The West Wing* and *Supernatural*. Bill Butler, who shot *Jaws*, and

Peter Hyams' similarly conspiracy-minded *Capricorn One*, was on his way into obscurity when he shot *Dark Skies*, but he hadn't forgotten how best to light a room. Aaron Sorkin's directorial team for *The West Wing* appear to have taken note of his approach to shooting the fake white house, as that show looks like it moved in the second this one was done filming and seven of the actors who appear in the pilot episode of *Dark Skies* later made appearances on the show.

The episode opens with a crudely animated run in between an air force pilot and a UFO. JT Walsh is Frank Bach, the official in charge of the switchboard when it happens. But forget about that for now. Eric Close is John Loengard and Megan Ward is his sweetheart Kimberly Sayers, and they've moved from California to work for the Kennedy administration in Washington. Hooper gets to indulge in the ironic '60s fetishism and his noir tendencies by letting Gregory Harrison as older John Loengard narrate his journey to their new apartment and his new job. Loengard rises in the ranks quickly, proving himself invaluable as a gopher in his new office, and impressing military higher-ups when he gets a chance to impress them. He's promoted to congressional investigator and tasked with looking into accounts of people who witness flying saucers, including notorious UFO witnesses Betty and Barney Hill (Lee Garlington and Basil Wallace). The veneer of respectability afforded by the name of his boss, congressman Charles Pratt (John M. Jackson), gets him in the door, but just barely.

Betty and Barney Hill were the most famous spotters of alien life in America. Hooper takes his time in taking their testimony. Wallace's performance as Barney in particular is quite stirring. The government is listening in through a wire a few blocks away. The story makes quite the impact on John, who, when driving home thinks he has his own close encounter with the unknown. Hooper rains blue light down on him from above, forcing him off the road and into a field. It's not aliens this time, it's government agents (filmed in darkness and shadow by Hooper and Butler) sent by Frank Bach, who beat him up and tell him to drop the Hills and their testimony.

Hooper's personality doesn't get released here beyond effects shots like the early UFO chase or when Loengard gets a look at artifacts from the covered-up UFO crash at Roswell, NM. He's adept at shooting in the prestige style—just a buttoned-up version of his louder TV work—but even his dynamic blocking feels underutilized working for NBC and their larger, broader and more abstractly conservative audience. Hooper's content to follow the script and certainly there's nothing more interesting than JT Walsh. Walsh was one of the great character actors in the US and he died two years after *Dark Skies*' pilot aired. His steely delivery of "does this look Russian to you?" while lording over the corpse of an alien kept in a morgue drawer is perfectly understated and sarcastic in a way only Walsh could have managed. He brings Loengard to Boise to investigate crop circles, which are another of Hooper's simple effects lovingly covered by Butler's camera in the sunbaked Idaho countryside. There's another crib from *North By Northwest* when the farmer Elliot Grantham (legendary character actor G. D. Spradlin) who owns the marked crop fields decides to try and kill Loengard with his truck and a brief chase ensues that ends with the farmer dead. Hooper shoots a lot of this from a helicopter—an indulgence he wasn't usually granted by producers or networks.

Hooper's finally back in expressionistic mode during patient zero's autopsy, filming from low angles as the doctor tries to buzz saw the top of his head open, but the procedure can't continue because the body moves. The doctor tries to jab his brain with a surgical instrument and something inside the Grantham's head grabs the tool and wiggles it around in the farmer's ear before letting it clatter to the floor. The building's put on lockdown as they try to extract whatever's inside his dome. The undead body strangles one of the doctors and then a tentacled critter crawls out of the farmer's mouth and attaches itself to the face of the nearest agent. Loengard extracts it with forceps and Bach seals it in a jar. This is one of Hooper's most dreadful sequences, made more so by the sturdiness of the grammar. Everything had seemed so normal and aboveboard, and then a Lovecraftian nightmare comes crawling out of a dead man's mouth.

Loengard is given a new office for his troubles but his detail hasn't much improved. He's placed in charge of an observational experiment: Bach and his team have placed the extraterrestrial creepy-crawly inside a monkey to see what it does. It breaks out of the office, beats up Loengard, steals his gun, shoots a man, and flees. Hooper, recognizing the patent absurdity of the situation, rewards us with a jazz cover of "Mack the Knife" by Bertolt Brecht to take us out of the scene. Kim finds out that John's been lying about working for the congressman, and he's already been drinking off the sight of a fellow agent gunned down by a chimp, so he's in a sore mood about being found out. He goes to the Lincoln memorial to clear his head and catches a glimpse of either a UFO or a shooting star, and that's all the sign he needs that he's got to come clean, but by then it's too late. Gorgeously designed but quite ugly Claymation aliens arrive, drip a grotesque secretion on the ground and envelope Kim in it—it turns to computer animation at that point as she's covered in that patented Hooper oil slick mélange. She wakes up with blood on her pillow and no memory of the abduction.

Loengard and Bach review an interview with a woman (an uncredited Amanda Plummer) who has also been invaded by the spider alien ganglion. Bach informs the stunned room that attempts to remove the alien surgically ended in her death. Driving home later, Loengard sees Kim wandering the streets by herself. He catches her in front of the window of an electronics shop where the TVs are playing Kennedy's speech about the Cuban Missile Crisis—Hooper captures their reflection on the screen, caught between the window and the TV, next to Kennedy's disembodied head, in one of the more lovely tableaux in the show. It makes literal the blurred lines between them and the tides of the world.

Loengard goes to Bach for answers. "Who appointed you god?"

"Ike," he replies.

Walsh is the iron backbone of the piece. It comes out in their discussion that President Kennedy has no idea what Bach's unit is up to in the search for extraterrestrial life, so Loengard feels especially vulnerable. He should be looking closer to home for his discomfort. While he's at work Pratt visits his wife and shows him a neat trick wherein he conjures an orb of glowing light (a psychedelic vision right out of *Eggshells*) from thin air. He, too, has been visited by the aliens, it seems. He bids her reach out and touch the orb. John arrives right after the orb shocks her to the floor. Loengard and Pratt tussle and he throws the old man out the window. Now he just has to perform his own procedure to save Kimberley from her infestation.

The exorcism of the alien is pretty disturbing. Loengard forces Kim to drink some awful concoction that raises the PH levels in her body, waking the creature up.

"It's moving in my head!" she shouts, horror rising in her voice.

He takes her to an abandoned building (light pouring in from the boards on the windows, as expected) to finish the job, but she attacks him, compelled by her visitor. He finally gets some acetone in her via syringe and she starts convulsing and shouting in an unnatural voice before she pukes the thing up and John mashes it underfoot like a bug. He tries to resign from his post but Bach doesn't let him, so he and Kim decide to shadow Bach to get into his house for hard evidence of his malfeasance to give to the public. Kimberly distracts his wife while John breaks into the house while Bach showers to retrieve his access key, granting him access to all of Bach's files. They give a dossier, complete with alien DNA samples, to the president (it's a wonder we don't hear another Brecht song during this part). RFK (James F. Kelly) calls Loengard to the Kennedy manor in Hyannis Port and tells Loengard he needs to keep his job and report back what he sees to the president.

Bach naturally learns of the meeting and two men come to kill John and Kim in their apartment, so they flee like Thomas Veil before them. Lying low in a hotel room in Norman, Oklahoma, they hear secondhand about the assassinating of JFK. Their futures uncertain, they drive off into the unknown while Buffalo Springfield plays on the soundtrack and the camera cranes up from their car to the skies and the cosmos above it. Hooper here is lapping himself historically here, returning to before the Vietnam war that animated the earliest entries of his body of work, from *The Song is Love* to *The Texas Chain Saw Massacre*. The distrust of the government had once again become part of a popular idiom, though this time it was on television, rather than in film. The world and Hooper have almost caught up with each other, and his episode of Spielberg's *Taken* would be the closest he came to capturing the zeitgeist the way he did with *Texas Chain Saw* and *Poltergeist*, but it wasn't to be. Hooper was doomed to be an outsider to the bitter end.

Perversions of Science, "Panic" (1997)

Perversions of Science had the same format as *Tales from the Crypt*, its programming mother ship. The original five producers of the first HBO show returned to see if lightning would strike twice, but the new series only lasted one ten-episode season. Each episode came from the pages of EC Comics's *Weird Science*, *Weird Fantasy*, and *Incredible Science Fiction* comic book series. The crypt keeper was replaced by a crudely rendered sex robot named Chrome (voiced by Maureen Teefy) who introduces this story by opening her metallic breast. Laraine Newman returns to the fold for a cameo in a cast also made up of a young Jason Lee and Jamie Kennedy, Chris Sarandon, Edie McClurg, and, in one of his last non-voice-over performances, Harvey Korman. Former Devo songwriter-turned-in-demand-composer Mark Mothersbaugh provides the jaunty synth score.

Sarandon plays Carson Walls, a deliberately obvious Orson Welles stand-in, about to unleash his version of the infamous *War of the Worlds* broadcast that listeners took for reality and so they shot up their town, believing aliens had invaded. Though it's mostly conjecture, I've said before that Hooper must have felt a kinship to Welles, but as noted earlier, their careers followed remarkably similar paths. Like Welles, he languished for most of his life with neither budgets nor critical approval commensurate with his experience, impact or talent. It's always a little strange watching the Welles story in anything other than the Welles style, but this at least has personality, aligning it more closely with something like Richard Linklater's *Me and Orson Welles* than Tim Robbins' *The Cradle that Rocked*, in which Welles is a minor character in a bland, pseudo-Marxist narrative.

Lee and Kennedy are young men preparing with excitement for Halloween, but only Lee makes any kind of stab at period behavior or dialect. They're throwing a holiday bash, unaware that Walls/Welles is about to unleash his broadcast about an alien invasion. When the broadcast begins, Hooper zooms around the cramped apartment for emphasis and pans and twists across the room at the costumed revelers horrified reaction, getting as close to cinematic as he can while only showing people listening to a radio—it's neat to watch him try to ace the challenge of filming people reacting to an exciting broadcast. The twist is also good fun. Lee and Kennedy don't give into the panic the way everyone else does—Lee simply bursts in from the kitchen with knives in his hand and murders every one of their guests. Turns out *they're* the aliens, and though the broadcast is fake, their invasion is real and they think the real one started without them.

Lee and Kennedy head into the countryside to the spot described by the broadcast to start their rampage, but the field is empty. They're furious when Sarandon admits that it was a radio play, not an actual news broadcast. Korman and McClurg show up armed, also believing that the invasion is real. They kidnap the aliens and bring them to their dungeon, which is outfitted with chains and another captive held in a box. Their intention is to do more than kill the Martians, it seems. They, like Walls, are from Jupiter and they were trying to flush the Martians out in order to make their *own* invasion easier.

The Apartment Complex (1999)

Hooper rekindled his relationship with Showtime, who'd previously funded *Body Bags*, for the 1999 *Apartment Complex*, one of his weirder experiments. This came on the heels of his shooting an unaired pilot for a short-lived TV show called *Prey*, about the discovery of a serial killer gene. Hooper's pilot featured Sherilyn Fenn in the lead, and the show recast her with Debra Messing and ran for one season. *The Apartment Complex* is similarly transfixed by the dark corridors of the mind, in this case a behavioral psychologist accidentally kills someone, which means that once more it's almost more noir than horror, and it's the kitschiest thing Hooper ever directed. Everything is in quotation marks. Every character is a caricature of the personality types that hero Stan Warden (Chad Lowe, brother of Rob, no one's favorite Lowe) sees in them. A close-up of a rat maze (all German expressionist angles, looking very *Cabinet of Dr. Caligari*, which gets name-dropped within) spins into the pool of the apartment set Hooper's going to spend the movie managing. The apartment is meant to look like a rat maze from the top. Hooper's camera work is fine enough, but his choreography is slow to match the syrupy pace and terrible comedy—he has to hold on people long enough for punch lines to creep across their faces, which means that his momentum suffers greatly.

Hooper cranes down (Jacques Haitkin is the DP this time out) from a god's eye view of the set to front door, looking like the demi-deco of *I'm Dangerous Tonight*. Chet (Obba Babatundé) shows Warden around and they quickly encounter skateboarders, adult twins, a loon played by R. Lee

Ermey, two combative models (Gina Mari and Tyra Banks), a foul-mouthed alpha male named Morgan (the always wonderful Patrick Warburton), a free spirited psychic (Amanda Plummer), and pug-like building manager Dr. Caligari (Jon Polito), who's also a plastic surgeon. The only resident Warden cares about is Alice (Fay Masterson) to whom he immediately takes a shine, who is naturally dating Morgan.

The problems start immediately. Stan finds a body in the disgusting pool. The two detectives who show up (Miguel Sandoval and Ron Canada) and immediately assume Stan is responsible. The real culprit is reclusive Charles Martin Smith, the tenant who's always hiding behind a locked door. Morgan is also a crook, so he's crushed by a snake as Freudian comeuppance so that Stan can have the moral high ground before moving in on Alice.

The Apartment Complex is fun in its subtext-free exploration of character types, but it's one of Hooper's least visually inventive films. He trades expressionistic set design (like Robert Weine, who directed *Caligari*, Hooper lets the walls do the talking) for his usual brilliant colors and inch-thick production design. Hooper ultimately doesn't have the interest in straight drama to make *Apartment Complex* work beyond the pleasure of watching its cast of famous faces spark off each other. The psychology of Hooper's work is always better explained in the environments he creates for characters to have blood-soaked meltdowns, finding themselves through utter chaos. Placing an entire movie on the shoulders of bland average guy Chad Lowe and killing his stylistic darlings was probably the least helpful thing Hooper ever did for himself. Even his next film (a straight-to-video schlock fest shot with no creative sets, hardly any unmotivated lighting, and a cast of desperately unlikable twentysomethings) is more fun than *The Apartment Complex*. The film's moral—people would help cover up a murder if they all agreed it was for the good of the community—is perfectly in keeping with Hooper's view of America, but he'd already said all of this more crazily and more eloquently. The film has no bite. *The Apartment Complex* was psychologically superfluous at this point in his artistic life. Maybe that's why he felt he needed a change to something dirty, cheap, and without even the slightest hint of subtext.

The Others, "Souls on Board" (2000)

The Others was just one more in a long line of short-lived cult TV shows for which Hooper directed the pilot. John Brancato and Michael Ferris created it in a brief successful run as in-demand writers—after writing the Sandra Bullock tech-thriller The Net and David Fincher's The Game, they became Jonathan Mostow's favorite screenwriters, writing the third Terminator film and later the heroin-addict hit man thriller Hunter's Prayer. The Others had a great cast and The X-Files's Glen Morgan in the writers' room but couldn't hold the finicky NBC audience captive for the length of the season.

Hooper starts with a slow-moving exploration of a crashed airplane while the audio from the black box plays, a cunning misdirect before revealing the crime scene crew photographing the wreckage. As in his Perversions of Science episode, he mines every drop of dramatic dynamism from the sight of people listening to an audio recording, their grave faces shattered as the recording nears the moment when the plane crashes, and then a ghastly moaning takes place of the flight record.

The episode proper starts by introducing some of the Others. Their paranormal investigators and they are waiting to board a plane. Hooper dollies back from Ellen "Satori" Polaski (Missy Crider) arguing with an airline employee to find Professor Miles Ballard (John Billingsley) reading up on his newest case in the reflection of Albert McGonacle's (John Aylward) sunglasses. The next shot is the McGonacle and Polaski is a split diopter shot. Sitting a short distance away from them is Elmer Greentree (Bill Cobbs) and Dr. Mark Gabriel (Gabriel Macht) arrives with everyone's coffee. Group oddball Warren Day (Kevin J. O'Connor) is in a drum circle with some Hare Krishnas and they're all taking bets about whether their youngest member, Marian Kitt (Julianne Nicholson), will show at all. Elmer is nervous and spills his coffee—he hates flying.

Hooper's largely back in prestige TV mode here, shooting everything from low angles but keeping the action ordinary and coherent in the sparely and beautifully lit airport and plane. Pockets of light abound. There's a kerfuffle on the plane when Ballard drops pictures from the plane crash in the opening and the stewardess sees them and thinks he's just a morbid rubbernecker trying to cause a stir on the plane. Marian recognizes one of the dead stewardesses (Casey Lluberes), however; she saw her alive in the airport before she got on the plane. Ballard deliberately booked them on the same route as the crashed plane. Hooper films their conversation as a series of close-ups, cutting every five or so seconds, but he finds excuses to move the camera when he can, as when one of the passengers call a stewardess over to complain that the Others won't stop talking about the plane crashing. Confining Hooper to a small space with no real room for a dolly track or a crane isn't the best use of his talents but if anyone can make a series of cut-up close-ups interesting, it's him.

Marian is the first to see something supernatural—white hands clawing at the outside of her window—but everyone's on their guard, especially when the plane starts experiencing turbulence identical to the kind that assailed the plane that crashed. Marian starts auto-writing, not aware what words she's forming, in the bathroom on every napkin she can put her hand to, before faces start screaming at her from inside the walls. They start bursting forth through the wall like it was made of fabric—an effect Hooper would have learned from *Repulsion* or *A Nightmare on Elm Street*. Hands start assailing her and she freaks out. She sees a dead man's reflection in the mirror and starts talking to him.

The pilot is played by Captain Dale Dye in his third turn for Hooper after *Invaders from Mars* and *Spontaneous Combustion*. Ballard gets one of the stewardesses to confess that there's something indeed supernaturally out of the ordinary on the flight. There's a great sped-up tracking shot from the cockpit back to Marian leaving the bathroom as she heads to the front of the plane to give a note from the ghost she encountered to the captain. The captain comes back to ask how Marian knew enough about him and aviation to write the note. Ballard notices his coffee sliding around his trey table in an unnatural pattern. Warren opens his window shutter and sees faces staring back at him outside the plane. Elmer tries to get Marian to open herself up to the spirit of the dead captain of the last flight. The dead captain alerts them to a hydraulic failure that will cause the plane to fail. As they scramble to fix it, everyone starts seeing the hands of the dead passengers out their windows. Hooper switches to a few second Steadicam shots to communicate the chaos up and down the fuselage of the airplane. When they begin their descent it's back to quick cuts between close-ups of the passengers and crew. They land safely and see the souls of the dead passengers on the runway, finally free.

Crocodile (2000)

It's fun to imagine a world where, by 1995, Hooper's brand of elaborate, sybaritic horror had become the norm in genre filmmaking—where mid-budget movies with a careful and enthusiastic an eye for visuals, sets, and colors came out once a month. The truth is, by the mid '90s, horror was all but out of the public eye. It wasn't until *Scream* that horror found new legs and a grim, new purpose. The slasher film came back and Hooper had to go underground, so to speak. Slasher movies were easy and predictable and he'd said everything he wanted to on the subject in the opening of *The Funhouse*, so he avoided it at first. Hooper, as was his wont, took a different course than his peers.

Maybe Hooper saw that the direct-to-video market had become huge enough to be considered a viable path. Or maybe he knew that in Nu Image, a production house founded by Avi Lerner (another Cannon group refugee), he could have a certain amount of creative freedom. Whatever the case, Nu Image partnered with the Sci-Fi channel (now Syfy) to produce and exhibit a series of monster movies in the early 2000s (Sci-Fi marketed them as a package deal) and Hooper was the only thing resembling a name attached to any of them. Unlike *Spiders* or *Octopus*, *Crocodile* (all three written by Cannon group star scribe Boaz Davidson) was a deliberately slight affair. It afforded Hooper the opportunity to return to his roots in more ways than one. First, there was the beast itself, a do-over for the shoddy puppet alligator in *Eaten Alive*, which splits its time between limited but effective puppetry and bad CGI (though, at that time and for that money, it was nothing to sneer at). The plot is also very much in the spirit of his early work—a bunch of twentysomethings on a road trip in a Southwestern backwater getting killed by something old, territorial, and violent. The crocodile stalking the mindless frat boys doesn't protect its *property*, but it does want revenge for the stealing/killing of its children.

The twentysomethings in the ensemble cast all act realistically, if unappealingly. Hooper and husband and wife screenwriters Jace Anderson and Adam Gierasch get the mannerisms, behavior, in-jokes, and sexual tension between the brain-dead college kids so right that it makes spending time with them a chore. They're as much a time capsule of late '90s upper-middle-class teens as *Chain Saw* is of teenagers in the mid '70s, but there's something less inherently compelling about the latter era as represented by their tasteless fashion, contemptible behavior, and conflicting sexual morality.

Shooting on the cheap meant that Hooper didn't have money to spend on lighting and production design, so *Crocodile* is less joyful visually (though his camera work was classically choreographed where possible). The attacks by the crocodile have to rely on shaking cameras and iffy edits to convince the audience that when the puppet strikes the edge of the houseboat in one shot, it causes the kids to fall off the roof in the reverse. It's dodgy and doesn't work nearly as well as the jump scares, which also have the benefit of keeping the CGI Croc out of view for the most part.

Five kids in their late 20s have rented said houseboat from husband and wife Kit and Annabelle (D. W. Reiser and Julie Mintz). Brady (Mark McLachlan) is dating Claire (Caitlin Martin), but Duncan (Chris Solari) has brought along Sunny (Sommer Knight), whom Brady slept with once upon a time. Hubs and Foster (Greg Wayne and Rhett Wilkins, later of *The Puffy Chair*) don't have personalities, so it's little shock when they get eaten first. Hooper's dolly and crane shots get healthy workouts during long shots of the boat in the river (including one with a sort of gothic hotel in the background—a matte painting poorly processed into the shot—which even gets its own ghost story in the form of a paraphrased version of the legend of Joe Ball and his pet gator, which inspired *Eaten Alive*) to the point that you could forgive the movie's tonal sins if you watched it with the sound off and perhaps while having a high fever.

Hooper concedes to the demands of the market—this film acts like its spring breaker characters (and presumably its intended audience). Bad dye jobs and obnoxious pop-punk music abound, and one begs for the crocodilian menace to hurry up already and put an end to these kids' vacuous nonsense.

There's plenty of Hooper in the movie, if you felt like looking for it, beyond just his camerawork. When the kids stop for food, they meet the sheriff (Harrison B. Young) and his little pep talk has exactly the same cadence as the old man warning Sally and her friends off of heading towards his property in *Chain Saw*. The momentum of the crocodile's first few attacks (both executed quite well, all things considered) have the same aerodynamic slicing across the frame as Leatherface jumping out of the dark to attack Stretch in *Chainsaw 2*. When the final trio of survivors tries to outpace the croc, Duncan winds up injured and in a wheelbarrow, whining all the while like Franklin in his wheelchair from *Chain Saw*.

Then there are the few peripheral characters and the world they inhabit. The two redneck fishermen who disturb the croc by smashing its eggs feel like refuges from Hooper's '80s films—both bemoan the loss of a bygone era just before they're murdered by the big beastie. The crocodile farmers responsible for letting the great reptile loose are right out of Hooper land. Their house is designed to within an inch of its life, full of taxidermy (of course) and in general hints at the film that could have been if it had just been about natives instead of tourists (a scene of the old crocodile hunter with the sheriff drinking and swapping stories is by far the best scene in the film, harking back to early Hooper). The younger of the two croc wranglers (co-writer Adam Gierasch) has just lost his hand trying to brush one of the croc's tails as if it were a horse. Neither they, nor the sheriff, live to see the final reel. In a bit of Hitchcock mimicry, Gierasch's prosthetic-endowed grotesque is killed by the editor—several different angles flash quickly to simulate the crocodile attacking to save having to film the mutilation. All of this has the perverse effect of giving this film, built on a core of mediocrity (the dog survives, as hack screenwriting teacher Robert McKee would have wanted) attempting to appease an audience that wouldn't have looked for any of Hooper's formalism, an old school sturdiness for which it had no use.

Crocodile bypassed critical appraisal by being released straight to TV and home video—not that it would have received good reviews. By the time Hooper returned to the big screen, he hadn't seen one of his films get even a token release in eight years. As good as his next feature films would be, it would hardly matter. To critics and distributors, it would appear as though he was no longer the director behind *Texas Chain Saw Massacre*. He was a guy who hadn't had a hit in over twenty years (I *barely* remember *Mortuary* and *Toolbox Murders* hitting the shelves of my local video store and I went every week during this period). Undeterred, Hooper rediscovered his stylistic acumen and returned as strong as ever.

If only anyone had paid attention...

Shadow Realm, "The Maze" (2002)
Shadow Realm, "Cargo" (2002)

The Maze was a short film that found two homes, first as part of an omnibus film released in 2002 called *Shadow Realm* with contributions from Keith Gordon, Paul Shapiro, and Ian Toynton. The films were then cut up and released as episodes of the anthology series *Night Visions* created by Dan Angel and Billy Brown, which was meant to be a twist on the *Twilight Zone/Tales from the Crypt* model, hosted by former Black Flag front man Henry Rollins. Hooper would then direct another episode called "Cargo" for the show once his first short film was incorporated.

Thora Birch, just before her departure from the spotlight, is Susan Thornhill (she shares a last name with Cary Grant's similarly befuddled hero in *North by Northwest*). We meet her on a run when she's accosted by admirer named Wes (Luke Edwards) who wants to take her to a concert, but she demurs.

Her friend Gail (Chiara Zanni) chastises her for not being more adventurous that day at lunch: "All you do is run and study. You've been here six months and you have exactly one friend on campus."

Their music teacher (Amanda Plummer, back after *Dark Skies*) stops by for a moment, to introduce her character so she won't come out of nowhere in the second act, but she leaves quickly, just as shy as Susan, evidently. Later, Susan will see Wes and to avoid him duck into a hedge maze on the school's campus. Hooper uses a variety of techniques to show that she's lost, including the obvious Kubrick-inspired winding Steadicam from *The Shining*, but he films her on a slowly panning crane and in medium-close-ups when she stops to look around.

Susan finally frees herself from the maze but is now in a kind of alternate dimension where there are no people on campus. She can't raise anyone on her cell phone and no one answers when she cries for help. Hooper films her in striking isolation against the brutalist architecture of the campus. The only noise she finally hears is music coming from Plummer's classroom, but everyone in the classroom has been murdered. She attacks Plummer and flees to another wing of the campus. She finds a white cat in the dining room, and then a dead man with his head in the oven. She grabs a butcher knife and then notices the date on the lunch special chalkboard is a year in the future.

Susan tries the library and hears a phone ringing. Wes on the other end of the line tells her she's going to die with or without the knife to protect her. The shelves start moving in the library, revealing Wes at the end of the corridor. He tells her to check the last newspaper she can find—turns out there's an asteroid headed for earth and she missed the mania about it. Most people are hiding out now, which is why she can't find anyone, and why her teacher went nuts: the world is about to end and it all seems to have happened during the few seconds she was in the maze. Wes is hiding out in the library waiting for the end. She hits on the idea to return to the maze just in time for Plummer's teacher to appear and stab Wes with the knife. The air raid sirens start to go off and Susan talks her teacher out of killing her. They run for the maze and get lost in it again. There isn't much in the way of a moral dimension or lesson in *The Maze* but as an excuse to see Hooper film a gorgeous location (Simon Fraser University in British Columbia) it's amiable company, indeed. The final seconds where the sky opens up and red light hits Birch (as it must in any Hooper film about a young woman's journey) the film obfuscates its own light weight and meaninglessness.

"Cargo" stars Jamie Kennedy once again and it's set in the bowels of an old commercial ship. A group of sickly European immigrants have stowed away on board, led by Joanna Pacula's steely-eyed matriarch. Something has killed one of them in their hideaway below deck. Kennedy plays Mark Stevens, an employee for the shipping company under the command of captain Dennis Brascom (Philip Baker Hall). Stevens hears the wailing of the bereaved and brings it to the captain's attention, to the chagrin of first officer Taferner (Johnny Cuthbert). Mark sneaks below deck and finds

Pacula and she insists he not tell Brascom about their presence. But she does request that he help them find the creature mutilating them in the cargo hold. The reveal of the body is stunning, viewed through a hole in the wall, dragged up for Mark to look at with its mangled limbs and carved up torso.

Hooper shoots this one fairly functionally as well, but the grim low light and atmosphere sell the desperation and horror. A seasick Steadicam follows Mark back up to Brascom's office as he tries to think of how to tell him about the murder without giving up the ghost for Pacula and her crew. Baker Hall sells the hell out of the short monologue about doing the right thing he feeds the haunted-looking Mark. A guest star with real gravitas is worth their weight in gold. Meanwhile the critter in the hold has claimed another victim. Hooper gets a ton of mileage out of the darkness down below—building unbearable tension in the cramped confines as Pacula waits for the critter to make its next move. Mark tries to blowtorch a hole in the side of the shipping container where she's hiding before the creature can get to Pacula and kill her. Of course the creature isn't what it seems to be. This nasty little morality tale is rife with claustrophobia and effective gore—not a revolutionary entry in his body of work, but on the more effective side of his work for television.

Taken, "Beyond the Sky" (2002)

Created by Leslie Bohem and executive produced by Steven Spielberg, *Taken* was appointment television, even though it aired on the slightly less respectable Sci-Fi channel instead of one of the major networks. It won an Emmy and a Golden Globe, the closest Hooper came to ordinary prestige. The directors chosen weren't big names, rather workmanlike hands who could handle spectacle at the show's budget and keep the pacing tight. The later episodes had nearly cult directors like John Fawcett, Jeremy Kagan, Michael Katleman, Sergio Mimica-Gezzan, Breck Eisner, and, of course, Hooper, who directed the impressive first entry in the miniseries. The music by Laura Karpman is a sweetly bombastic John Williams impression, and the whole thing has the impressive scale of Spielberg's brand of Americana.

Spielberg had perfected this mode of miniseries TV with the similarly lauded *Band of Brothers* for HBO a few years prior.

The show was about a brush with aliens as experienced by three families in three different eras. Hooper's entry was about the Keys family, and we're introduced to the world through an earnest voice over from Spielberg-favorite Dakota Fanning, later of his other Alien opus of the 2000s, *War of the Worlds*. She's Allie Keys and her grandfather Russell (Steve Burton) is a WWII bomber when we meet him during a dogfight that's interrupted by UFOs. Hooper directs the CGI-flight expertly, down to the grisly effect of enemy gunfire in the flesh of the American pilots. The aliens keep the ship from crashing. When we next see Russell he's back home in Bement, Illinois in 1945. He surprises his wife Kate (Julie Benz) at work and then has a heart-to-heart with his father (Fred Henderson). As Allie's narration tells us, there's something off about Russell and the white picket fences and suburban perfection that wait for him seem to gall him as he lies awake with memories of his fateful crash.

Hooper directs this in as straightforward a fashion as he'd ever attacked anything, part way between the prestige TV stylistic neutrality of most of *Dark Skies*, the deceptively calm suburban theatricality of *The Funhouse* and *Salem's Lot*, and Spielberg's sepia-toned nostalgia. We jump ahead two years to meet Captain Owen Crawford (Joel Gretsch) introducing his new recruits to the Enola Gay, hanging out like a museum piece in an airplane hangar in Roswell, New Mexico. Crawford decides to romance Anne Campbell (Tina Holmes), the daughter of his superior officer, Colonel Thomas Campbell (Michael Moriarty—who brushed up against Hooper when he starred in Larry Cohen's sequel, *A Return to Salem's Lot* in 1987), leaving his usual girl Sue (Stacy Grant) to drive home alone. She takes a long detour instead. The same UFO that helped Keys out of his bind flies over her stalled car and crashes just over the horizon.

Sue crawls after the downed spacecraft and discovers over a burning field just over a hill (in a scene is right out of *Invaders From Mars*). Amidst the embers and flaming trees she finds a piece of a ship right as a small alien espies her from the limb of a nearby tree. The next day she goes to tell Crawford what she saw, but two nuns who saw the same thing beat her to it. The media gets ahold of the story and Crawford and his commanding officers have no choice but to let the story stick—if they deny it they'll look guilty. Crawford tries to go back to work but an old man and his grandkids spot the enormous crashed flying saucer while on a hike one day—more *Invaders From Mars* déjà vu. Crawford can't help but climb back into it like he's been given the chance for experimental regressive womb therapy. We'll later learn there are four dead aliens (looking like clay sculptures laid out on a blanket) and five empty seats for them on the craft. One of them is still on the loose, though it takes only a few days for Campbell to deny to even Crawford that they ever existed.

Back in Bement Russell has tried his utmost to blend back in to regular life, but he still stares with envy at his wife's ease with their son, and at normal young boys playing together in the yard. He can no longer relate to people and he knows it. All he can see when kids are having a good time is being tormented in some half-formed memory of his time in the service, so he breaks up their fun time rudely. This sequence is fused with beautiful perspective tricks and ends with Russell alone at the front of the frame, with a party of horrified onlookers in the distance behind him looking at him and judging him, Hooper ever great with shorthand and isolated protagonists.

There's a great dream sequence that plays like a slight revision of a similar nightmare in John Landis' *An American Werewolf in London*. Russell wakes up in bed, looks to his left and sees a squad of Nazis standing in the corner of his room. That's how his brain made sense of his alien abduction—telling him it was the enemy. Though he can't explain the bruises on his arm when he wakes from them. He boards up the windows to keep his nocturnal invaders out, and Kate can no longer make sense of his behavior. He'll keep waking up in the middle of the night and checking on his son to make sure he's still there, and calling his old army buddies to see if they're experiencing the same symptom. They're all in even worse straits than him, so he packs up the car to go find out for himself what's happening to them all but he doesn't find anything helpful. The last surviving crew member of his bomber (Ryan Robbins) remembers more than he does. He reminds Russell that they were tortured for hours and only Russell saved them, further linking Hooper's TV work to *The Manchurian Candidate*. But there's one hitch: "You and I both know it wasn't Germans you killed that day."

The third narrative strand in *Taken* starts with Sally Clarke (Catherine Dent), a waitress in Lubbock, TX, and offers a chance for Hooper to return to his roots. The name Sally harks back to *The Texas Chain Saw Massacre* and her job at a diner fits the milieu of his early suburban settings—a shot of her leaving work and getting into her truck in her pink uniform with a neon sign over her shoulder would feel at home in any of his early horror features. She's married to traveling salesman Fred (Alf Humphreys) who kisses her head as she sits looking miserable in her vanity mirror as he leaves her for his next trip. The Clarke stuff feels pulled directly from Hooper's memories of life in the south as a boy, to say nothing of his own mother's lonely life after the death of her husband in 1961. After Fred leaves, Sally's up late by herself smoking a cigarette and reading science fiction stories on the couch when she hears something outside. She lights a lantern and heads out to investigate in the windy night, Hooper dollying with her as she walks across the brightly moonlit grass into her shed. Waiting for her in a corner is John (Eric Close back from *Dark Skies*), the last of the aliens from Crawford's crash site in Roswell, in human form—though naturally we won't "learn" that for a while. Sally gets a bloody nose from the encounter and afterwards has to have a cigarette—even just meeting a man who isn't her husband has had a borderline sexual effect on her. She even brings John breakfast in bed and they share a tender exchange as he talks around his circumstances and thanks her for her help. Being around him makes her physically sick.

Back in New Mexico, Crawford is trying his best to ignore that Campbell is slighting him in his quest for information about the crash by redoubling his efforts to woo Anne. There's a pretty sequence of the two of them horseback riding and necking at sunset. He proposes to her in the stables, and though she thinks it's just because they had sex and it *might* lead to pregnancy—a great little dissection of antique American sexual hang-ups—he persists and she says yes. He'd tell Campbell personally but he's running experiments on an alien that ends in the death of the little gray man and the doctor they brought in to study him. The aliens are dangerous to spend time with, which would have been good for the Clarke family to hear before letting John stay with them. When we rejoin their story he's working as a magician and making the young Clarke girl Becky (Shauna Kain) float six feet off the ground. Sally's son Tom (Kevin G. Schmidt) is less keen than Becky on the new visitor staying while his dad is away, recognizing that their mom is happier than she ever seems to be normally. Sure enough it isn't long before they're going on romantic rendezvous themselves, kissing passionately by the shed where she found him—Hooper filming earnest romance is a rare and wonderful thing; he's quite good at giving into his inner Sydney Pollack.

The good times are short-lived, naturally, as John goes right from loving mom to catching Tom and Becky going through his things and he gives them a stern talking to. Unmoved by his threat, they call in the sheriff's posse to come get John off their land. They're too late. After another moment of tenderness with mom, he sheds his skin and vanishes. The shot is spectacular—he frames Sally staring at the screen door and then John's transformation takes the form of strong light that overwhelms her, and when it relents she's still standing at the screen, sadness back in her eyes. A few weeks later the morning sickness starts. Crawford comes looking for him at Sally's house but knows he's missed his shot. His story is far from over, however. Sue comes back to him to give him the piece of saucer she collected on the night it crashed. At first he seduces her only to sneak into her trailer later and beat her to death with a rock. Now he can marry Anne without complications. He immediately blackmails the Colonel, his new father-in-law, into giving him the new rank of major and gives him the sample from the crash as collateral. Campbell's horrified by the man calling him dad, but there's a sense that he respects his cutthroat attitude.

In an interview with Mick Garris on his show *Post Mortem* in July of 2010, Hooper had a hard time coming up with an answer to the hypothetical question: if fully funded what genre would he most like to try out? His instinctual response was that no one would expect him to do anything but horror or sci-fi, so conditioned by his career and his dealings with producers was he, but then he thought about it a little and said "Dickens." Watching something like *Taken* which fuses his idiosyncrasies with a more widely acceptable form of mass-market entertainment, handsome and awed and more easily digestible than some of his personal projects, the mind reels at what his adaptation of *Bleak House* would have looked like with hundreds of millions of dollars at his disposal. It's one of the enduring tragedies that no one took a chance on him the way he really deserved.

Scout Tafoya

Chapter 6:
The Red Death (2004–2013)

Perhaps recognizing that his work for TV didn't allow him nearly the opportunity for stylistic growth he craved, Hooper returned to the big screen a changed man. His production problems remained (one of the three companies funding *Toolbox Murders* dissolved in the middle of production, cutting the shoot time by nearly a third), but he was back doing groundbreaking work with his camera and coining a new horror grammar along with Rob Zombie's *House of 1000 Corpses*, Eli Roth's *Cabin Fever*, Alexandre Aja's *High Tension*, and James Wan's *Saw*, all movies that showcased a pronounced debt to Hooper in their grim aesthetic, their antiauthoritarian bent, their plentiful gore, and their young countercultural heroes. Zombie and Hooper had become close friends by this point, and his wife Sheri Moon Zombie acted in *Toolbox Murders* as a favor to the older director. By the time Hooper's *Mortuary* saw its tiny release in 2005, the world was in the middle of a gore movie renaissance. Zombie's *The Devil's Rejects*, Roth's *Hostel*, Greg McLean's *Wolf Creek*, Neil Marshall's *The Descent*, and Darren Lynn Bousman's *Saw II* looked like the makings of a movement replete with stylish, high-key lighting to bring out the excruciating, grimy details of the film's creatively abject methods of torment and murder. Critic and author Alan Jones would, in 2006, call this young bunch of viscerally minded auteurs The Splat Pack, a term that's hung around in niche circles. Of course, it excludes older hands like Hooper in its cool classification, and that's stuck much more than a nickname.

Hooper was too old to be thought of as radical by then—in horror you're quickly written off as past your prime if you don't continue doing what made you famous. Hooper was historically as responsible for horror's new grammar as any of the Splat Pack members. They all stole from *Chain Saw* and its mix of the pastoral and the terrifying. The torture porn movies all restaged *Texas Chain Saw*'s narrative arc—men and women who seem innocent, who have their lives ahead of them, tortured and killed cruelly. They were dark reflections of the coverage of the bombings of the Middle East and the subsequent invasion of Iraq and Afghanistan by the US military following the terrorist attacks of 9/11. They made sure we couldn't run to the comfort of movie screens to escape from images of violence that were waiting for us on news networks. In making *Toolbox Murders*, which headed in the same dark, unsparing direction as Zombie, Roth, McLean, and Aja at the same time or before they did, he kept evolving. But no one made room at the newly set table for him. When the argument over "torture porn" would rage a few years down the line, Hooper's name would only be used in archival terms because critics hadn't seen or didn't care about his latest work.

In 2005, Hooper would be recruited by Mick Garris (who worked on a lot of Hooper projects from *Poltergeist* through to *The Others*) to make movies on Showtime's *Masters of Horror* series, which would seem to indicate that he'd received benediction for his long years innovating in the horror genre, but really all it meant was the *idea* of a Tobe Hooper film was more appealing than the genuine article. Of all the directors asked to participate (including John Carpenter, Dario Argento, Don Coscarelli, Stuart Gordon, John Landis, Joe Dante, and John McNaughton) only Hooper and Japanese master Takashi Miike experimented grammatically, making films off the beaten path of murder mysteries and creature features that looked and, more importantly, *felt* differently than the rest. While the bulk of the directors made films that behaved like mean-spirited horror, Hooper's work was arch and psychedelic, taking cues from the older source material (stories by Richard Matheson and Ambrose Bierce, respectively), having no clear heroes or villains, and beginning and ending in apocalyptic disarray.

And then Hooper would experience a longer creative draught than any of the rest of the "masters." Like Hooper, John Carpenter, Don Coscarelli, and John Landis all made one film a piece and then went quiet, but the others seem to have done so with more ease and with comparatively bigger budgets than Hooper, while Joe Dante and Mick Garris have worked steadily in film and TV. Dario Argento has made several films since and has another in production as of this writing. Hooper co-wrote the fiction book *Midnight Movie* with Alan Goldsher, in 2011, which was mostly well-regarded and wrapped up in his own mythology, but didn't do anything to resurrect his film career or help his reputation.

The gap between Hooper's second entry in the *Masters* series and his last film was nearly seven years, one year more than Coscarelli (2012's *John Dies At The End*), and even he has projects in the pipeline. Wes Craven, by comparison, made a film in 2010 and 2011 (*My Soul To Take*, which tanked, and *Scream 4*, a hit) then executive produced a TV show based on his film *Scream* and another little movie called *The Girl In The Photographs*. If he hadn't passed away in 2015, he'd likely still be working with more regularity than did Hooper. When Hooper did eventually make another film, 2013's *Djinn*, his last, the few critics who saw it panned it. Hardly seems like the respect due a "master," but respect was never what drove Hooper.

Hooper always did things his own way and this late phase in his career proved that even after everything he'd been put through, every budget cut, every production company shut down, every critical and commercial bomb, Hooper's interest was in making the most interesting film possible under whatever conditions presented themselves. If Hooper perfected the kind of bombastic film he'd plainly imagined as far back as *The Heisters* with *Lifeforce, Invaders From Mars, Texas Chainsaw Massacre 2, Spontaneous Combustion, Night Terrors,* and *The Mangler,* then it made perfect sense that his next action would be to search for a new outlet for his talent, a new grammar in which to work.

Toolbox Murders (2004)

We begin with a sly little joke—Hooper's thank you to the studios and producers for their hard work on his behalf all these years: "Every year thousands of people come to Hollywood to pursue their dreams. Some Succeed. Some move back home... And some just disappear." Quite a bit could be read into that opening text about Hooper's resilience in the face of indifference. On a dark rainy street, the body of a workman is loaded into an ambulance while perky Daisy Rain (Sheri Moon Zombie) buys groceries at a tarp-covered convenience store across from her apartment, the Lusman Arms, where lately a worker was electrocuted during renovations. Daisy's chat with the uncredited newsstand worker has a splendidly easy, lived-in chemistry.

Cinematographer Steve Yedlin, whom Hooper poached from Lucky McKee and who would become Rian Johnson's go-to cameraman, follows Daisy back to her apartment from a low-angle, Dutch tilt dolly, walking with her and observing as she's dwarfed by the apartment building with every step she takes towards it—the modern answer to the shot of Pam walking towards Leatherface's house in *Chain Saw*. She steps over tiles with odd Masonic symbols to get to the lobby, passing Luis the doorman (Marco Rodríguez), Ned the handyman (co-writer Adam Gierasch, once more playing the biggest creep in the film), and the newest tenant, Nell Barrows (Angela Bettis, another McKee veteran). Hooper frames Nell's first close-up in the lobby (in one of his fake split diopter shots) in a low angle, with Ned the handyman over her shoulder standing on a ladder fixing a light, his mop of greasy hair like a pair of curtains on either side of his face.

In *Toolbox Murders*, the colors and textures, not to mention the distance between camera and subject, are atypical for Hooper. His close-ups feel more pointedly isolating, the darkness malevolent and unplanned, his lighting grey, yellow, green, and dim. Skin tones are unflattering under this oppressive new light. Blood looks darker, walls are an ill hue, and everything looks damp. His momentum is different too. He follows Daisy when she leaves the rickety elevator in a medium close-up Steadicam shot for a few seconds, then cuts to a wider angle at her front door, slowly dollying in as she unlocks the door and lets herself in. Hooper's camera predicts where Daisy will be, waiting to pick her up and guide her to the next setup like a dance partner. If he loses her, he always finds her in complementary directions in the next cut. It's easy to wonder if it's Tobe Hooper in there at all, with the wall-to-wall yellows, and lightning pace of the edit, until lightning *really* strikes and Daisy's apartment turns *Eggshells* pink thanks to the dark red walls in her bedroom. There are insert shots—very un-Hooper—as the killer knocks a defensive pair of scissors out of Daisy's hand with his hammer, then beats her to death with it, her hair stuck to the hammer in as gross a fashion as possible with each blow to her head. Blood hits the windows, turning the Hollywood skyline into a collage of moist, psychedelic neon. When the building manager reminds Nell and Steven that not too many buildings in the area offer the same safety and security, we'll be remembering the hair on the killer's hammer.

Nell and her husband Steven (Brent Roam) quickly meet most of their neighbors through wacky chance encounters. The zany dynamic of the building's tenants make this appear to be a stylish, commanding redo of the relatively anemic *The Apartment Complex*, a way to tell that kind of story without giving the audience everything wrapped up in a bow. In *Toolbox Murders* the sprawling cast of characters includes Saffron (Sara Downing), a moody artist, who gets nail gunned early on. The Sterling family, Dora (Stephanie Silverman) and Philip (Alan Polonsky), live down the hall, and their son Austin's (Adam Weisman) web cam perving will prove integral to the plot. Chas Rooker (Rance Howard), a retired actor, befriends Nell in the laundry room and tells her he's lived here since the Lusman arms were built, which means he knows its secrets. Hudson (Jamison Reeves) is a struggling actor up for a role in a horror film, so when he rehearses, he sounds like he's being murdered. Julia Cunningham (Juliet Landau, daughter of Martin) is fitness obsessed and would be Nell's best new friend if she didn't vanish a few hours after their first meaningful conversation. She is also the girl Austin Sterling spies on with his webcam. Which brings us to the film's primary fascination: in the 21st century, women are constantly the object of unwanted attention, lust, and voyeurism, if not outright sexual violence.

Hooper makes it clear from the get-go that the women of the Lusman Arms would be unsafe with or without a serial killer. Ned the handyman, who creeps on every woman in the building? He's just a red herring. He isn't killing anyone, he just makes every woman uncomfortable by staring at them too long. Saffron is in a constant argument with her tattooed, bald boyfriend, who Nell encounters on the elevator. Hooper frames this perfectly to highlight Nell's comparatively diminutive stature next to the big, angry man, her eyes trying to see the menacing guy behind her after hearing him shout at a woman for ten minutes. When we meet Daisy, she's modeling her Taser for the convenience store clerk, as if it were a funny little keychain. Both of these women know it's nothing for them to be carrying weapons to put down male assailants, and yet it still doesn't save her. Nell doesn't object to her husband working long hours, but she is acutely aware that *her* being alone in this neighborhood isn't good for her.

The building itself, crookedly shaped with green light in its windows, seems to mock her. It looks as full of evil as it turns out to be. Like so many Hooper locations, it has consumed the bodies of its inhabitants. A cavity the length of the building has been the home of the supernaturally preserved Mr. Lusman, who has kept the bodies of hundreds of victims, over fifty years of murder, in there with him. Yes, he kills men *and* women, but the women are the ones whose bodies no one seems all that interested in finding. The police don't want to believe Nell when she calls after hearing Saffron get murdered—*two* women they don't want to help—and don't even look hard enough in her apartment to find her body nailed to the ceiling of the bedroom.

The world of *Toolbox Murders* is one where women are being spied and preyed upon. They can feel every eyeball on them, but they can't make anyone else understand their situation. Voyeurism has become a part of everyday life (just look at Austin Sterling, who actually comes to his lust object's rescue when he sees her being killed), so the police view Nell's constant refrain of having *heard* a crime take place as especially feeble. The evidence needs to be as shocking as possible now that the world has succumb to its most jaded self—which was also true of new horror films. Thankfully, at no point does anyone have to spell that out for us. Hooper lets the actions of his lead and the alternately empty, bemused, and sympathetic responses she receives speak for themselves.

When Julia goes missing, Hooper frames Nell dwarfed by the Lusman building. She waits to run into her on her morning run—their usual meet up—and when she doesn't show, the building is *right* over her shoulder with the answer to the riddle. She eventually figures out the connection between the disappearances and the strange Masonic symbols all over the apartment complex and goes on a treasure hunt, not taking her friend's vanishing lightly and knowing the police are as likely to help her as Ned the handyman. Not even her husband takes her seriously, not taking "I don't want to be alone right now" as enough cause to leave his job to be with her. In a masterfully upsetting touch, when she hangs up with Steven, construction begins overhead. So, she's left alone, curled up on the couch with blinding white light flooding in through the windows, and the sound of hammering drowning out even her sobs.

Trying to capture what it feels like to be a frightened woman with any kind of psychological realism is rare for male American directors, let alone a 60-year-old making a kind of slasher film, but Hooper takes Nell's condition—including her immense courage—very seriously. When she goes on her hunt for Julia in the hotel's "missing" rooms, Hooper captures her in both symmetrical and asymmetrical frames, dollies and pans, helping her cut a dynamic figure on screen, filling her journey with momentum even when she stands still. Hooper's direction and Andrew Cohen's editing may have been the result of a budget crunch and trying to stretch the footage they had before money ran out, but it works in the film's favor. *Toolbox Murders* is full of energy and has twice as many lovely compositions for having to use what may have just been coverage as the meat of a scene. Nell's journey is also, blessedly, full of hope, which makes her investigation even more thrilling on a second viewing. Unlike the *Saw* films or the films of Eli Roth (among other Splat Pack mainstays), *Toolbox Murders* has a happy ending with its heroine victorious.

Lusman's lair, when Nell finds it, is a typically marvelous Hooperian chamber of decrepitude. The set dressers, production designers and art directors did a mightily impressive job. Nell falls into the basement (like Stretch into Battle Land in *Chainsaw 2*) and enters the dungeon of horrors, a womb where the horrible Lusman gets to live forever spying on and killing all the women he pleases. The sheen of glamour has faded completely from the rotten core of the hotel. The building is like an organism with an infection or a tumor, dying from the inside out (the huge collection of dead bodies could be right out of *Chain Saw*, as could the elaborate killing methods. Though the building manager's demise, in which he's stabbed in the spine with shears and dances around like a puppet, feels a little more like *Chainsaw 2*). The ugliness of the rest of the hotel seems like an infection from the killer's hideout, not an unfamiliar concept in Hooper's cinema. The slight art deco influence of the building (built in the '40s, after all) is cut by the elaborate decay of the intervening years. There's a great shock moment where Nell encounters an ancient lit-up painting of old Hollywood with bright, colorful spotlights. The film's version of cannibalism involves the eating of the young and hopeful would-be starlets who came to the Lusman Arms in hopes of becoming famous. The cannibal demon in the bowels of the hotel can prey upon them with abandon because no one questions the fate of lost girls who go missing trying to be famous. Something has to keep the wheels spinning or Hollywood and the attendant magic and glory wouldn't mean anything. Tellingly, it's the killer's belief in mystical symbols that proves his undoing. Fame is like religion in Hooper's world. If we stopped believing in it, it would disappear.

Mortuary (2005)

Our first shot is of Jamie Doyle (Stephanie Patton), her face and surroundings blue to match her anxiety about moving to a new home. The new place is a very Californian version of a small town, surrounded by train tracks and stacks of shipping containers on the edge of town. Their new home is the mortuary. Jamie is freaked out by her mother's new job. Leslie (Denise Crosby) is an amateur mortician and she coolly responds to Jamie's question about the scariness of dead bodies with, "No, honey, not at all." But Jamie hugs her teddy bear tight all the same. Jonathan (Dan Byrd), the eldest child, is about as cool with moving to the palm-tree-flanked death house as Jamie. The Doyle family have the expected naturalistic chemistry Hooper has made his stock in trade. This is the last script Hooper used by Adam Gierasch and Jace Anderson and it's as full of archetypes as ever, though this one's a little different in an interesting way.

The grim, high-contrast, and detailed look of *Toolbox Murders* is further washed out by Jaron Presant in *Mortuary*, who worked as the second unit photographer on all those Rian Johnson films that *Toolbox* DoP Steve Yedlin worked on. Hooper also uses a lot of slow dollies-in as his establishing shots and edits out of them, using momentum to set a scene, which he'd done in the past but not with the regularity he does here.

Hooper dollies around a big mud slick to find the Doyle's minivan parked next to the realtor's sedan. The realtor (Greg Travis, a bit player from *Toolbox Murders*) can't stop laughing even as he explains the problems with the septic tank. The house (shown in full with another insistent dolly shot) has chipping paint and seems to lean—it looks like a haunted house set.

Hooper creeps over the organ in the lobby to greet his guests as they walk in the front door. The lights in the kitchen are green (literal flashes of classic Hooper lighting) and the taps run brown—the house is expressing its history of torment, talking to the family, like when one of the coffins in the showroom falls down in front of Jamie. Hooper's compositions here are frequently symmetrical, such as the shot of Jonathan alone in the attic room for the first time, obscuring the light, looking taller than he does in the rest of the film. He investigates the attic and notices, next to the big open windows, the name "Bobby F" carved onto a table corner.

The basement workshop is a little more inviting. The floor tile is black and white like the chessboard patterns from *I'm Dangerous Tonight* and *Spontaneous Combustion*. The most curious thing is what happens when Linda cuts herself on her new keys. Some black tendrils come out from the drain and drink it—one more carnivorous dwelling in a long line.

Hooper cranes down from the roof of the local diner as Jonathan drives up into the dirty parking lot. Inside, a group of kids, Sarah (Tarah Paige), Tina (Courtney Peldon), and Cal (Bug Hall), snicker as Jonathan tries to order food and apply for a job. Rita (Lee Garlington), the woman behind the counter, is an interesting twist on an established Hooper type: the survivor of the '60s. She's like a benevolent Choptop, a surrogate for Hooper himself, old enough to have the stories and asides that Rita tells her young charges. "You done as many drugs as I have, you'll eat anything," and "My memory's a complete blank between the Kennedy and Reagan administrations. CIA administered LSD tests," are two standouts. She agrees to let Jonathan start work the next day. Jonathan stops for a cigarette in his new cemetery backyard and in the cool mix of green and blue light is stalked by something fast and tall. He trips and discovers a piece of jewelry.

The following day, the mud frozen outside in the cool morning, and Leslie is still unpacking. The brief scene of her pulling things out of boxes and sorting them is hilariously grim, "Kitchen... kitchen... embalming... kitchen." When Jonathan comes to her and tries to explain the events of last night, she doesn't want to hear it. At the diner, Jonathan meets his only other fellow employee, Rita's niece Liz (Alexandra Adi), and just before he can start in with small talk, her boyfriend Grady (Rocky Marquette) walks in. This makes Jonathan sad enough to start a fight with Cal when he makes trouble. Just as he asks Liz and Grady about "Bobby F.," we cut back to Leslie discovering a crypt at the edge of edge of the cemetery. Another womb space, this time with moistened, organic-looking stone walls as in *Invaders from Mars*. This is where Fowler hides from the future and, when freed, tries to turn the world back into the Eisenhower-era paradise he last witnessed above ground. Leslie finds a strange keyhole complete with an eerie poem and discovers one of her new keys opens it. But the sheriff (Michael Shamus Wiles) arrives and distracts her before she can go inside. He wants to warn her about kids sneaking into the cemetery to have sex ("Together we can stop graveyard babies," he finally blurts).

Liz and Grady tell Jonathan the story of Bobby Fowler that night (Gierasch and Anderson's scripts are full of campfire tales). Liz's profanity-laden rendering is a thing of beauty. Bobby was apparently tortured as a kid when his father's farm wouldn't yield and, because of his deformities, stayed in the crypt on the edge of the property—the one Leslie unlocked. All of this backstory essentially makes the premise of *Mortuary* a spin on Harper Lee's *To Kill A Mockingbird* that asks, "What if Boo Radley was a zombie?" The film is notably absent the book's racial dimension but Jonathan, Grady, and Liz even have the Scout, Gem, and Dill dynamic.

Bobby claims his first victims when Cal, Sarah, and Tina show up to have a three-way in the graveyard and desecrate some headstones. Cal pisses on an old teacher's grave and then the crew traipse into Fowler's resting place, the labyrinthine crypt where Fowler's been living. They'd just gotten to taking their clothes off when Fowler wakes from his grave and attacks. Their thwarted three way is a little paean to the free love in the commune in *Eggshells*. Hooper won't let them co-opt someone else's idea of freedom without having suffered the same fear as his peers did when they were that age.

The Doyles get two pieces of good news the next day. Jonathan finds out that Grady is just Liz's gay best friend, *not* her boyfriend, and then Leslie gets her first corpses to embalm. Of course, both bits of fortune are tainted slightly when the first body belongs to Liz's piano teacher Mr. Barstow (Gierasch under a foot of makeup designed to make him look like Leatherface's grandpa). The machine she uses to fill him with fluid has a great sea foam green color—a nice piece of kitschy set decoration right out of *Spontaneous Combustion*. Leslie has a bit of a Jerry Lewis moment when she messes up the procedure and tries to stop embalming fluid from getting everywhere right when the sheriff calls. Hooper's sense of humor hadn't gotten this much of an airing since *The Apartment Complex*, and this scene actually works as a piece of filmmaking. There's another great little joke when Leslie finally answers the door and greets the sheriff.

"Nice landscape."

"Really livens the place up."

"Yes, it does," he says matter-of-factly when Hooper cuts to a patch of ugly grass surrounded by dirt and septic run off.

She leaves just in time to miss the creeping vine from the drain return to suck Mr. Barstow's blood.

The sheriff's arrival signals the beginning of the end for the Doyle's fresh start. He asks after Cal following his fight with Jonathan, then searches the property, predictably wandering into Bobby's crypt, the last we'll see of him. Jamie has a scare that night, imagining she sees Bobby Fowler in her closet—he's literally the monster in her closet like in a storybook—but Jonathan can only find a dirty shroud like one Liz described in her ghost story.

When Liz confesses she has feelings for Jonathan the next day, their happiness is *mighty* short lived because Sarah and Cal walk in, looking much the worse for wear after their encounter with Bobby. Their skin is pale and dirty and their brains seem stuck on repeat. They both start puking up black blood, Cal right on Rita's face. Back at the mortuary, Leslie has the same thing happen to her when two corpses stand up from off the operating table and attack. She seems to have gone slightly Stepford when Jonathan comes home with Liz and Grady in tow. The black blood has turned her into a perfect suburban mom—pieces of Bobby Fowler's never-lived perfect life. Her setting the table for a nice dinner with the family while the walls grow with the odd black vine and the green light over the stove flickers is a most unsettling scene. Hooper still finds nothing more upsetting than suburban "perfection," and the kids' fear of viewing their mother as a threat is potent and upsetting. Leslie sucks up her bowl of soup (more of the black bile) with the grotesque complacence of the Gardners sucking down bacon in *Invaders from Mars*. She even makes the family say grace. She starts puking up the black bile, and that's when Jonathan grabs Jamie and races off to hide in the cemetery (the Doyle's minivan is covered in the vine).

Inside the crypt, they find a still living Tina who shows them the way out—a passageway back to the Doyle's home. By this point, the house is surrounded by "zombies," so Jonathan hides Jamie in the attic—the most beautifully lit room of the set, even in its dilapidated state. When he returns downstairs, the coffins in the living room all burst open, dislodging their undead contents, a lovely, macabre set piece. Tina, by now infected, backs into a cabinet and knocks into a jar of salt, which melts her, giving the kids their solution to the problem: salt the zombies like snails.

Bobby finds his way into the attic and takes Jamie into his abattoir hideaway (it's full of ancient corpses and a pale yellow glow like so many Hooper mass graves), but all he wants is to play with the little girl. Like Leatherface, his intelligence is that of a child and he wants to make the world into his playroom. When Jonathan finds Bobby, he's about to feed Jamie into a hole in the ground (more hungry Earth), which looks like the pit from Stuart Gordon's 2001 adaptation of Lovecraft's *Dagon*, complete with tentacles. If Fowler can't have things the way he wants them, he'll destroy them (all of which sounds like a George W. Bush critique). The films ends bleakly, as any post-2004 election, liberally minded horror film must.

Mortuary is most haphazard dramatically, but its ideas and anger are understandable. It feels like an expression of Hooper's helplessness in a mudslide towards the surrendering of civil rights and a never-ending climate of war and invasion, a return to a time of apparent prosperity ('50s or '80s, a time when the government had the same nostalgia for wholesome '50s living that Fowler appears to) that itself marked by war, sexism, racism, and ignorance. His next film took the signs of encroaching doom and celebrations of violence from politicians and on TV at face value and created a world to reflect the chaos and madness that had become the national mood.

Masters of Horror, "Dance of the Dead" (2005)

There's no escaping the fact that while Jon Joffin was a director of photography willing to experiment along with Hooper, his visuals are murky and thin. So he couldn't quite bring Hooper's pair of career-tracing

TV movies to *look* as expansive and conclusive as they feel. The small budgets also got the better of him—allowing for only a glimpse of the catastrophes that should feel apocalyptic. *Dance of the Dead* and *The Damned Thing* capture the two different facets of Hooper's filmmaking—on one hand, a girl leaves home for the first time and discovers big, brightly lit carnival populated by a tightly knit group of killers and freaks. And on the other, a small town invaded by an ancient, evil force.

Dance of the Dead opens on an image of balloons bobbing in and out of view of a white sun, like those that played a part in the dream sequences all the way back in *Eggshells*. In both cases, they are symbolic of lost innocence, of being targeted by the big wide world and its dark agenda, of bubbles about to burst. Hooper has freak-out episodes aplenty in *Dance* and they're frequently announced by a triangulation effect where two shadows of an image dance around the concrete first image. In the opening, it signals the arrival of the wave of destruction that sets the plot in motion—the sky is crowded by waves of darkness and the guests at the little girl's birthday party run screaming, the frame a blur of primary and pastel colors. Hooper and editor Andrew Cohen jumble the images over top of each other in double and triple exposures to agitate the chaos further. Skin starts ripping and turning to rot. This is a flashback and a dream and it belongs to Kate (Marilyn Norry), who was the mother of two young girls at the party. Her world is considerably drabber now—though Joffin's colors make it hard to tell that that's an intentional juxtaposition. Her surviving daughter, Peggy (Jessica Lowndes), rouses her. Both wear dirty aprons, symbolic of the suburban life they pretend to still possess.

The film's second free-form freak-out (introduced with a slow motion shot of a woman walking in a backless shirt, like Pam approaching Leatherface's house) takes place at a topless metal bar called The Doom Room, the overstimulating converse of Kate and Peggy's diner. While a metal band plays (hand selected by music supervisor Billy Corgan), a crowd takes part in a full-on bacchanal. There's writhing, grinding, dancing, and Hooper's lighting works overtime, filling the vast industrial space with blues and whites. Cohen jumbles the images and plays with little jumps into fast motion. Out from the back, draped in lights, is the MC of the nightclub (Robert Englund, looking like a cosplay take on his Bill Gartley, in his last performance for his five-time director), who makes his wordplay-laden introduction to the evening's entertainment, which we'll see in the final act.

Back in Peggy and Kate's hometown, we see the film's futuristic equivalent of a mugging involving two young bikers named Boxx and Jak (Ryan McDonald and Jonathan Tucker, who'd just starred in the Michael Bay produced remake of *Texas Chain Saw Massacre*). When the panicked couple asks to be left alone, Box points a gun and smiles.

"We can't do that. We're the youth of America, endeavoring against insurmountable odds to eke out a living." He says it like he's heard it a thousand times.

The two bikers hook the woman up with needles and IVs and steal some of her blood. Between their tanned leather getups and barking eccentricity they're styled like postapocalyptic takes on Robert Englund and William Finlay in *Eaten Alive*.

At the diner (as in *Mortuary*, a diner represents lost innocence in a suburban setting), Peggy begs her mother to tell her stories of her father. Hooper frames them in silhouette and lets a sickly old woman creep up on them, her injuries hidden to the camera at first. Kate asks her to leave, her small town prejudices having soured even further in the wake of the attacks. Peggy follows her and gives the old woman food, and we see her wounds wrapped under a funeral shroud. When she returns, Jak and Boxx have shown up with two girls in tow (Erica Carroll and Lucie Guest). They make a big Marlon Brando in *The Wild One*-esque scene of themselves and Kate makes them leave. But Peggy is suitably enthralled by Jak to follow him out and he invites her to tag along during their evening run to the Doom Room to sell the blood they've collected. During this scene, Hooper cuts to images of two men in dirty jumpsuits burning the bodies of people infected with some illness in a dumpster, eyes turned white, skin gone pallid and bruised, as if to highlight what Kate thinks she's saving Peggy from when she tells her the world killed her father and sister Anna. It will be revealed that though Peggy's father was killed fighting in World War 3, Anna's fate was at least partly Kate's fault.

"Is it obscene...or is it science?" asks the MC. He's talking about the Doom Room's star attraction, the LUP. This is all borrowed from the source short story of the same name by the great Richard Matheson (who also wrote the story on which Hooper's *Amazing Stories* entry was based and just like on that episode, his son, Richard Christian Matheson, wrote the teleplay). The LUP (Living Undead Phenomenon) is when the MC drugs the bodies of overdosed teenagers into restless life and has topless women shock them with cattle prods until they stop dancing. Peggy witnessing this will be what finally draws her out of childhood.

Jak coaxes Peggy out of her bubble and into the backseat of Boxx's muscle car. As they drive at insane speeds, Hooper places the camera very close to their faces and has reams of color pass them—perhaps his most interesting cheat of the traditional rear projection highway. The colors whoosh past, all the brilliant reds and psychedelic greens he couldn't fit elsewhere in the lighting design, turning the car ride into another freak-out: a chugging, intoxicatingly off sequence redolent of the psychic carousel sequence in Byron Haskin's *The Power*, exacerbated by the drugs the gang takes on the road, which causes Peggy to have a flashback to the party that haunts her mother. There, she sees the chemical weapons drop for the first time ("Blizz," it's nicknamed), which maims and kills everyone it touches. This is another Hitchcock riff: a grislier, more disorienting take on Cathy's birthday party in *The Birds*. We learn that Kate refused to let the other mothers and children into her house, thus exposing them to Blizz and then watched as they perished. It's unsurprising when we learn the roll she had in Anna's death.

The town of Muskeet, where the Doom Room is located, is filled with freakish displays of costume and production design. There are fire dancers, a man pounding a drum built into his suit of armor, a shop selling charred, unidentifiable meat, drugged out whore hounds, and sex acts filling the outer reaches of the frame. Like the Marquis De Sade's jailhouse in *Night Terrors*, Muskeet and the Doom Room have an ornate busyness that bristles with perverse imagination—it too bears a faint resemblance to the frame stuffing of Max Ophüls' *Lola Montès* (which also had an MC character and chronicled a woman's sexual awakening during times of unrest).

Kate wakes up and finds Peggy gone, so she drives out to Muskeet to retrieve her before she sees her older sister Anna (Melena Rounis) on stage, one of the LUP dead bodies reanimated to dance for the public's sick delight. Englund's performance on stage introducing the LUP dancers is typically great, relishing every bad joke and theatrical laugh. The "spasmodic gyrations" of the dancers are another little paean to the mechanical dancing woman in Michael Powell's *Tales of Hoffmann*. Jak and Peggy steal Anna off the stage and the MC and Kate both find them at the same time, so the MC tells the story of Kate selling Anna's body to him after she kept escaping to Muskeet and OD'ing. So Peggy does the humane thing and trades her mother to the MC so that she can have Anna's body and bury it properly (in front of a beautiful matte painting of WW3-ravaged Muskeet, rendered a little fuzzy and thin thanks to Joffin's photography).

Dance of the Dead's alternate reality bikers and small town girls version of the 1950s is a sort of gallows humor imagining of America in the 2000s: it dreams of a time when war spilled onto American soil and our chemical weapons were used against us. The results of the third World War turned what little was left of the country into a goth/punk funhouse mirror of Eisenhower's America, the primary colors of that birthday party replaced with a whirr of Hooper's psychedelic palette. Violence and broken bodies are now how the survivors pass the time, which is not productive, but it feels less like a lie than Kate's death grip on suburban normalcy. She is, after all, the villain of the piece, the genuine throwback that Leslie Doyle becomes when infected by the mortuary. Hooper doesn't find anything productive or heroic in *Dance of the Dead*, but he knows which characters he admires more.

Masters of Horror, "The Damned Thing" (2006)

Hooper and a returning Jon Joffin introduce our setting magnificently by showing the reflection of a house in a lake's dark surface. They Steadicam around the Reddle dinner table swiftly, setting up their cozy chemistry. Kevin (Ryan Drescher) is a smart kid who's memorized a lot of arcane knowledge about the law. Mother Jodi (Georgia Craig) has gotten wind of some strange things happening in their little town, but dad John (Brent Stait) seems unfazed... until he hears something rumbling far away. Then he interrupts Kevin and Jodi preparing his surprise birthday cake by walking in and murdering his wife in cold blood. Maybe it has something to do with the oil-like substance leaking from the ceiling. Hooper and a returning Andrew Cohen once more overlaying the literally spinning shadows of the image over both John and Kevin as he turns on his son. John chases Kevin into the field outside their home. But before he finds and kills his son, something invisible grabs John and disembowels him, spinning him like a top on the side of his truck. The effect mimics the way the images spin and spasm, like they're being shaken by the hand of the editor. The deep greens of the grass in which Kevin hides are turned pale yellow by the heat lightning, Hooper stalking both father and son with a dolly like a big jungle cat.

Years later, Kevin Reddle (now played by Sean Patrick Flannery) has become sheriff of a town a few miles up the road from his family's massacre. We meet him in Clover County behind a billowing American flag. He seems permanently uncomfortable in his own skin. *The Damned Thing* is shot by Joffin in a yellow-orange tobacco-stained filter, the little pieces of the tiny town that Reddle polices make it seem like a Texas town that would have sat comfortably in Muerto County. For the first ten minutes after the attack, *The Damned Thing* is just about Reddle's fairly ordinary life and has a nice, ambling rhythm. He has run-ins with his ex-wife Dina (Marisa Coughlan), his son Mikey (Alex Ferris), his amateur cartoonist deputy (Brendan Fletcher), and his priest (Ted Raimi). The relative calm is shattered when local Gabe Green (Clint Carleton) smashes his face to bloody pieces with a hammer and then Reddle has a nightmarish vision of oil falling on his hand, reminding him of his father's murderous episode before his death. He begins hearing sounds and his CCTV goes haywire. So he runs away, fleeing in his jeep, the scenery flying by as in the ride to Muskeet in *Dance of the Dead*. He happens upon a bad accident but, when he tries to free the driver, accidentally yanks her torso free from her legs. Craziness has begun to follow him, it seems.

Atypically for Hooper, a lot of the Sheriff's encounters are shot in tight close-ups, which is paid off richly when he catches a glimpse of himself in a hospital mirror and the crack in his forehead releases what looks like a small creature living there. It could be a fantasy, but it's also a metaphor for the grief he carries around with him. It's the best moment in *The Damned Thing*, reveling in the handmade and grotesque, making literal the dark secrets our imaginations and past traumas can hide in our unconscious. The next day, nosy local journalist Joe Linton (Andrew McIlroy) finds Reddle and floats a theory that will of course turn out to be true: that Reddle's grandfather struck oil and when the oil dried up, the town went insane, leaving only a few people, including Jodi and John Reddle, alive. The damned thing followed John to his new home and possessed him and it has found Kevin again. It threatens to turn everyone mad around him.

The madness strikes that very night, hitting Dina and Mikey's trailer first (their yard is littered with colorful lights just like Mark Jackson's in *The Mangler*). Deputy Strauss calls while chaos rages in the background—an apocalypse on a budget—and, rather than helping anyone, goes to confession (the space between priest and confessor like prison bars). There's a slight, funny implication that when the priest kills him it's because he worships Mickey Mouse before God. The priest has gone mad, along with everyone else in town. The few survivors show up on Reddle's doorstep with guns and he locks them in his basement to keep them away from Dina and Mikey when they turn on each other. Reddle's house is filled with oppressive, sickly yellow/green floodlights. The damned thing comes for Kevin, but he pulls himself out of his murderous frenzy in time to stop the priest from murdering Mikey and Dina. He is then be eaten by the creature, which is visible thanks to the oil in Kevin's nightmares coating it and showing off its shape.

The Damned Thing is a classic Hooper idea: the ground unleashing an ancient evil to kill the people who've taken shelter over top of it. Its root cause? Capitalism. The oil drying up sends people into a panic (which plays like a critique of the Bush family and their ties to oil companies, not to mention the petroleum wells hiding behind the thin justifications for invading Middle Eastern countries), turning parents against their children and husbands against wives. The law only wants to keep everyone quarantined while they tear each other apart. The clergy decides a blood sacrifice is in order. When things turn to madness, authority is useless. The oil, like an extension of the malignant vine in *Mortuary*, is a harbinger of madness and death. *The Damned Thing* suffers from the limitations of its tiny budget and while it is a nice, efficiently nasty summation of Hooper's pet themes as well as a nifty Iraq War parable about oil driving people to heedless violence, fans could be forgiven for thinking he had at least one more great film in him.

Djinn (2013)

Horror directors flying to foreign countries to kick-start a filmmaking economy is nothing new. Another recent example would be Brian Yuzna, writer of *Reanimator* and director of *Society*, flying to Indonesia to make *Amphibious*, the country's first 3D horror film (not that the project paid off). Hooper made *Djinn* for Image Nation, a production wing based out of Abu Dhabi, with dozens of international credits including Steven Soderbergh's *Contagion* and Gus Van Sant's *Promised Land*. *Djinn* was one of their first horror films, one of the first horror films made in the United Arab Emirates, and may well be the first horror film in both English and Arabic. *Djinn* was also the first film Hooper shot digitally, and he utilizes its capability for capturing murky dark grays and greens as well as more picturesque sun-kissed tableaux It's an unusual work and not just for Hooper. It's a horror film about motherhood and religion and it sides unequivocally with freedom of expression. It's the indigenous cousin to the exoticism and othering of *Night Terrors*.

The film was released in a more polished state by the distributor but a director's cut has since surfaced that preserves a little more of Hooper's expressive colors and maintains a more traditionally effective shape. In the theatrical cut we are shown ancient Emirati ruins at sundown. The actress Ahd explains in voice-over that man was made from clay and a djinn is a demon made from fire. We join Salama and Khalid (Razane Jammal and Khalid Laith), an expat couple living in America. Joel Ransom, the director of photography, starts above the grave of Salama and Khalid's child, then sinks down to the couple grieving in the rain, America a dull grey compared to the rich oranges of the UAE prologue. Before getting in a cab to leave, they spy a mourner, a woman in black. She vanishes before they can get a good look at her.

At couple's counseling, their therapist (Soumaya Akaaboune) suggests reconnecting with their families in the old country. She's so insistent, it starts to bother Salama, who keeps giving reasons why they can't uproot.

Finally, the therapist, in Arabic, snaps and her voice turns supernaturally low. "You will not get in *my* way."

When Salama questions the outburst, Khalid jumps in, gaslighting her into believing she imagined it. "My way, she meant my way."

This film's understanding of the insidious sexism of marriage is remarkable.

"How can you deny a request from the man you love?" asks the counselor.

As in *I'm Dangerous Tonight*, Hooper once more sides with the browbeaten woman stuck in the tangled web of male suggestion and assumption.

We cut from a Dutch tilt of the doctor's office to a desert race. Hooper begins his director's cut here, which frames the rest of the film as a kind of expansion of the ghost story told to scare our POV character. He's a spoiled American (Paul Luebke) and his guides drive their big SUVs around villages abandoned thanks to the people's belief in the djinn. Hooper cranes down when the race ends and alternates between medium close-ups of the men talking and spying far off POV shots from the brush surrounding their campfire. The guide tells a campfire tale (a Hooper motif) of a child that was half-djinn and half-man. A couple's baby was replaced by a djinn child by a sorceress (it creeps into the baby's window like the black vine from *Mortuary*) and so the couple had it exorcised. The mother of the demon child searches the earth to this day looking for its child but cannot find it because it has had its evil drained from it. In Hooper's cut there's a flashback to the village, captured in a glowing orange hue. The djinn climbs into a young mother's second storey window aided by dark magic to replace a human child with its own half-demon child. A cleric is called to take the child away, and the djinn now waits to reclaim its grown changeling in the village.

The American scoffs at their tale and wanders off into the dark to relieve himself. But when he returns, his guides are missing. It seems they made a deal to feed the American to the djinn.

One of the guides warns him just before the spirit finds and disembowels the American, "She said they won't hurt me. But you...they are gonna hurt you."

The blood that covers the door of the American's car has Hooper's patented diagonal spray pattern. There's a degree to which this film acts as a corrective to the othering exoticized view of the Middle East found in *Night*

Terrors, the killing of its only white character a sort of blood sacrifice to start showing how other cultures experience horror absent a white perspective, though the outlines are similar to a lot of Hooper's American movies. The setting for most of the film is a high rise, which cannily contrasts the financial success of the indigenous populace, and also hints at the rotting capitalist core still present of society, as does the new developments in *Poltergeist*.

When Khalid and Salama arrive at the airport, they trade conspiratorial looks as they descend the escalator in front of his family, like they need the other's permission to wave and smile. This scene is our introduction to them in Hooper's cut, hinting that he felt dropping us into their family dynamic was the more efficient way to introduce us to them. The extent of their relationship problems is communicated without a word. Then we realize that Khalid's uncle and Salama's father are the same man, Nasser (Abdullah Al Junaibi), and their problems become compounded—by coming home, they're reminded that this was some kind of arranged marriage. Salama's younger sister Aisha (May Calamawy) is happy to have her back because her mother (Carol Abboud) has probably been asking her to have a child since her eldest moved to America.

Nasser drives them to Khalid's firm's new development (apparently they bought the village where the djinn legend originated and built over it) but stops when he nearly crushes a pedestrian in the fog. Khalid gets out to investigate, but only sees his firm's newest building, the building where he and Salama will be living, standing erect in the fog like a beacon of hopelessness. When they arrive, they're plainly among the only guests in the hotel. Hooper dollies and pans across the great empty hotel corridors and the married couple's luxury suite—their new home. Salama is overwhelmed by the spaciousness, the regality, and most of all the height. It's enough to give her a stress flashback to her child's death. She starts investigating a vent in her room when a bird crashes into her window, lost in the fog. The grey green of the fog all around the property is one of Hooper's methods of deglamorizing his portrayal of a foreign country. There is nothing othered about this place. It's drab, menacing, and ugly. Hooper sees the empty hotel as symbolic of capitalist excesses, a testament only to the loneliness of the rich who think they deserve to live here. It's the soulless, new modern equivalent of the Lusman arms: a place destined to die surrounded by no one and nothing.

In Hooper's cut, the dialogue and expository camera work are all given a little more room to breathe, the camera slowly dollying and panning around the apartment and the hallways of the hotel and around the conversations. The relationship between Salama and her family is more precisely drawn, and a scene where they give her gifts before leaving underscored by the gentle synth score leaves one with a kind of graceful high point from which the film can now more meaningfully fall. There's a lovely scene when Salama and Khalid are finally alone and she tells him not to speak Arabic, that she was just doing it for her parents. The expectations heaped on her make her feel even more exhausted than she is. By jettisoning the funeral, Hooper ensures we learn about the death of their firstborn more subtly, a bold but rewarding gesture.

Salama says goodbye to her family, who pile back into Nasser's SUV for the drive home. They don't make it far. The car breaks down and then the djinn attacks, scraping its nails against the windshield and climbing the roof. The camera shakes during the attack, a technique from Hooper's work in the early 2000s (Andrew Cohen is his editor once more). Nasser gets out to investigate, pride overcoming his sense of danger, and is distracted by a golden light emerging from the fog—the headlights on a truck that obliterates the family and their SUV. His masculinity traps and dooms his family.

Khalid leaves for work after arguing with Salama about their new life. She tries to go for a walk, but a big angry dog finds her in the fog mere steps away from the hotel lobby. She runs inside and happens to see something on the closed circuit TV—an eerie black shape crawling along the hallway on the floor outside her room (Hooper remained transfixed by CCTV monitors, the way images and appearances lie to us). It jitters and changes shape as she watches it—it's a simple effect and more frightening that it probably ought to be. The doorman (Malik McCall) doesn't believe her reports of an intruder, but she protests until he comes upstairs with her. She waits outside, stalked by ominous sound design and a pair of disembodied hands, while he checks her room. *Djinn* is probably Hooper's most frightening film since *Poltergeist* and much of that is thanks to the sound design.

As the doorman leaves her in peace, Salama meets her new neighbor, Sarah (Aiysha Hart), clad in a familiar-looking black dress. Her eyes are a brilliant shade of orange like a cat's, or Kurt Barlow's. She has answers ready for every piece of information she shouldn't know about Salama. Alone in her room again, Salama leaves her sister a voice message complaining that by coming home, she traded a job and purpose for the life of a housewife. As if in answer, a loud banging issues from the floor and travels the length of her apartment to the bedroom. There she sees handprints on the floor and in the ceiling, as if invisible people are walking all around her. It's especially clear in the director's cut, which retools the story to slice every extraneous limb (there is no stop in America, the rest of her family is dispatched early, there are fewer characters and they last an even shorter amount of time before being killed) from the story until all we're left with is Salama alone in her fancy apartment, that this is meant to be a study of unnerving isolation more than anything. The imprints of hands and feet on the ceiling are nods to Roman Polanski's 1965 movie *Repulsion*, another work about a woman unraveling alone in an apartment. In that film, phantom limbs and later big imposing men would emerge from the walls to attack and molest mentally fragile Catherine Deneuve. Polanski's later *Rosemary's Baby* (1968) also sacrifices a mother to a fraught religious conspiracy as Hooper does here.

Hooper frames Salama from a low angle when the banging stops, slowly dollying in, the rhombus-shaped ceiling behind her a faint echo of the art deco of Hooper's early '90s work. A room full of terrifying dead-eyed stuffed animals prompts a vision of her son, eyes black and malevolent, like the baby creature in Larry Cohen's *It's Alive*. At his office, Khalid is also having flashbacks mixed with visions of the woman who spied on their son's funeral.

Salama notices that the symbols on the air vents all look similar (like the Masonic symbols in *Toolbox Murders*) and throws on the shawl her mother gave to her before leaving. She starts praying, which calls the djinn into her room, an angry black spot over her right shoulder crawling ever closer to her as Hooper sinks beneath Salama to film her in a low angle, a reverse of the shot of Salama mourning. Her prayers are answered by the force that's been watching her all along. When Salama drops to her knees to pray, her mother's ghost appears to her (though Salama doesn't know her family has died). She speaks as if she knows something about the way Salama's child died. Or more that she knows Salama feels guilt over it, like she killed the child herself. Their reunion is short and soon Salama is left to freak out alone once more. Razane Jammal's performance is one of the best in all of Hooper's canon, at once adept at hysterical melodramatic surrender and a more modern blunted emotional reactions to everyday nuisances.

In the kitchen (after a few more failed attempts to contact Khalid), Hooper's red light returns after a decade without having resorted to it. Salama is about to go somewhere from which she won't ever be able to return. She goes to the fridge for something to drink and stuck to its door with a magnet is an ultrasound scan of a djinn fetus, its mouth open and cackling, its fingers long and spindly like claws. Khalid, too, is bathed in red light when Salama calls him on his way to the apartment; he's been asleep under a kind of spell in the backseat of his car all day under the care of a phantom limo driver in sunglasses. Khalid meets Sarah in the elevator and she gives him a pack of lies about moving from a nearby village. Khalid is so enchanted he forgets to push his floor button. When he walks in and starts talking about having another baby, it's clear that they were never going to solve their problems. Sarah rings their doorbell just when their conversation reaches an impasse.

Salama starts hallucinating as soon as she enters Sarah's apartment, where we meet some of her other neighbors—they include the guide who fed the American to the djinn in the first act and the four strange women dressed in black who spied on Khalid and Salama at the airport, glimpsed for only seconds. They aren't there because it's crucial we remember the moment, but rather to give the nagging feeling that the couple are being watched by uncanny forces. The party of conspirators feels very much in line with *Night Terrors* and *Texas Chain Saw*, a gathering of ghouls out to claim a life. Salama starts seeing visions of the guests eating grotesque organic matter, which combine with a dizzying intrusion of small red lights. This is the first time since *Eggshells* that Hooper has found himself using experimental collage a la Stan Brakhage's 1963 short *Mothlight*. It's little wonder this was downplayed in the theatrical cut. She has a woozy, out-of-focus conversation with the remaining guests who gently taunt her about her dead child.

Khalid leaves Salama alone with Sarah (she spills a drink on him as a gambit to leave, which backfires) and is flooded with visions of the djinn traipsing around his apartment. When he runs back to Sarah's apartment, all the furniture is gone and hundreds of birds crash into the window at the same time. He flees to the elevator and calls the police from the ground floor, dwarfed by the building like Nell and Daisy in front of the Lusman Arms in *Toolbox Murders*, and then the power fails. The police can't see him when they arrive anyway—the hotel has only opened for Khalid and Salama.

Salama wakes from her stupor and sees a vision of her murdered family and then of the four nearly identical women surrounding her in some kind of ritual. In the director's cut there's a vision of a black and white tiled floor, reviving his Deren-inspired décor one last time.

The djinn, sitting in a wheelchair like the ghost in Peter Medak's *The Changeling*, crawls over to her and says, "It's time."

Everyone wants her to give birth again, to tell her what to do with her body. When Khalid returns to Salama, he finds her wrapped in a red cloak, like the shroud from *I'm Dangerous Tonight*. He, he sees in a vision, is the djinn's halfling son. In the release version, the djinn possesses both of them, convincing Khalid that Salama murdered their infant son, and then finally compels him to throw his wife off the roof of the building. In Hooper's version the djinn throws her off and then the four women in black claim him in the lobby and murder the police officers who arrived to help as well. Neither ending is happy, but Hooper's feels bleak in a way that's of a piece with the rest of his work.

Djinn is all the sadder and more grim because it's so good, so frightening, and so economical. Hooper, had he been allowed to continue working, was plainly ready to meet the next generation of horror fan head on. His sense of the political cruelties of living hadn't dimmed and he was adapting with a changing sensibility. Unlike his *Masters of Horror* entries *Djinn* isn't a movie filled with Hooper's old hobbyhorses and aesthetics, he tries new things every chance he gets, from the darker digital color palette to the cultural circumstances. It will always haunt me that Hooper only got to make one new film post-2010 when international horror cinema became a much more well-funded and seen genre. Horror movies are currently being produced at maybe the highest rate in history, and there just wasn't room for one of its most exacting and exhilarating practitioners anymore.

Scout Tafoya

Additional reading:
The Sequels and Remakes

Hooper's legacy in pop culture is far-reaching to say the least, beyond the obvious. *Texas Chain Saw* became its own cottage industry, spawning a dreadful game for Atari that had you playing as Leatherface and carving up women on his property. It's an absurdly misogynist premise and the graphics are so bad it's borderline abstract. Jeff Burr directed the second sequel to *The Texas Chainsaw Massacre* in 1990 called *Leatherface: The Texas Chainsaw Massacre III*, and it's a modest success on its own oddball terms. Ken Foree and Viggo Mortensen duke it out in a Southern California hovel poorly masquerading as Texas. The trailer was a hoot, in which Leatherface draws a chain saw from a lake like he's King Arthur reaching for Excalibur. It's not got much to do with either of Hooper's films, but it's better for forging its own artistic identity. By contrast original co-producer and writer Kim Henkel made his own film in 1995 called *The Return of The Texas Chainsaw Massacre* and later redubbed *Texas Chainsaw Massacre: The Next Generation* on home video, and it's little but a sweatier, semi-modern update of the original. Representatives for co-leads Renée Zellweger and Matthew McConaughey lobbied hard for the film to head straight to video as their stars had risen in the time between shooting and editing it. McConaughey plays the puppet master pulling the new Leatherface's (Robert Jacks) strings. He'd later play a variation on this character in William Friedkin's *Killer Joe* to broad acclaim. Zellweger plays a girl on her way to prom waylaid by maniacs, who are themselves working on the behest of a shadowy corporation, which makes no sense at all except as a kind of aimless, undercooked metaphor. Certainly it's as grimy and gross as both of Hooper's films, it's just nowhere near as intense, frightening, funny, or interesting.

Not even a decade later, Michael Bay, director of *Armageddon* and *Pearl Harbor*, financed a remake of *Chain Saw* directed by music video director Marcus Nispel. It was the flagship film of Bay's Platinum Dunes production shingle, initially seemed to exist to give his other music video director pals from his days before he made *Bad Boys* in 1995 and moved to the big leagues, a shot at making big budget studio movies. Until the company started producing *Purge* sequels the 2003 *Texas Chainsaw Massacre* was their best film. Nispel gives the remake a kind of manicured rusty grotesquerie, which is dishonest but nevertheless winning as an aesthetic object. The cast is too pretty (Jessica Biel, who was at the time fresh off a stint as the elder sister on Christian sitcom *7th Heaven*, is the lead) but the look is impeccable (original photographer Daniel Pearl returned and makes a meal out of the higher budget) and it's reasonably tense. Jonathan Liebesman, who became Bay without the personality, directed the prequel, 2006's *The Texas Chainsaw Massacre: The Beginning*, which, apart from a performance by R. Lee Ermey as Leatherface's dad (returning from the 2003 film), is empty and useless, a transparent cash grab. In 2013 middling crime film director John Luessenhop directed *Texas Chainsaw 3D,* which ends with Leatherface and the final girl (Alexandra Daddario) on the same team, a novel and fun twist that helps keep the reasonably fun film above mediocre and expected. In 2017 French filmmakers Alexandre Bustillo and Julien Maury directed the excellent prequel story *Leatherface* about the killer's teen years. It's got the look and feel of a modern giallo, and the sweltering, unforgiving moral core of Hooper's original. As of this writing another remake is being planned.

In 1986 MGM financed *Poltergeist II: The Other Side* directed by Brian Gibson. It's quite poor, despite direction that is at least solid in a kind of William Girdler fashion, and like Girdler's *The Manitou*, this is a film with a ridiculous Native American mythology at its core. It's responsible for the common belief that the original film is set above a Native burial ground, one of horror's most enduring clichés. *Poltergeist III* followed two years later, directed by Gary Sherman, who made one of the other great '70s cannibal films, *Raw Meat* or *Death Line*, in 1972. It reset the action in an apartment high-rise and Heather O'Rourke was the only returning cast member. Her premature death makes the film almost unbearable to sit through, despite a hint of William Gibson/J. G. Ballard sociology introduced in the setting, and fine work from Tom Skerritt and Nancy Allen as Carol Anne's aunt and uncle. Sherman took the name and the idea to television for *Poltergeist: The Legacy* in 1996, created and written by Richard Barton Lewis, which lasted for four seasons. Animator Gil Kenan remade the movie in 2015, and despite an incredible cast—Sam Rockwell, Rosemarie DeWitt, Jane Adams, Jared Harris—it's dreadful. As of this writing another one's being planned, which may never happen, but the point is this is an idea that Hollywood won't ever tire of resurrecting.

Enterprising genre maverick Larry Cohen directed the unrelated but great sequel *A Return To Salem's Lot* in 1987 starring Michael Moriarty and shot by Daniel Pearl. People for a long time considered this one of Cohen's weaker films, but it's great fun, taking its cues from Moriarty's nervous presence in the lead and a scene-stealing turn from director Sam Fuller as a Nazi hunter turned vampire hunter. The book was readapted by Mikael Salomon in 2004 for the TNT network. It's reasonably effective and precipitated Salomon becoming a go-to for other made-for-TV remakes like 2008's *Andromeda Strain* and 2012's *Coma*. Rob Lowe is the lead and he's better suited for comedy. The supporting cast (Donald Sutherland, Samantha Mathis, James Cromwell, Andre Braugher, and Rutger Hauer) is more convincing.

The Mangler, despite poor reviews and box office, spawned two direct-to-video sequels. Michael Hamilton Wright's *The Mangler 2* is a highly tedious teen tech thriller starring an underutilized Lance Henriksen, and Matt Cunningham and Erik Gardner's 2005 *The Mangler: Reborn* is a highly tedious serial killer film starring an under-utilized Reggie Banister. *Crocodile* received a direct-to-Sci-Fi channel sequel directed by Gary Jones called *Crocodile 2: Death Roll* and later *Crocodile 2: Death Swamp*, also written by Jace Anderson, Adam Gierasch, and Boaz Davidson, who also helped produced *Leatherface* in 2017. Long-time makeup artist Dean Jones partly crowdfunded a *Toolbox Murders* sequel, also called *Coffin Baby*, which is certainly committed to its occasionally striking torture porn images, but is nevertheless a slog, only occasionally enlivened by a ten minute supporting performance by Bruce Dern. Hollywood never had time for Tobe Hooper when he was alive, but they never stopped picking the bones of his ideas.

Conclusion

Perhaps it's too much to ask for a happy ending to Hooper's career considering his work almost never had them. When Hooper passed away in August of 2017, there was no published critical appraisal of his work in English. *Djinn*'s prognosis for the future is grim, like most of Hooper's movies. From the start of his career, Hooper's characters have been consumed by forces beyond comprehension, eaten by buildings, earth, ghosts, and other people; the world is carnivorously resisting idealism and change for the better, turning wombs and caves, shelters from changing tides, into sarcophagi. *Djinn* does represent something of a bright spot in that it shows Hooper, even at age 70, was willing to keep making art, keep working under new circumstances, relearn how to frighten people, and keep making things with his usual thematic liberalism and exciting, enticing color palette. What difference does it make if the notices were poor when he'd been courting uproar, controversy, anger, and bad press all his life? If he were in this for good reviews, for understanding, he'd have gotten out of the game years ago. Instead, Hooper stayed true to himself and his artistic aspirations. The kid who directed *The Heisters* in that Texas basement all those years ago was still having fun with the medium he loves.

Maybe that's all the happy ending this story needs. Tobe Hooper never fit anyone's tidy definition of a horror director or an artist (in a country with a bad relationship to both). He was always more than what people wanted him to be, relying on his own rubric for success. In a career that spanned over forty years, he filled every blank canvas he was handed with his unmistakable, lavish brushstrokes, staying true to his artistic identity and ambition.

Acknowledgements

Dennis Tafoya and Jill Steelman for first renting *The Texas Chain Saw Massacre* for me and buying me my first books of film criticism all those years ago. Jon Wilton and Stan Giesea for their help with research. Scott "El Santo" Ashlin, the man who taught me that trash could be art and art could be trash. Sean Dillon and Mira Singer for editing this book into readable shape. Matt Zoller Seitz for starting me on my journey as a professional critic, and for always being there for me personally. Nell and everyone at Miniver for helping finally publish this book after a six-year journey to bookshelves. Patton Oswalt, my guardian angel.

CPSIA information can be obtained
at www.ICGtesting.com
Printed in the USA
LVHW081135140321
681503LV00008B/648